FIRST
THE LIFE AND FAITH OF
Emma Smith

JENNIFER REEDER

DESERET BOOK

Salt Lake City, Utah

© 2021 Jennifer Reeder

All rights reserved. No part of this book may be reproduced in any form or by any means without permission in writing from the publisher, Deseret Book Company, at permissions@deseretbook.com. This work is not an official publication of The Church of Jesus Christ of Latter-day Saints. The views expressed herein are the responsibility of the author and do not necessarily represent the position of the Church or of Deseret Book Company.

DESERET BOOK is a registered trademark of Deseret Book Company.

Visit us at deseretbook.com

Library of Congress Cataloging-in-Publication Data

Names: Reeder, Jennifer, author.
Title: First : the life and faith of Emma Smith / Jennifer Reeder.
Description: Salt Lake City : Deseret Book, [2021] | Includes bibliographical references and index. | Summary: "A biography of Emma Smith, the wife of the Prophet Joseph Smith"—Provided by publisher.
Identifiers: LCCN 2020056723 | ISBN 9781629728780 (hardback)
Subjects: LCSH: Smith, Emma Hale. | Mormons—United States—Biography. | LCGFT: Biographies.
Classification: LCC BX8695.S515 R44 2021 | DDC 289.3092 [B]—dc23
LC record available at https://lccn.loc.gov/2020056723

Printed in Canada
Marquis, Montreal, Quebec, Canada

10 9 8 7 6 5 4 3 2

To Emma,
for being a part of my heavenly host,
as I have been part of her earthly host.

CONTENTS

Acknowledgments ix

Emma Hale Smith Bidamon Pedigree Chart xi

Emma Smith Timeline xvii

Introduction 1
    Emma: First Woman of the Restoration

1. First Family and First Home 6
    Emma Hale of Harmony, Pennsylvania

2. First Love 16
    Emma's Marriage to Joseph Smith

3. First Mother of the Latter Days 37
    Emma and All Her Children

4. First Priestess 57
    Emma's Covenants, Ordinances, and Revelations

5. First Scribe 78
    Emma and the Scriptures

6. First Latter-day Saint Hymnal 90
    Emma and the Hymns

7. First Lady 104
    Emma as Wife of the President

8. First Presidentess of the Relief Society 121
    Emma as Elect Lady

9. First Partner 142
    Emma as a Woman of Property, Business,
    and Political Activism

10. First Widow 158
    Emma After Joseph

Abbreviations 183

Additional Reading 185

Index 189

ACKNOWLEDGMENTS

Just as Emma surrounded herself with friends, assistants, and helpers, I have done the same. This is my host:

Chére Jones Clarke, Matthew C. Godfrey, Gordon & Lesli Goodman, Tammy Uzelac Hall, Rachel Killebrew, Elizabeth Kuehn, Brooke LeFevre, Dave LeFevere, Karen & Gary Norton, Frank Rolapp, Julie A. Russell, Mark L. Staker, and Angela Townsend have helped with research, revisions, source-checking, and overall excitement.

The Church of Jesus Christ of Latter-day Saints Church History Archive, the Joseph Smith Papers, the Community of Christ Library and Archive, and the 2019 Latter-day Saint Theology Seminar with the Maxwell Institute at Brigham Young University provided documents and perspectives.

Authors, both published and unpublished, have provided valuable insight and resources, and they deserve the highest of praises: Valeen Tippetts Avery and Linda King Newell, Richard L. Bushman, Vesta Crawford and her collection at the University of Utah, Ron Romig, Lori E. Woodland, and Buddy Youngreen.

And deepest gratitude to Miriam with her timbrels and drums—a priestess and a midwife.

EMMA HALE SMITH BIDAMON PEDIGREE CHART

Family of Isaac and Elizabeth Hale (Parents)

ISAAC HALE
Birth: 21 Mar. 1763, Waterbury, New Haven County, Connecticut
Death: 11 Jan. 1839, Harmony Township, Susquehanna County, Pennsylvania

ELIZABETH LEWIS
Birth: 19 Nov. 1767, Litchfield, New Haven County, Connecticut
Death: 16 Feb. 1842, Harmony Township, Susquehanna County, Pennsylvania

Children:
  Jesse Hale
  Birth: 24 Feb. 1792, Harmony Township, Susquehanna County, Pennsylvania
  Death: 2 Dec. 1874, Amboy, Lee County, Illinois
  Spouse: Mary Elizabeth Ann McKune
  David Hale
  Birth: 6 Mar. 1794, Harmony Township, Susquehanna County, Pennsylvania
  Death: 16 Apr. 1878, Amboy, Lee County, Illinois
  Spouse: Rhoda Jane Skinner
  Alva Hale
  Birth: 29 Nov. 1795, Harmony Township, Susquehanna County, Pennsylvania
  Death: 18 Apr. 1881, Osceola, Polk County, Wisconsin
  Spouse: Clara Rouse

Phebe Elizabeth Hale
Birth: 1 May 1798, Harmony Township, Susquehanna County, Pennsylvania
Death: 25 Dec. 1836, Harmony Township, Susquehanna County, Pennsylvania
Spouse: Denison Root

Elizabeth Hale
Birth: 14 Feb. 1800, Harmony Township, Susquehanna County, Pennsylvania
Death: 18 May 1874, Amboy, Lee County, Illinois
Spouse: Benjamin Wasson

Isaac Hale
Birth: 11 Mar. 1802, Harmony Township, Susquehanna County, Pennsylvania
Death: 13 Sept. 1892, Osceola, Polk County, Wisconsin
Spouse: Nancy Agnes McKune

Emma Hale
Birth: 10 July 1804, Harmony Township, Susquehanna County, Pennsylvania
Death: 30 April 1879, Nauvoo, Hancock County, Illinois
Spouse: Joseph Smith Jr.
Spouse: Lewis C. Bidamon

Tryal Hale
Birth: 21 Nov. 1806, Harmony Township, Susquehanna County, Pennsylvania
Death: 3 June 1860, Amboy, Lee County, Illinois
Spouse: Michael Bartlett Morse

Reuben Charles Hale
Birth: 18 Sept. 1810, Harmony Township, Susquehanna County, Pennsylvania
Death: 17 Feb. 1891, Reading, Berks County, Pennsylvania
Spouse: Bethian Heartford

Family of Emma Hale and Joseph Smith Jr.

EMMA HALE
Birth: 10 July 1804, Harmony Township, Susquehanna County, Pennsylvania
Death: 30 Apr. 1879, Nauvoo, Hancock County, Illinois

JOSEPH SMITH JR.
Birth: 23 Dec. 1805, Sharon, Windsor County, Vermont
Death: 27 June 1844, Carthage, Hancock County, Illinois

Children:
  Unnamed son
  Birth: 15 June 1828, Harmony Township, Susquehanna County, Pennsylvania
  Death: 15 June 1828, Harmony Township, Susquehanna County, Pennsylvania
  Unnamed daughter
  Birth: 30 Apr. 1831, Kirtland, Geauga County, Ohio
  Death: 30 Apr. 1831, Kirtland, Geauga County, Ohio
  Unnamed son
  Birth: 30 Apr. 1831, Kirtland, Geauga County, Ohio
  Death: 30 Apr. 1831, Kirtland, Geauga County, Ohio
  Julia Murdock Smith (adopted 1831)
  Birth: 1 May 1831, Warrensville, Cuyahoga County, Ohio
  Death: 12 Sept. 1880, Sonora, Hancock County, Illinois
  Spouse: Elisha Dixon, ca. 1850
  Spouse: John Jackson Middleton, 19 Nov. 1856, Hancock County, Illinois
  Joseph Murdock Smith (adopted 1831)
  Birth: 1 May 1831, Warrensville, Cuyahoga County, Ohio
  Death: 29 Mar. 1832, Hiram, Portage County, Ohio

Joseph Smith III
Birth: 6 Nov. 1832, Kirtland, Geauga County, Ohio
Death: 10 Dec. 1914, Independence, Jackson County, Missouri
Spouse: Emmeline Griswold, 22 Oct. 1856, Nauvoo, Hancock County, Illinois
Children:
    Emma Josepha 1857–1940
    Evelyn Rebecca 1859–1859
    Carrie Lucinda 1861–1944
    Zaide Viola 1863–1891
    Joseph Arthur 1865–1866
Spouse: Bertha Madison, 12 Nov. 1869, Sandwich, Kendall County, Illinois
Children:
    David Carlos 1870–1886
    Mary Audentia 1872–1963
    Frederick Madison 1874–1946
    Israel Alexander 1876–1958
    Kenneth 1877
    Bertha Azubah 1878–1884
    Hale Washington 1881–1956
    Blossom 1883
    Lucy Yeteve 1884–1945
Spouse: Ada Rachel Clark, 12 Jan. 1898, Amaranth, Dufferin County, Ontario, Canada
Children:
    Richard Clark 1898–1969
    William Wallace 1900–1989
    Reginald Archer 1903–1974

Frederick Granger Williams Smith
Birth: 20 June 1836, Kirtland, Geauga County, Ohio
Death: 13 Apr. 1862, Nauvoo, Hancock County, Illinois
Spouse: Anna Marie Jones, 13 Sept. 1857, Hancock County, Illinois
Children:
    Alice Fredericka 1858–1932
Alexander Hale Smith
Birth: 2 June 1838, Far West, Caldwell County, Missouri
Death: 12 Aug. 1909, Nauvoo, Hancock County, Illinois
Spouse: Elizabeth Agnes Kendall, 23 June 1861, Nauvoo, Hancock County, Illinois
Children:
    Frederick Alexander 1862–1954
    Vida Elizabeth 1865–1945
    Ina Inez 1866–1945
    Emma Belle 1869–1960
    Don Alvin 1871–1904
    Eva Grace 1874–1893
    Joseph George 1877–1936
    Arthur Marion 1880–1965
    Coral Cecile Rebecca 1882–1968
Don Carlos Smith
Birth: 13 June 1840, Nauvoo, Hancock County, Illinois
Death: 15 Aug. 1841, Nauvoo, Hancock County, Illinois
Unnamed son
Birth: 6 Feb. 1842, Nauvoo, Hancock County, Illinois
Death: 6 Feb. 1842, Nauvoo, Hancock County, Illinois
David Hyrum Smith
Birth: 17 Nov. 1844, Nauvoo, Hancock County, Illinois
Death: 29 Aug. 1904, Elgin, Kane County, Illinois

Spouse: Clara Charlotte Hartshorn, 10 May 1870, Sandwich, DeKalb County, Illinois
Children:
    Elbert Aoriul 1871–1959

Family of Lewis Bidamon

LEWIS CRUM BIDAMON
Birth: 16 Jan. 1804, Smithfield, Isle of Wight County, Virginia
Death: 11 Feb. 1891, Nauvoo, Hancock County, Illinois
Spouse: Nancy Sebree, 1827
Children:
    Charles 1828–1830
    Almira Smith 1829–unknown (daughter of Nancy Smith)
    Zerelda Ann 1834–1879
    Mary Elizabeth 1835–1911
Spouse: Mary Ann Douglass, 1842
Spouse: Emma Hale Smith, 23 Dec. 1847, Nauvoo, Hancock County, Illinois
Spouse: Nancy Perriman Abercrombie, 20 May 1880, Nauvoo, Hancock County, Illinois
Children:
    Charles E. 1864–1944

EMMA SMITH TIMELINE

10 Jul. 1804	Emma Hale is born in Harmony Township, Pennsylvania
Nov. 1825	Joseph Smith arrives in Susquehanna County for work, begins to board on the Hale family property in Harmony
18 Jan. 1827	Emma and Joseph marry in South Bainbridge, New York; move to Smith family home in Manchester, New York
Aug. 1827	Emma's furniture is transported to New York
22 Sept. 1827	Emma goes with Joseph to receive the gold plates
Dec. 1827	Emma and Joseph move to Harmony
1828	Emma scribes for Joseph's translation of the Book of Mormon
Apr. 1828	Martin Harris comes to Harmony to help scribe the Book of Mormon
14 Jun. 1828	Martin Harris takes manuscript to New York
15 Jun. 1828	Emma gives birth to an unnamed baby boy; baby dies
Jul. 1828	Book of Mormon manuscript is lost
Feb. 1829	Joseph Sr. and Lucy Mack Smith come to Harmony to visit
5 Apr. 1829	Oliver Cowdery arrives in Harmony to scribe
15 May 1829	Restoration of Aaronic Priesthood
Jun. 1829	Joseph leaves Harmony to go with Oliver to Fayette, New York, to finish translation with assistance of Whitmer family

Emma Smith Timeline

1 Jul. 1829	Book of Mormon translation finished
4 Oct. 1829	Joseph returns to Harmony after securing printing contract
Dec. 1829	Joseph goes to Manchester to deal with publication problems
Jan. 1830	Joseph returns to Harmony
Feb. 1830	Joseph goes to Manchester to work with publishers
26 Mar. 1830	Book of Mormon published
6 Apr. 1830	Official organization of Church of Christ in Fayette; Emma not present
28 Jun. 1830	Emma baptized in Colesville, New York; Joseph on trial, in jail
Jul. 1830	Emma receives revelation through Joseph in Harmony—now D&C 25
Aug. 1830	Emma and Sally Knight confirmed in Harmony
Sept. 1830	Emma and Joseph move to Fayette to live with Whitmer family
Oct. 1830	Emma sews clothing for missionaries to the Lamanites
4 Feb. 1831	Emma and Joseph move to Kirtland, Ohio
30 Apr. 1831	Emma gives to birth to twins who die soon after birth
30 Apr. 1831	William W. Phelps begins to assist in editing Emma's hymn collection
9 May 1831	Emma and Joseph adopt Joseph and Julia Murdock
Jun. 1831	Emma's hymns begin to be published in *The Evening and the Morning Star* in Independence, Missouri

Emma Smith Timeline

27 Aug. 1831	Joseph returns to Kirtland; Smith family lives above Whitney store
12 Sept. 1831	Smith family moves to Hiram, Ohio
Oct. 1831	Joseph leaves Kirtland to go to New York City
24 Mar. 1832	Joseph is tarred and feathered in Hiram
29 Mar. 1832	Joseph Murdock Smith dies of measles and cold
1 Apr. 1832	Joseph leaves Ohio to spend the spring in Independence
2 Apr. 1832	Emma and Julia return to Kirtland
6 Jun. 1832	Joseph writes to Emma
Jun. 1832	Joseph returns to Kirtland
Oct. 1832	Joseph leaves Kirtland to travel to the Eastern United States
13 Oct. 1832	Joseph writes to Emma
6 Nov. 1832	Emma gives birth to Joseph Smith III; Joseph returns to Kirtland a few hours later
27 Feb. 1833	Joseph receives Word of Wisdom revelation based on Emma's concern
20 Jul. 1833	Independence printing office destroyed by mob; Emma loses hymns
5 Oct. 1833	Joseph departs Kirtland for mission to Canada
4 Nov. 1833	Joseph returns to Kirtland
12 Feb. 1834	Emma and Joseph move into their own home in Kirtland
5 May 1834	Joseph leaves Kirtland with Zion's Camp to Missouri
18 May 1834	Joseph writes to Emma
4 Jun. 1834	Joseph writes to Emma

12 Oct. 1834	Emma and Joseph ride to Willoughby, Ohio, for store goods
14 Sept. 1834	Emma assigned to make final hymn selection
16 Oct. 1834	Joseph leaves Kirtland for Michigan
Late Oct. 1834	Joseph returns to Kirtland
2 Dec. 1834	Emma and Joseph go to Painesville, Ohio, to do business
9 Dec. 1834	Emma receives patriarchal blessing from Joseph Sr. in Kirtland
14 Dec. 1834	Emma nurses Samuel Brannon
Apr. 1835	Joseph leaves Kirtland to seek economic resources
17 Aug. 1835	Joseph leaves Kirtland to go to Michigan
23 Aug. 1835	Joseph returns to Kirtland
14 Sept. 1835	Kirtland high council calls for publication of Emma's hymnal
24 Nov. 1835	Emma attends wedding of Newel Knight and Lydia Goldthwaite, performed by Joseph
Dec. 1835	Joseph Sr. and Lucy Mack Smith move into Emma and Joseph's home in Kirtland
1 Jan. 1836	Dispute between Joseph and William Smith resolved
7–9 Jan. 1836	Emma and Joseph attend three-day feast for poor and lame, given by Whitneys
Mar. 1836	Emma publishes *A Collection of Sacred Hymns*
27 Mar. 1836	Dedication of Kirtland Temple
3 May 1836	Joseph leaves Kirtland due to trouble with Kirtland Safety Society

Emma Smith Timeline

20 Jun. 1836	Emma gives birth to Frederick Granger Williams Smith in Kirtland
25 Jun. 1836	Joseph leaves Kirtland to travel to Boston and New York City
Sept. 1836	Joseph returns to Kirtland
Feb. 1837	Joseph leaves Kirtland to go to Michigan
Spring 1837	Joseph travels throughout Ohio in attempt to salvage financial loss
25 Apr. 1837	Emma writes to Joseph
3 May 1837	Emma writes to Joseph
19 May 1837	Joseph returns to Kirtland
28 Jul. 1837	Joseph travels to Toronto, Canada
27 Sept. 1837	Joseph travels to Missouri
Jan. 1838	Emma and Joseph and family leave Kirtland to move to Missouri
14 Mar. 1838	Emma and Joseph and family arrive in Far West, Missouri
28 May 1838	Joseph leaves Far West to go to Daviess County, Missouri
1 Jun. 1838	Joseph returns to Far West
2 Jun. 1838	Emma gives birth to Alexander Hale Smith, Far West
4 Jun. 1838	Joseph leaves Far West; travels to Adam-ondi-Ahman, Missouri
16 Jun. 1838	Joseph returns to Far West
Jul. 1838	Joseph leaves Far West to go to Adam-ondi-Ahman in Daviess County
9 Aug. 1838	Joseph returns to Far West

31 Oct. 1838	Joseph is taken prisoner: Independence, Richmond, Liberty, Missouri
4 Nov. 1838	Joseph writes to Emma
12 Nov. 1838	Joseph writes to Emma
1 Dec. 1838	Joseph writes to Emma
8 Dec. 1838	Emma visits Joseph in Liberty Jail
20 Dec. 1838	Emma visits Joseph in Liberty Jail
11 Jan. 1839	Emma's father, Isaac Hale, dies, age 75, in Harmony
Feb. 1839	Missouri governor Lilburn Boggs issues extermination order for Latter-day Saints
15 Feb. 1839	Emma and children leave Missouri, move to Quincy, Illinois, where they live with Sarah Cleveland family
Feb. 1839	Emma returns to visit Joseph in Liberty Jail
7 Mar. 1839	Emma writes to Joseph
21 Mar. 1839	Joseph writes to Emma
4 Apr. 1839	Joseph writes to Emma
22 Apr. 1839	Joseph joins Smith family in Quincy
10 May 1839	Smiths move to Commerce, Illinois; live in Smith homestead
30 May 1839	Joseph leaves Commerce to go to Quincy
5 Jun. 1839	Joseph returns to Commerce
Summer 1839	Malaria epidemic
29 Oct. 1839	Joseph leaves Commerce to go to Washington, DC
6 Dec. 1839	Emma writes to Joseph
29 Feb 1840	Joseph returns to Commerce

Emma Smith Timeline

Summer 1840	Emma assists the sick in a malaria epidemic in Nauvoo, Illinois
13 Jun. 1840	Emma gives birth to Don Carlos Smith in Nauvoo
1841	Emma baptized by proxy for her father, Isaac Hale, in Nauvoo
15 Mar. 1841	Emma's second hymnal printed
15 Aug. 1841	Young Don Carlos Smith dies in Nauvoo
5 Jan. 1842	Emma and Joseph open the Red Brick Store in Nauvoo
6 Feb. 1842	Emma delivers an unnamed baby boy who dies in Nauvoo
20 Feb. 1842	Elizabeth Hale, Emma's mother, dies, age 75, in Harmony
17 Mar. 1842	Founding of Nauvoo Female Relief Society with Emma as president
Jul. 1842	Emma leads the women of the Relief Society to sign a petition to Illinois governor Thomas Carlin to protect Joseph; travels to Quincy to deliver petition
10 Aug. 1842	Joseph leaves Nauvoo to escape extradition to Missouri; remains in hiding until Jan. 1843
16 Aug. 1842	Emma writes to Joseph; Joseph writes to Emma
19 Aug. 1842	Joseph writes to Emma
17 Aug. 1842	Emma writes to Gov. Carlin requesting protection for Joseph
5 Oct. 1842	Emma baptized for health in Mississippi River
1843	Emma baptized by proxy for her mother, Elizabeth Hale, in Nauvoo
10 Jan. 1843	Joseph returns to Nauvoo

18 Jan. 1843	Emma and Joseph celebrate their sixteenth anniversary with a jubilee
28 May 1843	Emma and Joseph sealed in the new and everlasting covenant
13 Jun. 1843	Smith family travels to Dixon, Illinois, to visit Emma's sister Elizabeth Wasson and her family
23 Jun. 1843	Joseph arrested in Dixon
30 Jun. 1843	Joseph returns to Nauvoo
12 Jul. 1843	Hyrum Smith reads plural marriage revelation to Emma—now D&C 132
31 Aug. 1843	Smith family moves to Mansion House in Nauvoo
28 Sept. 1843	Emma receives her temple endowment in Nauvoo
16 Mar. 1844	Final meeting of the Nauvoo Relief Society
7 Jun. 1844	*Nauvoo Expositor* printed
23 Jun. 1844	Joseph writes to Emma
25 Jun. 1844	Joseph writes to Emma
27 Jun. 1844	Joseph writes to Emma; Joseph and Hyrum are assassinated in Carthage, Illinois
17 Nov. 1844	Emma gives birth to David Hyrum Smith in Nauvoo
9 Mar. 1845	Brigham Young disbands the Nauvoo Relief Society
May 1845	Emma welcomes Joseph's brother William Smith and family into her home in Nauvoo
Sept. 1846	Emma rents out the Mansion House, takes her children to Fulton, Illinois
Feb. 1847	Emma and children return to Nauvoo
23 Dec. 1847	Emma marries Lewis Bidamon in Nauvoo
14 May 1856	Lucy Mack Smith dies in Emma's home in Nauvoo

6 Apr. 1860	Emma joins the Reorganized Church of Jesus Christ of Latter Day Saints in Amboy, Illinois; Joseph III elected president; Emma visits her sister Tryal Hale Morse in Amboy
1861	Emma publishes a hymnal for the RLDS church
Apr. 1862	Frederick Smith dies in the Mansion House in Nauvoo
1865	Emma brings Charles Abercrombie into her home to raise
1866	Emma releases Joseph's Bible translation manuscript to the RLDS church
1871	Emma and Lewis move into the Riverside Mansion in Nauvoo
10 Jan. 1877	David Smith committed to Illinois Hospital for the Insane in Elgin, Illinois
30 Apr. 1879	Emma dies in the Riverside Mansion in Nauvoo

Introduction

EMMA: FIRST WOMAN OF THE RESTORATION

One of my favorite things about being a historian is to pull all the strands of detail together into a grand, whole finale. Take Emma Smith, the first woman of the Restoration. She played an integral part in the early days of the Church. Like many other women, Emma may have acted mostly behind the scenes, but from my twenty-first century perspective—my ability to look around corners and under rugs—I see how she supported Joseph in receiving the gold plates and translating the Book of Mormon, and in so many other ways. She helped him in his journey to prophethood. And yet there was much more to Emma than being Joseph Smith's wife. She created the first Latter-day Saint hymnal and left a truly remarkable worship-music legacy. She was a gracious First Lady. Most of us are aware of her foundational work with the Relief Society. As the first woman in the Restoration to receive her temple blessings and to bestow them on others, perhaps I could trace my temple priesthood ordinance line back to her. She engaged in business and political activism. By examining the different genres of her life—wife, mother, host, hymnodist, Relief Society president, activist—I can see on paper how tremendous Emma was individually, and I recognize more clearly, through her eyes, the overall role women played in the Restoration, including us today. I love that—sign me up to be a part of this!

But I also see the complexities of Emma's life. It certainly was not a smooth road. There were long periods of time in between Emma's "accomplishments," like the twelve arduous years between 1830—when she was invited by revelation to expound scripture and exhort the Church—and 1842, when, as the first Relief Society president, she was actually able to fulfill those roles. Those were years of movement, homelessness, losing babies, and raising children, often on her own while her prophet husband watched over the Church. It took nearly six years to compile the hymns that would be published in the first hymnal, and those were years of persecution, relocation, and constant restarting and rebuilding. And we cannot forget the deep heartache she experienced with the revelation of plural marriage and the discovery of her husband's sealings to some of her dearest friends without her knowledge. Plural marriage seeped into nearly every aspect of her complex life. And oh! the loss of Joseph at his death and her estrangement from the Church thereafter.

Emma's life was not a smooth trajectory of progress. It was one step forward, two steps backward, then a little to the left. I know what that is like—I am very familiar with that pattern of progression. That makes me love Emma even more deeply. She was complicated and had real struggles, like I do. She feared for the health and safety of her children, her husband, and herself. She walked across frozen rivers and trod deep in mud as she figured out how to hold it all together. She expanded her definitions of home, family, and relief—something that I, too, am learning to do with my own situations. At times she was measured and diplomatic, but when pressed, she could become outwardly defensive, even a bit feisty. I believe that she and Joseph talked through a lot of things, not only in their marital relationship, but in understanding his visions and revelations. I like to say that Heavenly Father and Jesus Christ did not give Joseph a handbook binder in the Sacred Grove during the First Vision. Joseph—along with Emma and many others—had to figure out what it meant to restore the Church. Together they learned how to create Zion, often *because* they experienced malaria and mud, business failure and loss of property. Ideas, relationships, culture, and practices evolved. They did the best they could with what they had in their weeds and thistles of mortality.

I imagine Emma learning with Joseph about priesthood—the power of partnership with God—the pattern of both Heavenly Father and Heavenly Mother. In fact, I see Emma and Joseph in the same way I see Eve and Adam, or Sarah and Abraham, or Sariah and Lehi, or Mary and Joseph. Each of them faced impossible situations, and yet each learned how to access the Atonement of Jesus Christ and the power of the priesthood, simply because they *needed* it. As they discovered how to work together as companions, they drew upon each other's strengths and covered each other's weaknesses. I love that I, too, access that same priesthood as I recognize my impossible situations as well as the infinite blessings associated with my temple ordinances that enable me to become at one with my Heavenly Parents. This, my friends, is a perfect, complete, whole partnership. Emma's life shows me what that means.

As I studied Emma's life, I felt a responsibility to both her and to the rest of us to get her story right. I searched for primary, contemporary sources. Unfortunately, Emma did not leave a journal or even much correspondence. I found some letters she wrote to Joseph in *The Joseph Smith Papers*, and I poured over letters she wrote her son, Joseph III, in the Community of Christ (formerly Reorganized Church of Jesus Christ of Latter Day Saints) library. But I have no idea how much she knew about Joseph's plural wives, for example, or when she learned about them. Beyond Emma's own words, I worked to incorporate the words of those closest to her in *The Joseph Smith Papers* and other archival collections, to get an idea of her actions and reactions. I hesitated to use reminiscences because they often reflect the time in which they were written, rather than the actual moment. I also gave pause to secondary sources lacking proper documentation. Much has been written about Emma Smith, and I did my best to use credible sources, to track down each story. Every statement is made accountable in the footnotes—and yet many of my ideas are conjectural; I pieced together events and words of others to understand possible explanations for Emma. This was a monumental task.

On Sunday, March 17, 2019, the 177th anniversary of the founding of the Relief Society, I stood on the grass at a site marked for a temple to be built in Independence, Missouri. The land is owned today by the Church of Christ Temple Lot, or Hedrickites. On August 3, 1831, Joseph Smith dedicated the area as a center place for the New Jerusalem and the location of a temple in Jackson County, Missouri. Emma never saw this sacred space; the closest she came to Independence was in visiting Joseph in Liberty Jail a few miles away, while she and the children lived in Far West, Missouri. Yet as I stood barefoot in the middle of that grassy field, hoping the sacredness of the location would seep through the bottom of my feet, I felt Emma all around me. In every direction I turned, I could see remnants and reminders of Emma in the brick and stone buildings of the Church of Christ, the Community of Christ (RLDS), The Church of Jesus Christ of Latter-day Saints, and the Remnant Church of Jesus Christ of Latter Day Saints. Numerous faith groups claim connection to this historic ground, many with small churches around the corner or down the streets of Independence.

We are all cousins, fragmented and splintered as we may be, individually and collectively. We share a history—and oh! that history is glorious! I love how the *Oxford English Dictionary* defines *restoration*: to renew, revive, re-establish; the act of returning something to a former owner, place, or condition; restoring to a former state. Restoration is a recovery, even a resurrection. The spirit of restoration is not locked in one moment of time. It is a story of resilience and strength in the latter days. And we, too, all play a part of the Restoration.

This is the story of Emma.

Chapter 1

FIRST FAMILY
AND FIRST HOME

Emma Hale of Harmony, Pennsylvania

The Susquehanna River winds from upstate New York, through eastern Pennsylvania, to the Chesapeake Bay in Maryland. Native Americans hunted along its banks, competing for access to beavers in a thriving fur trade. The Onondaga, "People of the Hills," lived in the Susquehanna Valley, a bend in the river as it crossed back and forth between New York and Pennsylvania. The river was named using Indian words: the Onondaga word *susqe* may have meant muddy or serpent-like, while *hanna* referred to the rapids. Early white settlers on the Pennsylvania side created Willingborough Township, with the later development of Harmony in the eastern portion of the valley. The scenic area surrounding Harmony was heavily wooded and mountainous, making it difficult for farming, but prime for hunting.[1]

Emma Hale was no stranger to wilderness. In this rugged and yet protected cradle between wooded mountain and flowing river, she began her life within a supportive, eventually successful family. All the Hales—mother and father, brothers and sisters, aunt and uncle and cousins—worked together for survival, despite primitive conditions, to build a veritable Eden. They found a natural wealth in each other—supporting, protecting, celebrating, mourning, sharing burdens, marrying, raising children together—along the banks of the Susquehanna. Here, in Harmony, Emma learned resourcefulness—how to survive the wild frontier—which prepared her for the difficult tasks of moving and building new settlements later in her life. In Harmony, she met and married Joseph Smith and scribed for his translation of the Book of Mormon. In Harmony, she received a noteworthy revelation directed to her from God in which she was taught about her important role in the Restoration. In Harmony, she gave birth and buried her first baby, a tragedy that she carried with her the rest of her life. The Susquehanna Valley became a foundation for her life and role in the Restoration of The Church of Jesus Christ of Latter-day Saints.

Beginnings

The large and winding Susquehanna River provided ready access to transportation and commerce. Because of these factors, Isaac Hale and his future brother-in-law Nathaniel Lewis settled here, deep in the fresh new land of the United States in 1790.[2] Their new brides, Elizabeth Lewis Hale (Nathaniel's sister) and Sarah Cole Lewis, joined them a year later from New York (now Vermont).[3] In this wild but bountiful valley, sparsely populated by white settlers from the northeast, they found wild grapes and flax pleasantly situated between the mountains and the river.[4] Indeed, it was an Edenic valley of abundant resources and beauty.

Isaac and Elizabeth Lewis Hale settled on the north bend of the Susquehanna in a rough log cabin, eager to create a home and family.[5] They built their first home and farm at the foot of a mountain, where panthers, bears, and wolves crept at night.[6] The Hales were known for their honesty, integrity, and hospitality, working hard to claim their land, to raise their family, and to look out for their neighbors who slowly claimed land in the area.[7] Isaac and his oldest son,

Jesse, hunted wild game, including deer, bear, elk, and small animals, and shipped fresh meat down the river.[8] A "man of forethought and generosity," Isaac was known for anonymously leaving meat on a neighbor's table. His brother-in-law Nathaniel Lewis considered Isaac "a man of truth and good judgment."[9] Emma patterned her life after these traits she saw in her father.

The nearby Harmony Turnpike was the quickest overland route for travelers between western New York and the urban areas of southern Pennsylvania.[10] In this remote crossroads, Elizabeth provided food and lodging for travelers and workers, contributing to the family income. An acquaintance described her as an approachable and knowledgeable woman.[11] She used natural herbs for nursing.[12] Emma learned valuable skills from her mother, hosting countless people in her home and caring for the sick with natural remedies as was appropriate for her time.

Emma was born in the Hales' log cabin near the Susquehanna River on July 10, 1804, the seventh of nine children and third of four daughters. Later, six years of hard work allowed the Hale family to transition from their cabin to a comfortable frame house, known then as a "mansion"—evidence of their efforts to fit into an emerging middle class.[13] Upon visiting the home in 1829, Lucy Mack Smith was impressed. She remembered, "the ma[n]sion in which they lived [was] a neatly framed home with <every> convenient appendage necessary."[14] Internalizing this example from her parents, Emma would later find it important to create a home of refinement when she moved into the Mansion House in Nauvoo, Illinois.

Growing up, Emma's brothers adored her and taught her how to ride horseback and row a canoe on the river. Her two oldest brothers, Jesse and David, were drafted and left home to fight in the War of 1812 when she was eight years old, but thanks to them, Emma grew up to be an accomplished horsewoman.[15] After the war, Jesse hunted with his father and became a local tax assessor.[16] Her two older sisters, Phebe and Elizabeth, taught her how to keep house.[17] Emma became the family cook, an ability she would use throughout her life in hosting dignitaries and visitors in Kirtland and Nauvoo.[18]

Harmony: Emma's Eden

On the rural Pennsylvania frontier, the Hales were a religious family. Daniel Buck, a family friend who arrived in the Susquehanna Valley at the same time as Isaac, was a pastor in the Congregational Church; Emma was baptized by Buck not long after her birth.[19] As the religious fervor of the second Great Awakening expanded, George Peck, a Methodist circuit rider, described the Harmony community as exhibiting "such weeping and shouting [as] I have seldom heard or witnessed." A neighbor claimed that when Emma was young, like many others with new, intense, religious fervency, "she often got the power."[20] Young Emma was among those at camp meetings who, caught up in spiritual emotion, shouted, wept, or spoke in tongues. Emma's uncle Nathaniel converted to Methodism and became a preacher in Harmony. His congregation worshipped outdoors or in private homes.[21] Emma began attending a Methodist Sunday school when she was seven years old. She read the Bible and gained religious instruction from Sunday sermons and the weekday preaching of circuit riders.[22] Father Isaac was slower to join; he considered himself a Deist, believing God was not active in the affairs of the world. One day, according to family tradition, he happened upon Emma, seven or eight years old, praying for him in the woods. His hard heart softened, and he converted to Christ.[23]

Elizabeth Hale was an educated woman; she made sure her daughters were schooled as well. Emma was known as a girl of unusual intelligence.[24] The settlers of Harmony built a log school where students, including Emma, learned to read, write, and do math. Affluent young women in the community attended the Female Seminary in Great Bend Township, roughly two miles west of Emma's home. She may have studied there for a short period, gaining exquisite penmanship skills. Some believe she later taught school as a young adult and acquired several cows as salary.[25] The cows allowed her to run a dairy, later a means of financial support.[26] Harmony became a central location for the Hale siblings when they reached adulthood and started families. Oldest son Jesse married a neighbor in 1815, then built a small home on his father's property. He became a successful exporter of lumber and owned a sawmill.[27] David, a practicing Methodist, was known in the community for his integrity.[28] Fourth child and oldest sister Phebe married a poor, uneducated farmer who was a widower from the mountain hollows south of the Susquehanna Valley; they lived with his family until November 1820, then settled on the south side of the river, near brother Jesse. Second sister Elizabeth married a carpenter with little education, in Colesville, New York, across the river about thirty-five miles northeast. They moved into the Hale home in Harmony in 1819, and a year later, built their own home. Youngest sister Tryal married an uneducated Methodist carpenter who had grown up in the Susquehanna Valley. They moved into a log cabin on the north side of Jesse's farm on the steep edge of Oquago Mountain and worked in David's store.[29] These were Emma's people—a tightly connected family whom she loved and respected.

In the Susquehanna Valley, Emma grew to adulthood, a tall, attractive, olive-complexioned woman with brown eyes and black hair.[30] Her attraction to Joseph Smith, an uneducated farm boy from New York who had seen great visions, proved problematic with the Hale family. Isaac forbade their marriage—not because Joseph was poor and uneducated, like his other sons-in-law—but because of his unorthodox religious ideas. Emma followed her heart, choosing a life with Joseph rather than the comfort of her Edenic home and family. They were married on January 18, 1827, in Bainbridge, New York.³¹

The End of Hale "Harmony" for Emma

Emma left Harmony when she married Joseph; they lived with the Smith family in Manchester, New York. The two came back to live near her family in Harmony for one and a half years, from late 1827 to late summer 1830, but then left for good to join the Saints in Fayette, New York, Joseph having gone first to attend to Church business. When he came back for Emma in August 1830, Isaac was done trying to reconcile with him. He told his son-in-law, "You have stolen my daughter and married her. I had rather have followed her to her grave."³² When Emma left Harmony for the last time in 1830, little did she know that she would never see her parents again. How she must have looked back on that day.

Reunion

After Isaac's death in 1839, Emma's nephew, twenty-one-year-old Lorenzo D. Wasson, son of her sister Elizabeth, came to Nauvoo to share news of the loss. Only then did Emma renew contact with her family after a decade-long rift. She wrote to her mother about each of her children—some of them named after her brothers. She invited the Hale family to move to the Nauvoo area even if they did not accept her religion. Some did; the Wasson family had relocated to central Illinois a few years earlier. In 1841 Lorenzo moved in with the Smith family in Nauvoo, and he was baptized by Joseph in 1842. Mother Elizabeth was too ill to travel; Emma's brother Alva remained in the valley to care for her.³³ She died in 1842 at the age of seventy-five and was buried in Harmony next to her husband and Emma's first child.

Emma reunited her splintered family with letters and visits. By 1843, six of her siblings lived in Illinois. In June, Emma's sister Elizabeth, mother of Lorenzo, invited Emma and Joseph to visit her family in Dixon, about 175 miles northeast of Nauvoo. The visit was cut short as Illinois governor Thomas Carlin issued a writ for Joseph's arrest and extradition to Missouri. Officers arrested him in Elizabeth's front yard in a dramatic effort to once again separate Joseph and Emma from Emma's family.[34]

Not long after Joseph Smith was killed, Emma received a letter from her dear older brother Jesse, seeking to repair their relationship after years of silence. She must have found this letter to be a great comfort in a time of deep mourning. Fifty-three-year-old Jesse wrote, "My grey hairs and the failing of my eyesight and many other things admonish me that my time is fast hastening to a close and that my obligations should all be fulfilled so far as I am able." He thanked Emma for a friendly visit before Joseph died.[35] In 1845 Jesse and David moved their families near the Wasson family in Temperance Hill, almost two hundred miles northeast of Nauvoo; Alva followed that fall.[36] Tryal's family moved to Amboy in northern Illinois in 1859. Emma visited her in 1860—the first time she had seen her younger sister in almost thirty years, and just two months before Tryal's untimely death.[37] Having her family close to her later in life renewed relationships.

Separation and reunion. Loss and compensation. Poverty and refinement. Fierce protection of family. These would become recurring themes in Emma's life. Although marriage to Joseph and membership in the restored Church of Christ took her away from her family of origin, Emma's Harmony upbringing provided her with a foundation of fervent religion, tenacious love for family, and resourceful skills and talents that would assist in powerful ways with the coming forth of the Restoration.

Notes

1. Mark Staker, "Isaac and Elizabeth Hale in Their Endless Mountain Home," *Mormon Historical Studies* 15, no. 2 (Fall 2014): 13–17, 58; see also Mark Staker, "Joseph and Emma Smith's Susquehanna Home: Expanding Mormonism's First Headquarters," *Mormon Historical Studies* 16, no. 2 (Fall 2015): 69–70.
2. Seraphina Gardner, ed. *Recollections of the Pioneers of Lee County* (Dixon, IL: Inez A. Kennedy, 1893), 96.
3. David Hale, *Amboy Journal*, May 1876; Gardner, *Recollections*, 142; Vesta Crawford Collection, biographical notes on Emma Smith, 24, UofU.
4. Lucy Mack Smith, History, 1844–1845, bk. 7, p. [11], see josephsmithpapers.org; Vesta Crawford and Fay Olloerton, *The Elect Lady: A Yankee Woman Who Married the Prophet Joseph Smith,* manuscript, 3, Crawford Collection.
5. Larry C. Porter, *A Study of the Origins of The Church of Jesus Christ of Latter-day Saints in the States of New York and Pennsylvania*, dissertation, Brigham Young University, 1971 (Provo, UT: BYU Studies, 2000), 45.
6. Staker, "Isaac and Elizabeth Hale," 76; Crawford and Olloerton, *The Elect Lady*, 6.
7. Gardner, *Recollections*, 96; Emily C. Blackman, *History of Susquehanna County, Pennsylvania* (Philadelphia: Clayton, Remsen & Haffelfinger, 1873), 103–4, 579.
8. Staker, "Isaac and Elizabeth Hale," 40–42.
9. Blackman, *History of Susquehanna County,* 103–4, 579; Gardner, *Recollections*, 96.
10. Staker, "Isaac and Elizabeth Hale," 1–2.
11. Blackman, *History of Susquehanna County,* 103.
12. Crawford and Olloerton, *The Elect Lady*, 5.
13. Staker, "Joseph and Emma Smith's Susquehanna Home," 7.
14. Staker, "Isaac and Elizabeth Hale," 76; Crawford and Olloerton, *The Elect Lady*, 6; Lucy Mack Smith, History, 1844–1845, bk. 7, p. [11]; see josephsmithpapers.org.
15. Gardner, *Recollections*, 96.
16. Blackman, *History of Susquehanna County*, 104; Staker, "Joseph and Emma Smith's Susquehanna Home," 4–6.
17. Crawford and Olloerton, *The Elect Lady*, 7.

18. Mark Staker surmised Emma Hale's role as a cook in a BYU Education Week class on 20 Aug. 2019. His careful research in an unpublished manuscript places Emma serving breakfast. Mark Staker, "Murder on the Susquehanna: The Execution of Jason Treadwell," 2012, copy in author's possession.
19. Staker, "Isaac and Elizabeth Hale," 56, fn171.
20. Mark L. Staker, *Hearken, O Ye People: The Historical Setting of Joseph Smith's Ohio Revelations* (Salt Lake City: Kofford, 2009), 126.
21. Vesta Crawford Collection, biographical notes, p. 24.
22. Mark Staker, "A Comfort Unto My Servant, Joseph," *Women of Faith in the Latter Days, Volume 1,* Turley & Chapman, eds. (Salt Lake: Deseret Book 2011), 348, fn20; see also Mark Hill Forscutt, "Commemorative Discourse on the Death of Mrs. Emma Bidamon," *The Saints' Herald* 26, no. 14, (15 Jul. 1879): 209.
23. Forscutt, "Commemorative Discourse," 209; W. W. Blair, "Correspondence," *The Saints' Herald* 26, no. 11 (1 Jun. 1879): 191.
24. Gardner, *Recollections*, 96; Crawford and Olloerton, *The Elect Lady*, 1, 7.
25. Staker, "A Comfort Unto My Servant, Joseph," 344, fn4, 350; Isaac Hale, "Affidavit, March 20, 1834," in Eber D. Howe, *Mormonism Unvailed* (Painesville, OH: E. D. Howe, 1834), 263; Susquehanna County Assessor, Tax Assessment Records, 1827–29.
26. Staker, "Joseph and Emma Smith's Susquehanna Home," 100–103.
27. Staker, "Joseph and Emma Smith's Susquehanna Home," 70, 73, 79, 80; Gardner, *Recollections*, 141.
28. Gardner, *Recollections*, 141; Blackman, *History of Susquehanna County, Pennsylvania*, 104.
29. Staker, "Joseph and Emma Smith's Susquehanna Home," 82–86.
30. Abel, "Scraps of History, April 12, 1867," David H. Smith Documents and Reference, CCLA.
31. Joseph Smith Family Bible, private possession; Joseph Smith History, vol. A-1, 8, JSP.
32. Howe, *Mormonism Unvailed*, 234–35.
33. Staker, "Isaac and Elizabeth Hale," 96–97; Gardner, *Recollections*, 57–58; Lorenzo D. Wasson to David Hall, 12–19 Feb. 1841, typescript, CHL; Wilford Woodruff, "Sabbath Scene in Nauvoo," *T&S* 3 (15 Apr. 1842): 751–53.
34. Lorenzo Wasson to Emma Hale Smith, Undated [ca. December 1840–April

1841], BYU. See Staker, "A Comfort Unto My Servant, Joseph," 361; Staker, "Joseph and Emma Smith's Susquehanna Home," 82; Joseph Smith, History, vol. D-1, 21 June 1843, p. 1581, CHL; josephsmithpapers.org.
35. Jesse Hale to Emma Hale Smith, 30 Mar. 1845, photograph of holograph, CHL.
36. Staker, "Joseph and Emma Smith's Susquehanna Home," 73; Gardner, *Recollections*, 141.
37. Linda King Newell and Valeen Tippetts Avery, *Mormon Enigma: Emma Hale Smith* (Urbana, IL: University of Illinois Press, 1994), 273.

Chapter 2

FIRST LOVE

Emma's Marriage to Joseph Smith

The Susquehanna River flows southwest from central New York, through the village of Bainbridge, just north of the Pennsylvania border, then doubles back to Harmony. The river led Joseph Smith to find Emma Hale. Life with this hard-working visionary farm boy transformed her Garden of Eden in Harmony into a lifetime of briars and weeds in Kirtland, Far West, and Nauvoo, followed by a "crown of righteousness" and a "mansion in heaven" in the presence of the Lord.[1] Their partnership intermingled with physical and emotional separation, babies lost and children grown, itinerant wandering and deeply rooted commitment, religious exhilaration and severe Abrahamic sacrifice. Together they forged their way through persecution and celebration, poverty and abundance, betrayal and reconciliation. A partnership cut short at the early death of Joseph left Emma determined to preserve their family, sealed with eternal promise.

A Chance Meeting

In October 1825, Joseph was hired by wealthy South Bainbridge farmer Josiah Stowell to search for a lost Spanish silver mine across the river in Pennsylvania.[2] Gossip about Joseph's ability to discern things unseen by the natural eye reached Josiah over one hundred miles southeast of Manchester, and he enticed Joseph with a high wage he could not refuse.[3] Money-digging was popular in New York and Vermont at the time, blending Christianity with old world magic traditions.[4] After arriving in Harmony and ascertaining the situation, Joseph persuaded Josiah to abandon the endeavor and focus on farming; nevertheless, this experience gave Joseph the negative reputation of being a "money digger." Joseph worked on the farm for several months and boarded on Isaac Hale's property, where he met Emma.[5] He considered her a woman of "decidedly correct mind and uncommon ability of talent and judgment."[6]

Joseph returned home to visit his beloved family. He missed them, especially his older brother Alvin, who had died in 1823.[7] He told his parents—Joseph Smith Sr. and Lucy Mack Smith—about Emma: "I have been very lonely ever since Alvin died," he said, according to Lucy. "I have concluded to get married; and, if you have no objections, Miss Emma Hale would be my choice before any other woman I have ever seen." Lucy and Joseph Sr. were pleased and gave their consent.[8] However, Emma's father was not impressed with the "stranger;" when Joseph requested his daughter's hand, Emma remembered, "My folks were bitterly opposed to him," based on gossip about Joseph and not knowing his family.[9] She must have felt deeply conflicted—she sensed a strong attraction to the farm boy and believed his account of divine interaction.

Traditionally, couples married at the bride's home.[10] Due to Isaac's indignation, Joseph wrote, "I was therefore under the necessity of taking her elsewhere."[11] When her father was away, Emma went to visit Joseph at the Stowell farm in South Bainbridge, where he persuaded her to marry him immediately.[12] They were wed at the home of Zachariah Tarbell, a local justice of the peace, on January

18, 1827. While Emma did not have the permission of her parents, under New York state law, the union was legal based on their ages—she twenty-two and he twenty-one.[13]

From Hale to Smith—Blending of Families

The disparity between the Smiths and Hales was great. While the Smiths had fared poorly financially, moving from Vermont to New York because of failing farms and business ventures, the Hales had established roots in Pennsylvania, building a respectable reputation among their neighbors, establishing a successful business, and constructing a fine home. Joseph and Emma blended their diverse backgrounds into a complementary partnership. When speaking of Emma and their marriage, Joseph referred to the scripture, "they twain shall be one flesh," considering the way Emma had accompanied him, "against the wishes and advise of her relatives, to a land of strangers." He gratefully recognized that even as she had acted against the will of her family in marrying him, "her character stands as fair for morality, piety and virtue as any in the world."[14] Emma remembered that he "usually gave some heed to what I had to say."[15]

The Smith family welcomed Emma with open arms. They knew she was Joseph's chosen wife; Joseph's family became Emma's family. Immediately after marriage, Emma and Joseph lived with them in Manchester, New York. Later in Kirtland, Ohio, Lucy and Joseph Sr. lived with Emma and Joseph.[16] The loving welcome may have worn off when Emma witnessed Smith family tension in the fall of 1835. A string of disagreements between Joseph and his brother William came to a head over a Kirtland court case with the brothers on opposing sides. The conflict spilled over into church councils, community events, and at home, even becoming physical at times. Older brother Joseph and younger brother William expressed age-old grievances. Emma saw a tender reconciliation on January 1, 1836, something she had not seen within her own family. Joseph called their repentance and forgiveness a covenant "in the Sight of God and the holy angels and the brethren." He began to see family as an expanded network—and harmony among the people he loved as holy. "While gratitude swelled in our bosoms, tears flowed from our eyes." He continued, "It was truly a jubilee and time of rejoicing."[17]

After Joseph's death, Emma generously opened her home to the Smith family—they had, after all, become her family. Joseph's brother William and his family came in May 1845 after his excommunication, and she nursed his wife Caroline, who died of heart failure two days later.[18] For a time, Emma lovingly cared for Lucy, her mother-in-law, with the help of her niece, Mary Bailey Smith, orphaned daughter of Samuel Smith.[19] Even after Emma's marriage to Lewis Bidamon, Lucy, afflicted with arthritis, returned to Emma's care in 1852 until she died in 1856.[20] A decade later, Emma, unable to see her own parents' graves in Harmony, made arrangements to mark and protect those of Joseph Sr. and Lucy.[21] Emma's care for Joseph's parents and siblings extended her love for him and her desire to care for her own family.

"Spreading prairies that separate us"—Disruptions and Relocations

In an 1830 revelation, the Lord counseled Emma about her relationship with Joseph: "Thou shalt go with him at the time of his going."[22] Joseph and Emma's married life was somewhat nomadic and unsettled as persecution and revelation uprooted them time after time, and they often relied on the generosity of others. Very rarely did they have time alone as a couple and as a family. The constant change surely must have weighed on Emma. When they first lived with

Joseph's family in Manchester, his mother Lucy exerted great efforts to make their small home comfortable.[23] That spring of 1827, Emma wrote her father, asking if she could retrieve her clothing, furniture, and cows. Isaac consented, and the furniture arrived in New York in August.[24] While having her own belongings might have brought Emma some comfort, her heart must have been torn between her own family in Harmony and her new family in Manchester.

In December 1827, to escape persecution and due to Emma's difficult first pregnancy and a desire to return to her mother's assistance, her brother Alva helped them move back to Harmony.[25] Despite the tensions between them, Emma's father Isaac graciously supported Joseph's land purchase, and the couple settled into a home once owned by her brother and sister-in-law, Jesse and Mary Hale.[26] After eighteen months in that home, Emma said goodbye to her parents for the last time when she and Joseph left for the Whitmer farm in Fayette, New York, in late August 1830. That began several years of being dependent on others for a place to live. In February 1831, they arrived in Kirtland, Ohio, where they lived with Newel and Elizabeth Ann Whitney, then moved to Isaac Morley's farm just outside Kirtland, and from there, to Hiram with John and Elsa Johnson's family in September. In April 1832, when Joseph left Ohio to go to Missouri for the summer, Emma returned to Kirtland, where she and the children rotated through the homes of Thirza and Reynolds Cahoon, Rebecca and Frederick G. Williams, and Joseph Sr. and Lucy Mack Smith. The constant change and disruption must have been disheartening to Emma as she and Joseph never seemed to have the time or space to become their own distinct family.

In Kirtland, the Smith family finally obtained their own home near the temple in February 1834. Four years later, in January of 1838, a several-months-pregnant Emma and her family left Kirtland to join Joseph and the Saints in Far West, Missouri. After a year there fraught with persecution, Emma moved the children to Sarah Cleveland's home in Quincy, Illinois, while Joseph languished in Liberty Jail. The family finally reunited in April 1839. By May, they moved to the Homestead in Nauvoo, then eventually to the larger and much more comfortable Nauvoo Mansion House in 1843.[27] Emma and Joseph lived in five states over twelve years, only some of that time in their own home. Emma must have yearned for the space and stability of a physical foundation, her own furniture, a favorite quilt or the good dishes, a desk for her own study and writing, trunks and chests for children's clothing. Those would come with time.

Separation and trouble were ever present. In 1838, Joseph wrote to Emma: "My dear and beloved companion of my bosom, in tribulation and affliction."[28] Those two—tribulation and affliction—were constant partners in Emma and Joseph's marriage. They were often separated due to persecution or ecclesiastical matters. Joseph's first trial and imprisonment for public disturbance in June 1830 must have been terrifying for Emma. In 1832, Emma witnessed a tarred and feathered husband, who at first appeared dead. She cleaned him up and he preached to a congregation of Saints the following morning.[29] She wept with her children and clung to her husband as guards took him into custody in Far West on October 31, 1838.[30] Each separation seemed endless. Two days after his Far West arrest, Joseph wrote to Emma, "I cannot express my feelings; my heart is full."[31] Four months later, while Joseph remained in Liberty Jail, Emma took every opportunity to write him of her immense loss without him. "I make an attempt to write, but I shall not attempt to write my feelings altogether, for the situation in which you are, the walls, bars, and bolts, rolling rivers, running streams, rising hills, sinking vallies and spreading prairies that separate us, and the cruel injustice that first cast you into prison and still holds you there, with many other considerations, places my feelings far beyond description."[32]

On his way to Washington, DC, just a year later, Joseph wrote to Emma: "I shall be filled with constant anxiety about you and the children until I hear from you."[33] She responded a month later: "Dear husband in the midst of the confusion of my own family . . . I shall endeavour to write." Much was happening at home, including sick children, but she wanted him to be aware of her concern for him: "There is great anxiety manifest in this place for your prosperity and the time lingers long that ~~you~~ is set for your return, the day is waning and night is approaching so fast that I must reserve my better feelings untill I have a better chance to express them."[34]

It was not only Joseph who was in trouble; Emma experienced her own bouts of illness. On at least two occasions she lay near death: after giving birth to their first child in Harmony, and again in Nauvoo. Joseph often recorded in his journals about Emma's physical ailments.[35] He cared for her, prayed for her, called upon trusted doctors, and nursed her back to health, often with fresh air and horseback rides or carriage rides. Emma relished his time and attention.[36]

"I am ready to go with you"—
Affection between Emma and Joseph

Even amid physical separation, Joseph and Emma expressed terms of endearment in their correspondence. Perhaps it *was* separation that strengthened their love. Joseph addressed Emma as "Dear Wife," "My dear and beloved companion," "My dear Emma," and "Dear and affectionate Wife." He closed his letters with "O my kind and affectionate Emma. I am yours forever." "Yours forever your Husband and true friend," and "Your affectionate Husband until Death."[37] Emma wrote to Joseph "Dear Husband," or "Ever Affectionate Husband," then signed them with "Yours affectionately forever" or "Yours affectionately."[38] Feelings were mutual.

In the fall of 1832, Joseph went with Newel Whitney to the Eastern United States, leaving Emma, in the advanced stages of pregnancy and busy with toddler Julia, in Kirtland. He yearned for his family. Feeling overwhelmed in New York City, Joseph returned to his room to write, "The thought of home, of Emma and Julia, rushed upon my mind like a flood." He continued, "My breast is filled with all the feelings and tenderness of a parent and a Husband." He closed the letter with the hope that Emma's burdens would be lifted, "for I know your state and that others do not."[39] He understood her concerns about pregnancy and childbirth; at this point they had lost three babies in childbirth and one in sickness.

When Joseph left Kirtland unexpectedly to find economic resources in April 1835, Emma wrote him, "I cannot tell you my feelings when I found I could not see you before you left, yet I expect you can realize them."[40] A week later, she confessed, "It is my anxiety for your company at home," claiming "things would be much bettered by your presence."[41] That physical presence was missed often throughout Emma's life.

Even in Joseph's darkest experiences, such as Liberty Jail in the winter of 1838–39, he expressed great love for Emma. At the beginning of their separation while in Independence, Joseph wrote her with a plea: "Oh! Emma, for God's sake do not forsake me nor the truth." He closed the letter: "I am yours forever your Husband and true friend."[42] Joseph referred to a letter from her as "a sweet morsal," then endeavored to send his wife comfort. "Oh my affectionate Emma, I want you to remember that I am a true and faithful friend to you." He reminded her, "My heart is intwined around yours forever and ever, . . . I am your husband in bonds and tribulation."[43] Five months later, those bonds were stretched even further as his incarceration seemed to have no end. Joseph wrote Emma, "If you want to know how much I want to see you, examine your feelings, how much you want to see me, and judge for yourself." He described the lengths to which he would go to see her: "I would gladly walk from here to you barefoot, and bareheaded, and half naked, to see you and think it a great pleasure, and never count it toil."[44]

Separation continued to plague Emma and Joseph, even as it strengthened their marriage. While he was in hiding to escape extradition to Missouri in August 1842, Emma wrote to him, "I am ready to go with you."[45] He responded with gratitude that she was "my Wife, even the wife of my youth, and the choice of my heart." He remarked on their "commingling of thought," a tender description of their union.[46] In a letter following her visit, he wrote, "Tongue can not express the gratitude of my heart, for the warm and true-hearted friendship you have ministered in these things toward me." He confessed, "My safety is with you."[47] Safety. Ministry. Anxiety for your comfort. Bettered by your presence. Intertwined hearts. These honest, sweet words illustrate their "commingling of thought" amid affliction and tribulation.

"That I may be able to comprehend the designs of God"—The New and Everlasting Covenant of Marriage

Joseph and Emma certainly had an affectionate marriage; they also had a working relationship—an economic and emotional contract to each other, something very progressive for their time. Their relationship contributed to Joseph's evolving understanding of the theology, priesthood, and sacred rites regarding family and the Abrahamic Covenant. These new practices, particularly plural marriage, both bolstered and troubled Emma.

Joseph received significant revelation, translated sacred records, and restored the Aaronic and Melchizedek Priesthood in Harmony. Emma's relationship with her husband was delineated in one of these revelations: she was to go with him "at the time of his going" and to be a scribe. Joseph's Church calling would then support Emma, the revelation stated, creating a relationship of interdependence. Her "soul"—her deepest part—was to delight in her husband and his potential glory. Together they worked to build the Church. She was to comfort him "in his afflictions, with consoling words."[48] The noun *comfort* suggests relief from pain or distress of mind. The verb means to strengthen.[49] These were powerful, even holy charges for Emma—not auxiliary or passive support, but assertive, salvific activity. Christ promised His disciples the gift of the Holy Ghost: "I will not leave you comfortless." He continued, "I will come to you."[50] Emma could do that for Joseph: come to him and comfort him. As well, when Christ suffered in Gethsemane, an angel appeared from heaven, "strengthening him."[51] Emma could be an angel, that comfort for Joseph, to reach down and wrap arms of relief around him, to cover him. As a helpmeet, she helped, protected, and rescued her husband.[52]

Seven years after their own marriage, Joseph performed three wedding ceremonies in Kirtland with Emma in attendance. Each one reveals an expanding concept of marriage and his relationship with Emma. He told Newel Knight and Lydia Goldthwaite on November 24, 1835, to "covenant to be each others companions through life," then pronounced upon them "the blessings that the Lord conferred upon adam & Eve in the garden of Eden; that is to multiply and replenish the earth, with the addition of long life and prosperity."[53] A week later, Joseph officiated at the marriage of Warren Parrish and Martha H. Raymond. He pronounced them "husband and wife in the name of God according to the articles and covenants of the church of the latter day Saints."[54] The next month, Joseph performed the marriage of John F. Boynton and Susan Lowell "after the order of heaven." He said, "I pronounced upon them the blessings of

Abraham, Isaac and Jacob, and such other blessings as the Lord put into my heart."⁵⁵ Joseph was in the process of restoring an ancient order of marriage to the institution of a restored Church. By this time, he and Emma, like Adam and Eve, had experienced enough of their lone and dreary wilderness that speaking of marriage as "an institution of h[e]aven," solemnized "by the authority of the everlasting priesthood" was a significant reminder of their own divine order.⁵⁶

Over time and through experience, Joseph came to understand ancient doctrine regarding the Abrahamic covenant. In Kirtland, Moses and Elias had appeared to Joseph and Oliver Cowdery, delivering keys or authority to gather Israel, participate in the Abrahamic covenant, and bless the seed of all generations.⁵⁷ In Nauvoo, Joseph continued to study, ask, and receive prolific revelation to expand his understanding of an eternal connection or bond extending beyond earth into heaven. On May 16, 1843, he taught Benjamin and Melissa Johnson that an everlasting covenant of marriage was required for exaltation.⁵⁸ Less than two weeks later, Emma and Joseph were sealed on May 28 in the new and everlasting covenant—eternal husband and wife.⁵⁹

At the same time, Joseph studied Elijah's keys of uniting parents and children. He learned from both Moroni, every year from 1823 until 1827, and from Elijah himself in 1836, that the hearts of children and parents would turn to each other, "lest the whole earth be smitten with a curse."⁶⁰ He and Emma both dearly loved their families and friends, those living together and those distant or dead, and Joseph was increasingly drawn to the idea of strengthening kinships. On April 2, 1843, a month before he instructed the Johnsons about the everlasting covenant of marriage, he taught: "That same sociality which exists among us here will exist among us there, only it will be coupled with eternal glory."⁶¹ Joseph believed such relationships could expand posterity as suggested in the Abrahamic covenant—as the sands of the sea and the stars in the sky. He saw this as his responsibility to seek a way in which the whole human family could be saved. An ordinance of sealing or binding allowed him to create a great family or heavenly structure—the fullness of the priesthood, in time and throughout eternity. Saints could be gathered together to create the material connections of heaven within their own community. This perspective led Joseph to restore Old Testament practices with an understanding of family and patriarchal priesthood.[62] Surely Joseph discussed and processed these ideas with Emma, his companion and partner; most likely they considered their marriage to be an eternal one—Joseph wrote to her on August 16, 1842, "Your affectionate husband untill death, through all eternity forevermore."[63] Surely Emma agreed wholeheartedly and contributed to the conversation, especially considering the distance over time and space from her own family.

Joseph's visionary concept of family developed even further with sealing through plural marriage, a term applied later. As with many other ideas, Joseph worked through scripture, personal revelation, and obedience over time in order to understand the Lord's will regarding the restoration of plural marriage and the sealing of eternal families—he developed insight and practices over time.[64] Many of the women Joseph chose were friends and acquaintances of Emma, or those who lived with their family both in Kirtland and in Nauvoo, such as Zina Huntington and Eliza R. Snow.[65] Emma was cognizant of some of them; she even selected and witnessed Joseph's sealings to Emily and Eliza Partridge and Maria and Sarah Lawrence. Both sets of sisters were orphaned and lived with the Smith family.[66] Emma may have seen it as extending their family under the Abrahamic covenant. After her acceptance of Joseph's sealings to the girls, she and Joseph were formally sealed for eternity by priesthood power.

As the sealing ordinance and practice developed over time, Emma must have experienced great confusion. Joseph's earlier revelations defined marriage between one man and one woman, and on the second floor of the Red Brick Store she had covenanted with him and to him alone to head their own house of Israel, to multiply and replenish the earth.[67] She could accept the idea of extending their family network with Joseph's sealings to other women, but at the same time, whisperings of illicit sexual activity filtered through Nauvoo. Scurrilous men took advantage of rumors and approached both married and single women, using Joseph's name and supposed consent. And then there was the idea that Joseph's sealing relationships with these other women could include sexual relations. Things changed for Emma, and she regretted accepting her husband's sealings to the young women. She understood the continuing role of revelation, but discernment was difficult. Social norms and personal feelings are hard to remove from prophetic instruction. Emma experienced deep emotional trauma due to betrayal, distrust, embarrassment, and anger.

The Lord counseled Emma in 1830 to "murmur not because of the things which thou hast not seen, for they are withheld from thee and from the world."[68] At first glance, this seems to refer to the gold plates, which she never saw. But at a later period in her life, it could have referred to her understanding of the plural marriage commandment given to Joseph. In a private conversation with Maria Jane Johnston, a young woman working and boarding at the Mansion House, Emma confessed, "The principle of plural marriage is right, but I am like other women, I am naturally jealous hearted." She admitted the need to be humble and repent.[69] One plural wife, Lucy M. Wright, recalled Joseph's demand for respect for Emma, his "first love." When any other wife complained of Emma, Joseph made a simple request: "If you desire my love you must never speak evil of Emma."[70] It is not easy to ascertain Emma's reactions, because they changed over time and there are no contemporary sources in her own words. Very few people wrote definitively and clearly about Nauvoo polygamy while it was happening, both because it was not something culturally accepted and because they had pledged to keep sacred and secret this newly revealed practice.[71]

Because of the private tension in the Smith home, on July 12, 1843, just two days after Emma's thirty-ninth birthday, her brother-in-law Hyrum Smith read to her a revelation Joseph had received from the Lord, a direct commandment about plural marriage as a restoration of Old Testament patriarchal practices.[72] The revelation promised kingdoms, principalities, and glories—even godhood—within the new and everlasting covenant. It was also a personal chastisement addressed to both Emma and Joseph. She was commanded to accept his plural wives, and he was commanded to seek her approval before taking other women, which he had not always done.[73] Emma responded with anger, refusing to acknowledge any divine hand in something that caused her so much heartache.[74]

The secrecy and redistribution of intimacy for Emma rent her heart and brought deep enmity to what had been so intimate. Joseph, on his part, had to navigate between God's command and his love for Emma.[75] The inertia forced the two to engage in serious discussions, and Emma threatened separation or divorce in August 1843, just six weeks after the revelation was read to her. William Clayton, a scribe and confidant to Joseph, recorded in his personal journal that Emma became very angry about letters found between Joseph and Eliza R. Snow. The following day, William reported that Joseph and Emma had more tense conversations.[76]

For Emma, the practice of plural marriage could be equated with an Abrahamic sacrifice. In 1833, Joseph proclaimed the Lord's word concerning the persecution of the Saints in Missouri: "They must needs be chastened and tried, even as Abraham, who was commanded to offer up his only son," that is, to lay on the altar one's deepest personal feelings or expectations.[77] While Liberty Jail was a catalyst for Joseph to experience a type of Abrahamic sacrifice, it may well be that plural marriage opened the door to Emma's personal Abrahamic sacrifice, namely her own marriage.[78] The two had been sealed for eternity, a deep, intimate bond between them, but a bond that was severely tested in unimaginable ways. Over time, Emma expressed her hope to understand: "I desire a fruitful, active mind, that I may be able to comprehend the designs of God, when revealed through His servants without doubting."[79] Somehow, sometime, before Joseph died, Emma was reconciled in her own way. Although very little is sure about Joseph's practice of plural marriage and Emma's experience, two things are certain: no children resulted from Joseph's plural wives, and Emma was pregnant with Joseph's son when he died.[80]

After Joseph's death and the migration of Brigham Young and the Saints to Utah, the issue of plural marriage continued to plague Emma. Though she never spoke of it to her children, they heard about it. It was not until 1852 in Salt Lake City that apostle Orson Pratt publicly acknowledged the practice of plural marriage, long after Emma's involvement.[81] Unfortunately, Emma never wrote about her own experience—early participants in Joseph's time vowed to keep their participation confidential. Records of interviews with Emma by visitors or by her sons allude to her inner conflict. Over time, and with no one in whom she could trust to process her thoughts, maybe she convinced herself. She told visitor Julius Chambers in her later years that "Joseph Smith never suggested or practiced polygamy." She believed Joseph was "a devoted and faithful husband."[82]

Shortly before Emma's death, Joseph III interviewed his mother, asking direct questions about the practice. Emma quickly asserted that Joseph had received no revelation on polygamy or spiritual wifery. She confirmed the rumors but affirmed that they were without foundation or doctrine. "I know that he had no other wife or wives other than myself; in any senses; either spiritual or otherwise."[83] A month later and shortly before Emma's death, in March 1879, the son of Thomas Marsh, a close friend to Joseph and Emma, visited Nauvoo. When he asked Emma if Joseph had been a polygamist, she "broke down and wept, and excused herself from answering directly." She reasoned "that her son Joseph was the leader of the Re-organized Church."[84] At that time, she deemed it more important for her to support Joseph III, whose church was partly founded on the idea that his father did not practice plural marriage. And perhaps it was important to her for the Reorganized Church to stand untarnished or without the "blemish of polygamy engrafted on Mormonism" by the stain of the Utah Saints.[85]

"Why am I a widow?"—Death of Joseph

In June 1844, many questions of civic and ecclesiastical authority things came to a head, contributing to divisions within Church membership and leadership, and the private practice of plural marriage led to dissension among many close to Joseph and Emma. Before her husband's hasty departure for Carthage, Emma described her feelings for Joseph: "I desire with all my heart to honor and respect my husband."[86]

After hearing word of his death, Emma mourned deeply. John P. Greene, the Nauvoo city marshal, came to comfort the family. She sobbed, "Why? O God! am I thus afflicted? Why am I a widow and my children orphans?" Marshal Greene assured her—perhaps unknowingly—with a phrase from her 1830 revelation, that her affliction would become a crown. Emma replied, "My husband was my crown; for him and my children I have suffered the loss of all things, and why, Oh God, am I thus deserted, and my bosom torn with this ten-fold anguish?"[87]

Somehow, in unrecorded ways, Joseph and Emma came to an understanding. They struggled over and through many things throughout their marriage—the blending of families, financial trouble, physical displacement, loss of children, persecution, and the gradual development of restoration. Plural marriage added another layer to their complicated relationship. Over time, with continued revelation, the Smiths' marriage was sanctified with unity despite separation. Years of affection, partnership, spiritual manifestations, eternal promises, and children bound the two together eternally. At the end of her life, Emma remained true to Joseph: she considered him a prophet and his work in the Restoration "a marvel and a wonder."[88] Emma's son Alexander was at her deathbed at the Riverside Mansion in Nauvoo. He heard her speak, "Joseph, Joseph, Joseph," then a few moments later, "Yes, yes, I'm coming," before she slumped back on her pillow and died.[89] Joseph came for Emma at the Susquehanna River, and he came for her again from the spirit world at her death on the Mississippi River.

Notes

1. D&C 25:15; Alexander Hale Smith, "Sermon at Bottineau, N.D.," 1 Jul. 1903, *Zion's Ensign* 14, no. 53 (Dec. 31, 1903): 7.
2. Lucy Mack Smith, History, 1845, p. 95, JSP; Larry C. Porter, *A Study of the Origins of The Church of Jesus Christ of Latter-day Saints in the States of New York and Pennsylvania*, dissertation, Brigham Young University, 1971 (Provo, UT: BYU Studies, 2000), 48.
3. Lucy Mack Smith, History, 1845, 95, JSP.
4. Richard Lyman Bushman, *Joseph Smith—Rough Stone Rolling: A Cultural Biography of Mormonism's Founder* (New York City: Knopf, 2005), 48–50.
5. Joseph Smith History, vol. A-1 [23 Dec. 1805–30 Aug. 1834], p. 8, JSP.
6. Joseph Smith History, 1834–1836, 102, JSP.

7. Joseph Smith History, 1834–1836, 10, JSP.
8. Lucy Mack Smith, History, 1845, 97, JSP.
9. Isaac Hale, "Statement of Mr. Hale," *Susquehanna Register and Northern Pennsylvanian* 9, no. 21 (1 May 1834); Joseph Smith III, "Last Testimony of Sister Emma," *The Saints' Herald* 26 (1 Oct. 1879): 289.
10. Mark Staker, "Joseph and Emma Smith's Susquehanna Home: Expanding Mormonism's First Headquarters," *Mormon Historical Studies* 16, no. 2 (Fall 2015): 85.
11. Joseph Smith, History, vol. A-1, January 1827, 8, JSP.
12. Hale, "Statement of Mr. Hale;" Mark H. Forscutt, "Commemorative Discourse on the Death of Mrs. Emma Bidamon," *The Saints' Herald* 26, no. 14 (15 Jul. 1879): 209.
13. The age of consent for males was seventeen and for females was fourteen.
14. Joseph Smith History, 1834–1836, 102, JSP. See Mark 10:8, Matthew 19:5–6, and D&C 49:16.
15. Smith, "Last Testimony of Sister Emma," 289.
16. Joseph Smith, Journal, 17, 29 Dec. 1835, 75, 92 JSP.
17. Bushman, *Joseph Smith—Rough Stone Rolling*, 299–302; Joseph Smith, Journal, 1 Jan. 1836, 94–96, JSP.
18. Linda King Newell and Valeen Tippetts Avery, *Mormon Enigma, Emma Hale Smith* (Urbana: University of Illinois Press, 1994), 215.
19. Mary Bailey Norman to Ina Coolbrith, 27 Mar. 1908, CCLA.
20. Julia M. Dixon to Emma Smith Bidamon, 25 Mar. 1852, Lewis C. Bidamon papers, CCLA; Joseph Smith III to Emma Knight, 16 May 1856, CCLA.
21. Emma Smith Bidamon to Joseph Smith III, 2 Dec. 1867, CCLA.
22. D&C 25:6.
23. Lucy wrote, "I set myself to work to put my house in order." She continued, "I felt all that pride and ambition in doing so, that is common to mothers upon such occasions." Lucy Mack Smith, History, 1845, 97; see also Lucy Mack Smith, History, 1844–1845, 1–4, JSP.
24. Hale, "Statement of Mr. Hale," [1].
25. Joseph Knight, Sr., Reminiscence, circa 1835–1837, "Manuscript of the History of Joseph Smith," CHL.
26. Staker, "Joseph and Emma Smith's Susquehanna Home," 73–78, 89.
27. Joseph Smith, Journal, Book 3, 31 Aug. 1843, 80, JSP.
28. Joseph Smith to Emma Smith, 4 Nov. 1838, CCLA, JSP.

29. Joseph Smith, History, vol. A-1, 25–26 May 1832, 205–7, JSP.
30. Joseph Smith, History, vol. B-1, 849, JSP.
31. Joseph Smith to Emma Smith, 4 Nov. 1838, CCLA, JSP.
32. Emma Hale Smith to Joseph Smith, 7 Mar. 1839, JSP.
33. Joseph Smith to Emma Smith, 9 Nov. 1839, CCLA, JSP.
34. Emma Smith to Joseph Smith, 6 Dec. 1839, JSP.
35. See for example, Joseph Smith, History, vol. D-1, 8–9 Jun. 1843, 1571; Joseph Smith, Journal, Book 3, Dec. 1843, 186; Joseph Smith, Journal, Book 4, 137, JSP.
36. See Joseph Smith, Journal, 1 Nov. 1842; 14 Jan. 1843, 244, JSP.
37. Joseph Smith to Emma Smith, 4 Nov. 1838, CCLA, JSP; Joseph Smith to Emma Smith, 9 Nov. 1839, CCLA; Joseph Smith to Emma Smith, 4 Nov. 1838, CCLA; Joseph Smith to Emma Smith, 16 Aug. 1842, Book of the Law of the Lord, 173; Joseph Smith to Emma Smith, 4 Apr. 1839, Beinecke Rare Book and Manuscript Library; Joseph Smith to Emma Smith, 13 Oct. 1832, CCLA, JSP.
38. Emma Smith to Joseph Smith, 16 Aug. 1842, Book of the Law of the Lord, 175; Emma Smith to Joseph Smith, 3 May 1837, Joseph Smith, Letterbook 2, 35; Emma Smith to Joseph Smith, 6 Dec. 1839, Charles Aldrich Autograph Collection, State Historical Society of IA, Des Moines, IA; JSP.
39. Joseph Smith to Emma Smith, 13 Oct. 1832, CCLA; JSP.
40. Emma Smith to Joseph Smith, 25 Apr. 1835, Joseph Smith Letter Book, 35, JSP.
41. Emma Smith to Joseph Smith, 3 May 1835, Joseph Smith Letter Book, 35–36; JSP.
42. Joseph Smith to Emma Smith, 4 Nov. 1838, CCLA, JSP.
43. Joseph Smith to Emma Smith, 12 Nov. 1838, CCLA; JSP.
44. Joseph Smith to Emma Smith, 4 Apr. 1839, Beinecke Rare Book and Manuscript Library, Yale University, New Haven, CT; JSP.
45. Emma Smith to Joseph Smith, 16 Aug. 1842, JSP.
46. Joseph Smith, History, vol. D-1, 1372, JSP.
47. Joseph Smith to Emma Smith, 16 Aug. 1842, Book of the Law of the Lord, 173–75, JSP.
48. D&C 25:5, 6, 9, 14.
49. "Comfort," Noah Webster, *American Dictionary of the English Language* (1828).
50. John 14:18.

51. Luke 22:43.
52. See Angela Ashurst-McGee, "'Help Meet': Women's Power to Serve," *Ensign*, Sept. 2020, 29–31.
53. Joseph Smith, Journal, 24 Nov. 1835, 49, JSP.
54. Joseph Smith Journal, 3 Dec. 1835, 55, JSP.
55. Joseph Smith, Journal, 20 Jan. 1836, 132–33, JSP.
56. Joseph Smith, Journal, 24 Nov. 1835, 49, JSP.
57. D&C 110:11–12.
58. William Clayton, journal, May 16, 1843, in *An Intimate Chronicle: The Journals of William Clayton*, ed. George D. Smith (Salt Lake City: Signature Books, 1995), 102; see also D&C 131:1–4.
59. Joseph Smith, Journal, 28 May 1843, JSP.
60. D&C 110:14–16; Malachi 4:5–6; Joseph Smith—History, 1:38–39; D&C 27:9–10.
61. D&C 130:2.
62. Jonathan Stapley, *The Power of Godliness: Mormon Liturgy and Cosmology* (New York City: Oxford University Press, 2018), 37–38, 40–41; Danel W. Bachman, "A Study of the Mormon Practice of Plural Marriage Before the Death of Joseph Smith," thesis, Purdue University, 1975, 94.
63. Joseph Smith to Emma Smith, 16 Aug. 1842, in Book of the Law of the Lord, 173–5, CHL. William W. Phelps wrote several letters to his wife, Sally Waterman Phelps, describing Joseph Smith's teachings on eternal marriage in 1835. See "Writing to Zion: The William W. Phelps Kirtland Letters (1835–1836)," ed. Bruce A. Van Orden, *BYU Studies* 33, no. 3 (1993): 542–94.
64. See "Plural Marriage in the Church of Jesus Christ of Latter-day Saints" and "Plural Marriage in Kirtland and Nauvoo," GTE.
65. Many historians have compiled lists of Joseph Smith's wives, including a comprehensive study by Brian and Laura Hales at https://josephsmithspolygamy.org.
66. Emily Dow Partridge, "Incidents," Dec. 1876, 4–5, UofU. See Brian Hales, https://josephsmithspolygamy.org.
67. See D&C 42:22 and D&C 49:16, both revealed in 1831.
68. D&C 25:4.
69. Maria Jane Johnston Woodward, statement, Joseph F. Smith, Correspondence, CHL.
70. Lucy M. Wright, "Emma Hale Smith," *WE* 30, no. 8 (Christmas 1901): 59.

71. "Plural Marriage in Kirtland and Nauvoo."
72. Emily Partridge Young, Diary and Reminiscences, 1874–1899, 7, CHL; Emily Partridge Young, "Incidents of the Early Life of a Mormon Girl," CHL; William Clayton, Journal 2, 23 Jun. 1843, in *An Intimate Chronicle*, 108. See Bushman, *Joseph Smith—Rough Stone Rolling*, 495–96. See also D&C 132:40, 45.
73. D&C 132:19–20, 26–27, 51–56, 61, 64.
74. See Newell and Avery, *Mormon Enigma*, 151–56; Bachman, "A Study of the Mormon Practice of Plural Marriage," 205–6.
75. See Bushman, *Joseph Smith, Rough Stone Rolling*, 458–81.
76. Clayton, 16, 21–23 Aug. 1843, *An Intimate Chronicle*, 117–18.
77. D&C 101:4.
78. See D&C 121–123; Jeffrey R. Holland, "Lessons from Liberty Jail," Sept. 7, 2008, Brigham Young University devotional, https://speeches.byu.edu; Valerie Hudson, "A Reconciliation of Polygamy," FairMormon Conference, 2011, https://fairmormon.org.
79. Emma Smith, blessing, 1844, CHL.
80. Brian Hales, "Did Plural Marriages Include Sexual Relations?" *Joseph Smith's Polygamy*, https://josephsmithspolygamy.org.
81. Orson Pratt, discourse, 29 Aug. 1852, *Deseret News*, Extra ,14–20.
82. Julius Chambers, *The Mississippi River and Its Wonderful Valley* (New York: G.P. Putnam's Sons, 1910), 183, 187–88.
83. Interview between Joseph Smith III and Emma Bidamon, handwritten notes, CCLA.
84. Lorenzo Snow to Francis M. Lyman, 10 Aug. 1901, Correspondence to the First Presidency, v. 36, CHL.
85. Chambers, *The Mississippi*, 183, 187–88.
86. Emma Smith, blessing, 1844, CHL.
87. "The Prophet's Death!," *Deseret Evening News*, 27 Nov. 1875. See chapter 10.
88. "Last Testimony of Sister Emma," 289.
89. Alexander Hale Smith, "Sermon," 7.

Chapter 3

FIRST MOTHER OF THE LATTER DAYS

Emma and All Her Children

Eve was the "mother of all living;" Mary was the mother of Christ; and Brigham Young titled Lucy Mack Smith "a mother in Israel." Emma is probably most often known as the "elect lady."[1] But when John Taylor set apart Emma as president of the Nauvoo Relief Society on March 17, 1842, he "blessed her, and confirm'd upon her all the blessings which have been confer'd on her, that she might be a mother in Israel."[2] Like Lucy, Emma certainly was a mother in Israel, fiercely devoted to her own children and to others she welcomed into her home—perhaps to all Saints of this dispensation.[3]

Emma had great examples of motherhood: her mother taught her vital domestic and nursing skills, and her mother-in-law demonstrated a strong sense of love and support in her sons and daughters and their families. Emma and Joseph loved their children, rejoiced with them, and grieved over them. When Emma received her patriarchal blessing in 1834 from her father-in-law, she had lost four babies and had a two-year-old—Joseph III, and a three-year-old—Julia Murdock. Joseph Smith Sr. must have recognized the sorrow she had borne over lost children. Perhaps she wondered if her body was even capable of carrying and delivering a healthy baby. Through the blessing, the Lord told her that she should not blame herself. Rather, the Lord acknowledged her "pure desires to raise up a family," and that she would, in fact, "bring forth other children, to the joy and satisfaction of [her] soul."[4]

Emma lived in a period of high infant mortality rates.[5] Over sixteen years, she delivered nine babies and adopted two. One was stillborn. Three died shortly after birth. An adopted son died at eleven months. Another son died at fourteen months. One adult son died at the age of twenty-six. One was committed to a mental institution. Only four of them outlived their mother. She buried six babies and one adult child. As Emma multiplied and replenished the earth, she found both joy and anguish in her posterity, and she expanded her family well beyond the blood lines to include many who needed her love and care as much as she needed them.

"Pure desires to raise up a family"—Emma's Joys and Afflictions

When Joseph and Emma left Manchester, New York, in December 1827, nearly a year after their marriage, she had begun her first pregnancy—one that proved extremely difficult. Perhaps she sought respite and care from her own mother in Harmony. Emma scribed for Joseph's Book of Mormon translation, but due to her advancing pregnancy, she passed her duties to Martin Harris, who was in Pennsylvania from April to June 1828.[6] Emma delivered her first baby on June 15, just a day after Martin's departure with the first section of the Book of Mormon manuscript.[7] The unnamed baby boy died soon after birth, and Emma struggled to recover, physically and emotionally.[8] Lucy Smith reported that "for two weeks Joseph slept not an hour in undisturbed quiet" until Emma felt better.[9] Their son was buried nearby in the McKune family cemetery, just thirty feet from where his Hale grandparents would be laid to rest.[10]

Following time in Harmony and Fayette, when Emma and Joseph arrived in Kirtland in early 1831, she was again pregnant. Lucy wrote that despite Emma's delicate health at the time, she remained active and "whatever her hands found to do, she did with her might." Her hard work exhausted her so much "that she brought upon herself a heavy fit of sickness, which lasted for weeks."[11] In April, the Smiths lived in a small frame home on the Morley farm, where at the end of the month, Emma endured another difficult labor. Joseph became frightened and sent for a doctor in nearby Willoughby, Ohio.[12] Twin babies survived about three hours and were probably buried somewhere on the Morley farm—yet another devastation for Emma and Joseph.

The next day, May 1, 1831, about twenty miles away in Orange, Ohio, Julia Clapp Murdock died after delivering twins, leaving her husband John with five small children. Overwhelmed, John Murdock did not want his in-laws to help raise the children, as they staunchly opposed the Church.[13] According to Emma, Joseph Murdock asked her to raise the twin babies, a blessing for both the Murdocks and the Smiths.[14] By May 8, shortly after arriving in Kirtland from New York, Lucy Mack Smith was delighted to meet her new adopted grandchildren, Joseph Murdock Smith and Julia Murdock Smith.[15]

Emma did everything she could to make the Murdock-Smith twins part of her family. She asked John to not make himself known to his birth children. "It was a hard request," Murdock wrote. "She wanted to bring the children up as her own and never have them know anything to the contrary, that they might be perfectly happy with her as their Mother."[16] Four months later, in September, Joseph and Emma moved with the twins to John and Elsa Johnson's farm in Hiram, Ohio, where Joseph worked with Sidney Rigdon on a new translation of the Bible. Again, the Smiths lived on the generosity of friends.

In March 1832, the babies, less than a year old, contracted measles. Baby Joseph was exposed to the cold night air when a mob broke into the home on March 24 and dragged his father outside. Emma and Elsa Johnson nursed both the sick babies and their injured father. Joseph Murdock Smith never recovered; he died on Thursday, March 29. The family sat with the dead child all night in the Johnsons' formal parlor, then buried him the same day Joseph departed for Independence, Missouri.[17] This time Joseph was gone until September. Meanwhile, Julia and her pregnant mother returned to Kirtland. Emma seemed destined to birth, raise, and lose her children, often on her own as Joseph attended to Church responsibilities. She had been warned of the high priority his prophetic role would take in their family: the Church was "his calling."[18]

In September 1832, Joseph moved his little family to the apartment over the Whitney store. During her third pregnancy, Emma had her friend Elizabeth Ann Whitney close by. In October, Joseph went east with Newel, Elizabeth Ann's husband, to New York City so that Newel could purchase goods for his store. After walking the streets of the large city (then around 200,000 inhabitants), Joseph wrote a letter to Emma, stating, "The thoughts of home, of Emma and Julia, rushes upon my mind like a flood and I could wish for a moment to be with them. My Breast is filled with all the feelings and tenderness of a parent and a Husband."[19] He returned on November 6, just a few hours after Emma had given birth to a son whom they named Joseph III.

By early 1833, Emma had a newborn (Joseph III) and a toddler (Julia) when Joseph conducted the School of the Prophets in Kirtland. Joseph invited John Murdock, Julia's birth father, to live with them.[20] Following Emma's request, John did not interact with her as her father. Julia remembered having a happy childhood until around age five, when she learned from another young girl that she had been adopted. "From that hour on," she wrote, "I was changed. I was bitter even as a child. O how it stund me when persons have inquired, 'Is that your adopted daughter?' of my foster mother."[21] And yet Julia loved her mother Emma. She remembered that Emma had been "more than a mother to me and loves me as one of her one."[22] Joseph had great admiration and high hopes for Julia; he wrote to Emma in November 1838 about their daughter. "Julia is a lovely little girl, I love her." He continued, "She is a promising child, tell her Father wants her to remember him and be a good girl."[23] Later in Nauvoo, Joseph enjoyed riding out of the city to their farm with Julia, just as he did with Emma.[24]

A period of rapid Church growth occurred over the next couple of years in Kirtland. On June 20, 1836, Emma gave birth to a third son, Frederick Granger Williams Smith, named after his father's counselor and friend, and the man who owned the press that printed Emma's hymns around that time. Joseph was home for this birth, but he left five days later to travel to Boston and New York to seek funds for the recently dedicated Kirtland Temple.[25] Emma cared for Julia, Joseph III, and Frederick in Kirtland while Joseph traveled. The single-parent strain was real. She wrote Joseph in April 1837: "The children feel very anxious about you because they dont know where you have gone."[26] Emma probably felt anxious, too.[27]

Emma provided for her children by taking in boarders, including a "Brother Baldwin" who contracted the measles in May 1837. She wrote to Joseph that the situation "makes much confusion and trouble for me, and is also a subject of much fear and anxiety unto me"— understandable, given baby Joseph Murdock's death from the disease in 1832. Neither Joseph III nor Frederick had been exposed to the illness. Emma continued, "I wish it could be possible for you to be at home when they are sick." It was a heavy burden. She pleaded with Joseph: "You must remember them for they all remember you, and I could hardly pacify Julia and Joseph when they found ou[t] you was not coming home soon."[28] Emma did the best she could in each situation, but the burden of both raising the children and supporting the family continued to fall on her. An absence of husband and father continued to be the pattern for her and the children.

During the spring and summer of 1837, Joseph traveled around Ohio in attempts to salvage financial loss. He then went to Toronto and to Missouri in the fall. After visiting Far West, Missouri, in November 1837, Joseph decided to move his family there, away from the increasing persecutions due to the failed Kirtland Safety Society. In January 1838, he and Sidney Rigdon left in the middle of the night, and three days later, Emma and the children, along with the Rigdon family, departed to join them in New Portage, Ohio, having left most of their worldly possessions behind.[29] The Smiths and Rigdons found the Salt River in Missouri frozen solid; pregnant Emma carefully walked across the ice.[30] After arriving in Far West, Joseph left again to care for Church settlements throughout Missouri. On June 1, having received word of Emma's impending delivery, he returned to Far West, where Emma delivered a baby boy the following day. Alexander Hale Smith was named after Alexander W. Doniphan—an attorney employed by the Church during the 1833 expulsion from Jackson County, Missouri, who later prevented the execution of Joseph in November 1838.[31] Joseph returned to Adam-ondi-Ahman three days after the birth, on June 4.[32] Alexander's early life was rocked with persecution. Five months after the baby's birth, Joseph was imprisoned, and Emma was left to fend for herself and her four young children under the age of eight at a dangerous time of uncertainty and ill treatment by Missourians. Joseph wrote Emma, "Those little children are subjects of my meditation continually.

Tell them that Father is yet alive, God grant that he may see them again."[33]

In February 1839, Missouri governor Lilburn W. Boggs issued an extermination order to the Saints, and Emma and the children fled Missouri for safer ground in Illinois. Joseph III, age seven, recalled the cold weather and the family's precarious position on the frozen Mississippi River. As they walked across the river, Joseph III later wrote: "Carrying in her arms my brothers Frederick and Alexander, . . . with my sister Julia, and myself holding onto her dress at either side, my mother walked across the frozen river."[34] Such incidents seared a powerful memory of Emma into her young children; she did what she could to protect them, albeit often on her own.

While Joseph was in Liberty Jail from December 1838 to April 1839, Emma again relied on the hospitality of friends, this time with the Cleveland family in Quincy, Illinois. Facing parenthood and personal struggles alone, Emma sought light amidst Julia's tantrums and Frederick's illness, writing to Joseph on March 7, 1839, "Little Alexander who is now in my arms is one of the finest little fellows, you ever saw in your life, he is so strong that with the assistance of a chair he will run all around the room."[35] Joseph recognized his wife's efforts. From Liberty in April 1839, he wrote concerning their children: "My Dear Emma there is great responsibility resting upon you, in preserving yourself in honor and sobriety before them." He viewed Emma as a parent who, because of her own character and experience, could teach their sons and daughter "to form their young and tender minds, that they begin in right paths."[36] Joseph trusted his wife to nurture their children. He loved that she loved them and that she sensed her responsibility as their mother.

Joseph joined his family in Quincy later in April, and they moved to an old homestead in Commerce, where they would build the city of Nauvoo. Again, as before, Joseph traveled extensively. On October

29, 1839, he and other Church delegates departed for Washington, DC, to seek redress and reparations from property loss in Missouri, returning at the end of February 1840. Before he left, three-year-old Frederick became ill with malaria. The worried father wrote Emma about his anxiety for the children, particularly Frederick: "It was so painful to leave him sick I hope you will watch over those tender offspring."[37] Well-trained by her mother in natural medicine, Emma was able to break his fever, though Joseph III also caught the disease.[38]

The tyranny of Missouri never left the Smiths. Joseph III was clearly aware of the constant threat of violence; in Nauvoo, he remembered living in such a manner that quick escapes were built into their homes to protect his father. In the old homestead, between the original structure and an addition in back, a hidden cellar was constructed under the breezeway. He recalled how his father hid in the space a few times. Another time, Emma coolly met some assailants at the front door while Joseph quietly hid in the cellar. Later, after the family moved into the Mansion House in 1842, Joseph III remembered the careful construction of a room hidden between a closet and the chimney.[39] Separation and reunion became a normal part of the Smith family's lives, and these patterns and fear of mortal danger and or imprisonment surely influenced the psyches of both Emma and her children.

On June 13, 1840, Emma gave birth to a fifth son, Don Carlos Smith, named after his uncle, Joseph's younger brother. Unfortunately, due to the swampy environment, malaria was a significant issue. Uncle Don Carlos succumbed to respiratory issues in August 1841, and little Don Carlos died eight days later. The Nauvoo *Times and Seasons* recorded the death: "Died—In this city, on the 15th ultimo, Don Carlos infant son of Joseph and Emma Smith, aged 14 months and 2 days—Like the bud of a beautiful flower, ere it had time to expand twas cut down, but it rests in peace."[40] Emma was in her seventh pregnancy at the time.

The winter of 1841–42 was busy. In December, Emma assisted Joseph in unpacking loads of goods for their new store, which opened in early January. At the end of the month, he asked her for help in the office, and on February 6, Emma delivered a stillborn baby. With Don Carlos, Emma buried two babies in just five months, and Joseph lay sick in bed on February 10.[41] Two weeks later, Emma's mother, Elizabeth Hale, passed away. And three weeks after that, Emma became president of the Female Relief Society of Nauvoo. Within six months, she lost two sons and gained a new identity as Elect Lady, leader of the women in the Church. She had a people to care for, physically and spiritually. Emma's progeny expanded even as it contracted.

"Why are my children orphans?"—Loss of Husband and Father

Even through the complications of polygamy, the continual threat of extradition back to Missouri, and the mounting persecution against Joseph from his closest associates, Emma and Joseph continued to expand their own family. In early 1844 Emma became pregnant again. Joseph was killed on June 27; David Hyrum Smith was born on November 18.

The tragedy of the death of a father was palpable for the Smiths. One observer noted the children mourning: "Julia and Joseph were on the floor with Alexander and Frederick, leaning over them, mingling their grief in one wild scream of childish despair."[42] Due to contemporary state laws, as a woman, Emma had to take legal action to gain custody of her own children.[43] She lived in fear of continued violence, so the children slept near her room so she could protect

Emma Smith with son David Hyrum. Photograph, unknown photographer, 1845. Courtesy Community of Christ Library-Archives, Independence, Missouri.

them, but perhaps it was they who could protect her.[44] Always a believer in God, she taught them to pray. David poetically wrote: "Remember how she taught us five / In faithfulness to pray / That God would guard us through the night / And watch us through the day."[45] Emma relied on God as her children grew. She wrote Joseph III in 1867, "If there is any thing in this world that I am, or ever was proud of it is the honor and integrity of my children but I dare not allow myself to be proud, as I believe that pride is one of the sins so often reproved in the good book. So I am enjoying the better spirit, and that is to be truly and cinserely thankfull and in humility give God the glory, not trying to take any of it to myself for it is him that has led my children in the better way."[46]

"Sister Emma was like a mother"—Emma's Other Children

While raising her own children, Emma welcomed other young people to live in her home, mothering them as they helped her in the Smith home. Zina Huntington lived with the Smiths for three months in 1839–40 after her mother died of malaria. Emma nursed the sick eighteen-year-old and her siblings back to health. "Sister Emma was like a mother," Zina remembered.[47] Twenty-year-old Eliza and sixteen-year-old Emily Partridge lived in the Smith home after their father, Bishop Edward Partridge, died unexpectedly in 1840. Joseph Smith was appointed guardian for the Edward Lawrence family after their father died in 1841, and Maria and Sarah joined the Smith household.[48] In 1842, sixteen-year-old Lucy Walker's mother died, leaving her father with ten children. Joseph and Emma took in the four oldest, and Lucy remembered how they introduced the girls as their adopted daughters.[49] These young women, as well as others who lived in the Smith household at different times, were sealed to Joseph as plural wives—perhaps in an effort to extend the Smith family and include them in an eternal family.

After Joseph's death, Emma continued to care for young people as she welcomed many into her home. She opened her doors to Elizabeth Kendall, a young orphaned English girl who later married Emma's son Alexander.[50] When Emma married Lewis Bidamon in 1847, she received his daughters, thirteen-year-old Zerelda and eleven-year-old Mary Elizabeth, into her home.[51] Later, in the summer of 1860, Emma took in then-adult Mary Elizabeth Gibson and her eight-year-old son Charles, as well as another Bidamon relative, Rosanna.[52] While married to Emma, Lewis had an affair with Nancy Abercrombie, a local young woman, who gave birth to Charles Bidamon on March 16, 1861. When Charles was four years old, Nancy had no means to raise the boy, so Emma brought him into her home and raised him. As an adult, Charles remembered Emma's even temper and her kind demeanor. "She had a queenly bearing, without the arrogance of a queen." He continued, she was "a noble woman, living and showing a charity for all, loving and beloved."[53] Later Emma hired his mother Nancy to work and board in her home. Before she died, Emma called Lewis and Nancy to her bedside and had them promise her that they would marry each other, thus making Charles a legitimate child.[54] Perhaps this was one way that Emma demonstrated her understanding of the expansion of family, possibly even polygamy.

"Not large enough to take all I would like to send"— Adult Children and Grandchildren

In her later years, Emma did everything she could to care for her children as they grew up. She had much to say in a letter to Joseph III, but not enough room to write it all: "This sheet is longer than a gnats wing but not large enough to take all I would like to send."[55] She assertively protected family finances and properties in order to preserve her family, and stood up to men seeking to protect the Church, its property, and its finances over the well-being of her family.[56] As her sons and daughter grew into adulthood, Emma maintained strong relationships with them, both through correspondence and in person. She loved them, their spouses, and her grandchildren. She mirrored the warm, accepting tone she had seen with her own in-laws, the Smiths. Emma lived for her family, admitting loneliness when they were not around. She wrote to Joseph III in 1868, "If kind Heaven lets my children, or some of them live either with me or near me I shall begin to see some of the good I am living for."[57] Each one relished time with her and cared for her as she aged. And she had a distinct relationship with each of them, children and grandchildren.

Nauvoo drew Julia back again and again. Like her own parents had done, Emma initially disapproved of seventeen-year-old Julia's first marriage.[58] When Julia became a widow in her early twenties, she returned to her mother in Nauvoo. In 1856, Julia married John Middleton and was baptized into the Catholic church in 1857.[59] After twenty years of abuse and finally abandonment, Julia moved back to Nauvoo in 1877. She and her brothers Joseph III and Alexander were with Emma when their mother died in 1879. A year later, Julia died of breast cancer at age forty-nine on September 12, 1880. Her obituary stated that she "was an advocate of all the graces and virtues and had a strong loving disposition." Like her mother, Julia was "considerably above the medium of intelligence and of an indomitable spirit."[60]

Joseph III was elected president of the Reorganized Church of Jesus Christ of Latter Day Saints (RLDS, now Community of Christ) on April 6, 1860, the thirtieth anniversary of the day his father founded the Church in Fayette, New York, at the Whitmer farm. Joseph III vehemently preached against plural marriage, both in Utah as an RLDS missionary, and to his church membership in the Midwest. But when his first wife Emmeline (or Emma) died young, and then his second wife Bertha died as well, he married a third wife—Ada. Emma loved each daughter-in-law. In 1867, she wrote Joseph III: "Tell Emma and the childrens Thare not forgotten then hug a thousand times. So good night to you all God bless my dear children."[61] She wrote Joseph III in 1871, "How I would like to just call into your house every day or two as I do into Alex and David and see Bertha and the Children." She finished her letter, "Give my love to her and the little ones and hugs God bless you all."[62] Altogether Joseph III was the father of seventeen children. His oldest daughter, Emma's first grandchild, was also named Emma. She lived with her grandmother for a few years in Nauvoo and remembered the cookies and doughnuts always on hand.[63]

Frederick grew up with a love for nature. As teenagers, he and Alex would explore the nearby woods when they were done with farm work.[64] He lived in Nauvoo for many years as a merchant and a farmer; he and Joseph III farmed on land east of Nauvoo. In 1856, a man visiting the Smith family noted that even as a six-foot-tall man, Frederick was "very affectionate to his mother, and often saluted her with a loving kiss." He continued, "Everybody loved him."[65] Fred's niece, Vida E. Smith, noted his "generous nature," that he was "the merriest heart of all the merry household."[66] He married Anna Marie Jones in 1857, and they had one daughter, born in Nauvoo in 1858. The family moved to the Smith farm outside Nauvoo, where Frederick became very ill. Joseph III stopped by the farmhouse and found him in a dangerous state, probably tuberculosis, his wife and daughter having returned to Nauvoo without him. Joseph III took Fred to the Mansion House where Emma nursed him—just as she had when he was young—until his death in April 1862, at nearly twenty-six years old.[67] Frederick's younger brother David wrote a memorial poem, indicating the effect his death had on Emma: "Then weep, mother weep, and bow thy head, / O'er the corpse so still and white; / Yes, give to thy grief a little sway, / E're they bear him from thy sight."[68] Emma had buried her fifth child.

Alexander married Elizabeth Kendall; they had four sons and five daughters. He was a skilled wrestler, hunter, and marksman. He went on a mission to Utah as a representative of the RLDS church and left his pregnant wife and two children with Emma in Nauvoo. Later, Alex and his family stayed close to Nauvoo, and Emma loved being near her grandchildren. In a letter to his older brother, Joseph III, Emma wrote, "I have been very lonely since Alex folks left here, but I am comforting myself with the idea that they will come back in the spring. I should have been thankfull indeed if they could have stayed here and not went to teach at all but so it is, I cannot have my will always."[69] Alexander served as an apostle and counselor in the RLDS church and spent the last years of his life as its presiding patriarch, a calling held by his grandfather, Joseph Smith Sr., and his uncle, Hyrum Smith. He died in the Nauvoo Mansion House in 1901.[70]

David Hyrum Smith, born six months after the death of his father, became a preacher, hymn writer, poet, and artist. He married Clara Hartborn in 1870, and their only child was born in 1871 in the Mansion House in Nauvoo. David served in the presidency of the RLDS church but suffered from debilitating mental health, including psychotic episodes, perhaps as a result of the trauma experienced in utero when his father died and his mother mourned and strained to care for the family. He desperately wanted to explain his "infirmities of flesh and spirit," he wrote to his brother Joseph III. "My talk is astounding to myself and I marvel whence it cometh." He continued, "It proceeds not from my heart nor is it David that speaks thus."[71] He wrote to his mother, "If ever I have added a sorrow to your heart, it has been doubly troubled mine." He continued, "Dear Mother, remember me as if I had been all to you I might have been."[72] After a relapse in the late summer of 1874, he returned to Nauvoo, where Emma, age seventy, again cared for her thirty-year-old son. She confided in Junius Wells, who visited her from Salt Lake City, that "David's imbecility was her greatest trouble," and considered his frequent missions to Salt Lake City the cause of his mental illness.[73] David's moments of clarity decreased.[74] On January 10, 1877, he was committed to the Illinois Hospital for the Insane in Elgin, where he remained until his death on August 29, 1904.[75] Emma's inability to nurse her son back to health broke her heart.

Even when her children and grandchildren were not close by, their thoughtful correspondence meant everything to Emma. "I do not know that any one really envies me the satisfaction I enjoy in receiving so many such kind good letters," she wrote to Joseph III in 1867. "One thing I do know that there is a great many parents that would be proud if not thankfull of their Children, and grand children had the affection, and talent to write to them, as mine have does to me." She then referred to a recent letter from her oldest granddaughter: that "new year letter that Emma sent me is a gem. I shall preserve it as long as I live."[76]

Shortly before Emma's death, she had a noteworthy dream, recorded by her nurse. Her husband Joseph appeared and took her to a beautiful mansion. There she found a nursery with a baby—Don Carlos. She excitedly took him up in her arms and asked Joseph about the others. He told her that she would have them, all of them.[77] And they would have them together. This would be compensation for a lifetime of loss, grief, separation—a glorious reunion.

Notes

1. Genesis 3:20; Lucy Mack Smith, General Conference, 8 Oct. 1845, Historian's Office, General Church Minutes, 6–8 Oct. 1845, pp. 7–13, CHL; see Jennifer Reeder and Kate Holbrook, *At the Pulpit: 185 Years of Discourses of Latter-day Saint Women* (Salt Lake City: Church Historian's Press, 2017), 23; see churchhistorianspress.org.
2. Nauvoo Relief Society Minutes, 17 Mar. 1842, 9, *FFYRS*, 32–33.
3. On the historical use of "Mother in Israel," see Carol Cornwall Madsen,

"Mothers in Israel: Sarah's Legacy," in *Women of Wisdom and Knowledge: Talks Selected from the BYU Women's Conferences*, ed. Marie Cornwall and Susan Howe (Salt Lake City: Deseret Book, 1990), 179–201.
4. Joseph Smith Sr., blessing, to Emma Smith, 9 Dec. 1834, Patriarchal Blessing Book 1, 4–5, JSP.
5. Infant mortality rates were 51.4% in 1830 and 48.3% in 1840. Michael R. Haines, "The Relationship Between Infant and Child Mortality and Fertility: Some Historical and Contemporary Evidence for the United States," in *From Death to Birth: Mortality Decline and Reproductive Change*, ed. Mark R. Montgomery and Barney Cohen (Washington DC: National Academy Press, 1998), 232.
6. Joseph Smith, History, vol. A-1, 9, JSP.
7. It is often assumed that this was 116 pages, but recent research questions the actual number of pages. See Michael Hubbard McKay and Gerrit J. Dirkmatt, *From Darkness unto Light* (Provo, UT: Religious Studies Center, Brigham Young University and Salt Lake City: Deseret Book, 2015), 101–2, fn46.
8. A relative wrote the name "Alvin" in the Smith family Bible to identify the baby, but the gravestone on the Hale family property in Harmony, Pennsylvania, simply reads "In Memory of an Infant Son of Joseph and Emma Smith," and Emma later confirmed that the infant was never named. See "Joseph and Emma Hale Smith Family," CHTE.
9. Lucy Mack Smith, History, 1845, 127, JSP.
10. Larry C. Porter, *A Study of the Origins of The Church of Jesus Christ of Latter-day Saints in the States of New York and Pennsylvania*, dissertation, Brigham Young University, 1971 (Provo, UT: BYU Studies, 2000), 55.
11. Lucy Mack Smith, History, 1845, 190, JSP.
12. Mark L. Staker, *Hearken, O Ye People: The Historical Setting of Joseph Smith's Ohio Revelations* (Salt Lake City: Kofford, 2009), 309.
13. John Murdock, autobiography, circa 1858, 104, CHL.
14. Joseph Smith III, "Last Testimony of Sister Emma," *The Saints' Herald* 26, no. 19 (1 Oct. 1879): 289. John Murdock remembered that Joseph approached him about adopting the twins. Murdock, 104.
15. Lucy Mack Smith, History, 1845, 206, JSP.
16. Murdock, 104.
17. Joseph Smith, History, vol. A-1, 205–9, JSP. Staker, *Hearken, O Ye People*, 354–55.

18. D&C 25:6, 9.
19. Joseph Smith to Emma Smith, 13 Oct. 1832, CCLA, JSP.
20. Joseph Smith, Minute Book 1, 22–23 Jan. 1833, JSP.
21. Julia M. Middleton to John R. Murdock, 2 Nov. 1858, in Murdock, 99–100.
22. Julia Murdock Middleton to John Riggs Murdock, 2 Nov. 1858, cited in the journal of John Murdock, BYU.
23. Joseph Smith to Emma Smith, 12 Nov. 1838, CCLA; JSP.
24. Joseph Smith, History, vol. E-1, 21 July 1843, 1679, JSP.
25. Oliver Cowdery to Warren Cowdery, 4 Aug. 1836, in *LDS Messenger and Advocate* 2 (Sept. 1836): 373.
26. Emma Smith to Joseph Smith, 25 Apr. 1837, JSP.
27. Emma Hale Smith to Joseph Smith, 3 May 1837, JSP.
28. Emma Smith to Joseph Smith, 3 May 1837, in JS Letterbook 2, 36, JSP.
29. Joseph Smith, History, vol. B-1, 780, JSP.
30. Linda King Newell and Valeen Tippetts Avery, *Mormon Enigma: Emma Hale Smith* (Urbana, IL: University of Illinois Press, 1994), 70.
31. Gregory Maynard, "Alexander William Doniphan: Man of Justice," *BYU Studies* 13, no. 4 (Oct. 1973): 463–67.
32. Joseph Smith, Journal, 1 June, 4 Jun. 1838, 45–46, JSP.
33. Joseph Smith to Emma Smith, 4 Nov. 1838, CCLA, JSP.
34. Mary Audentia Smith Anderson, "The Memoirs of President Joseph Smith (1832–1914)," *The Saints' Herald* (6 Nov. 1934): 1416.
35. Anderson, "Memoirs," 1416, Emma Smith to Joseph Smith, 7 March 1839, copied into Joseph Smith, Letterbook 2, 37, JSP.
36. Joseph Smith to Emma Smith, 4 Apr. 1839, Beinecke Rare Book and Manuscript Library, Yale University, New Haven, CT; see JSP.
37. Joseph Smith, History Draft, 30, JSP. See John Smith, Journal (1836–1840), 20 Feb. 1840, 58, CHL.
38. Emma Smith to Joseph Smith, 6 Dec. 1839, Charles Aldrich Autograph Collection, State Historical Society of Iowa, Des Moines, IA; see JSP.
39. Anderson, *Memoirs*, 1611–12.
40. Joseph Smith Family Bible, ca. 1831–1866, private possession, copy of genealogical information, CHL; "Obituary," *T&S* 2, no. 21 (1 Sept. 1841): 533.
41. Joseph Smith, Journal, 22 Dec. 1841, 36; 1–5 Jan. 1842, 44; 31 Jan. 1842, 10 Feb. 1842, 60, JSP. See also Newell and Avery, *Mormon Enigma*, 103.

42. B. W. Richmond, "The Prophet's Death!" *Deseret Evening News*, 27 Nov. 1875.
43. Appointment of Guardianship, 17 Jul. 1844, Lewis C. Bidamon Papers, CCLA.
44. Emma Smith McCallum, reminiscences, in Buddy Youngreen, *Reflections of Emma* (Orem, UT: Keepsake, 1982), 69.
45. David Hyrum Smith, Diary (1853–1864), 17 Feb. 1862, CCLA.
46. Emma Smith Bidamon to Joseph Smith III, 2 Feb. 1867, CCLA.
47. Zina D. H. Young, Biographical Sketch, Zina Card Brown Collection, CHL; Martha Sonntag Bradley and Mary Brown Firmage Woodward, "Plurality, Patriarchy, and the Priestess: Zina D. H. Young's Nauvoo Marriages," *Journal of Mormon History* 20, no. 1 (Spring 1994): 89–90.
48. Gordan A. Madsen, "Joseph Smith as Guardian: The Lawrence Estate Case," *Journal of Mormon History* 36, no. 3 (2010): 172–73, 181–87.
49. Lucy Walker Kimball, "Statement," CHL.
50. Thomas Ward, "Lines on the Death of Brother John Kendal," *The Latter-day Saints Millennial Star* 3, no. 7 (Nov. 1842): 128; Death Records, Hancock County, IL; 1860 US Census, Hancock County, IL.
51. Linda King Newell, "Emma's Legacy: Life After Joseph: 2010 Sterling M. McMurrin Lecture," *The John Whitmer Historical Association Journal* 31, no. 2 (Fall/Winter 2011): 9.
52. 1860 US Census, Nauvoo, Hancock County, IL.
53. Charles E. Bidamon to L. L. Hudson, 10 Aug. 1940, CCLA.
54. Interview with Leah Bidamon McLean, Lewis Bidamon's granddaughter, in Valeen Tippetts Avery, "Last Years of the Prophet's Wife: Emma Hale Smith Bidamon and the Establishment of the Reorganized Church of Jesus Christ of Latter Day Saints," thesis, Northern Arizona University, 1981, 91.
55. Emma Smith Bidamon to Joseph Smith III, 20 Jan. 1867, CCLA.
56. See chapters 9 and 10.
57. Emma Smith Bidamon to Joseph Smith III, 17 Dec. 1868, CCLA.
58. 1850 US Census, Nauvoo, Hancock Co., IL, 395 [A].
59. Hancock Co., IL, Birth Certificates, Death Records, Marriage Records, Applications for Marriage Licenses, 1829–1947, record no. 2813, 19 Nov. 1856, microfilm 1, 533,000, US and Canada Record Collection, FHL. "Records of Early Church Families," *Utah Genealogical and Historical Magazine* 28 (April 1937): 63.
60. Obituary, *Nauvoo Independent*, 17 Sept. 1880. Reed Murdock, *Joseph*

and *Emma's Julia: The Other Twin* (Salt Lake City: Eborn, 2004); S. Reed Murdock, *John Murdock: His Life and His Legacy* (Layton, UT: Summerwood, 2000).
61. Emma Smith Bidamon to Joseph Smith III, 2 Dec. 1867, CCLA.
62. Emma Smith Bidamon to Joseph Smith III, 5 Dec. 1871, CCLA.
63. Emma Smith McCallum, reminiscences, in Youngreen, *Reflections of Emma*, 53.
64. Richard P. Howard, *Joseph Smith III Memoirs* (Independence, MO: Herald Publishing House, 1979), 38.
65. Edmund C. Briggs, "A Visit to Nauvoo in 1856," *Journal of History* 9 (Oct. 1916): 458.
66. Vida E. Smith, "Biography of Patriarch Alexander Hale Smith," *Journal of History* 4, no. 1 (Jan. 1911): 14.
67. Ronald E. Romig, *Emma's Family* (Independence, MO: John Whitmer Books, 2008), 110–11.
68. David H. Smith, "A Memorial to Frederick G. W. Smith," David H. and Clara Smith Papers, CCLA.
69. Emma Smith Bidamon to Joseph Smith III, 27 Dec. 1868, CCLA.
70. "Presiding Patriarch Alexander H. Smith Called Home to Rest," *The Saints' Herald*, 18 Aug. 1909, 771–72.
71. David Smith to Joseph Smith III, n.d., 1874, CCLA.
72. David Smith to Emma Bidamon, 4 Jan. 1874, Vogel Collection, CHL.
73. Junius F. Wells, diary, 13 Nov. 1875, CHL.
74. Joseph Smith III to Dr. E. A. Kilbourne, 4 and 11 Jan. 1877; Joseph Smith III to Charles Derfy, 24 Jan. 1877, CCLA.
75. "Editorial," *The Saints' Herald* 51, no. 36 (7 Sept. 1904): 825–26.
76. Emma Smith Bidamon to Joseph Smith III, 20 Jan. 1867, CCLA.
77. Alexander Hale Smith, "Sermon at Bottineau, N.D.," *Zion's Ensign* 14, no. 53 (Dec. 31, 1903): 7.

Chapter 4

FIRST PRIESTESS

Emma's Covenants, Ordinances, and Revelations

Emma experienced a great number of losses in her life: babies, husband, homes—even her own family. One thing she gained that held together all those dear to her: the priesthood, or power of God. Her covenants and ordinances connected her individually to heavenly parents as well as to her beloved husband and children. "In the ordinances thereof, the power of godliness is manifest," she learned from a revelation her husband received in Kirtland in 1832.[1] She, too, participated in the priesthood—the power of God—beginning when she was baptized and confirmed, making covenants to take the name of Christ and become His daughter, to join the community of Saints and to renew those covenants with the sacrament. She received blessings of the priesthood with her 1830 revelation and her 1834 patriarchal blessing. And she joined in the priesthood when she received her temple endowment. These priesthood covenants bonded her to God and to her family.

Emma was not in attendance at the formal organization of the Church of Christ in Fayette, New York, in April 1830. Word was sent out, inviting interested people to come, but she remained at home in Harmony, about one hundred miles southeast of Fayette.[2]

Perhaps she was in poor health and needed rest: over the past year she had hosted numerous friends and family in her small home, including Lucy and Joseph Sr., Joseph's brother Samuel, Lucy and Martin Harris, Oliver Cowdery, and others. Joseph had been extremely busy with the publication of the Book of Mormon, yet her father did not support Joseph and his religious endeavors. She also had her cows and dairy, the only means at the time of the family's financial income.[3]

Emma may have been torn between her well-established Hale family and Joseph, who did not make enough money to support their new little family. She had a decision to make between the security of her family and her visionary, priesthood-bearing husband. Later she recalled that she believed Joseph: "I know Mormonism to be the truth; and believe the Church to have been established by divine direction. I have complete faith in it."[4] Their close relationship suggests that Joseph described to her his evolving ideas of the development of the Restoration.

"All those who receive my gospel are my sons and daughters"—Emma's Baptism

Joseph returned to Fayette in early June 1830 for the first conference of the organized Church. Again, he must have come back to Harmony and told Emma about the meeting: singing, prayer, and sacrament; priesthood ordination; additional baptisms; an outpouring of the Holy Ghost and visions of heaven.[5] Though Emma had been baptized as a baby, Joseph received a revelation requiring all those who desired to unite with the new Church receive a new baptism, even a "new and everlasting covenant."[6] So at the end of June, Emma traveled with Joseph, Oliver Cowdery, and John and David Whitmer about twenty miles north to Colesville, New York. Joseph

Knight, a friend of the Smiths who had provided financial support in their times of need, requested the establishment of a branch of the church there and baptism for his family.

On Friday, June 27, in preparation for the upcoming meeting and baptism, the men erected a dam in a pond on the Knight farm. The dam was destroyed by angry neighbors that night. Early Saturday morning, the men repaired the dam. Oliver Cowdery then baptized Emma and others, with the plan to confirm the new members. Instead, neighbors intervened and had Joseph Smith arrested for public disturbance. They took him to South Bainbridge, about twelve miles away, for a trial, followed by another trial back in Colesville.[7]

Obviously worried, Emma immediately gathered a group of women to pray for Joseph.[8] After all, she, like the people of Alma, was desirous to "come into the fold of God, and to be called his people," and had covenanted to comfort and mourn with fellow Saints as a witness of God, to support them in their afflictions.[9] Emma also needed that comfort and community for herself. After his release, Joseph found his wife "awaiting with much anxiety" at the home of her sister Elizabeth Hale Wasson.[10] Opposition seemed to follow every step Emma took, even as she received her first ordinance in the restored Church.

June 28, 1830, was not the only time Emma participated in the baptism ordinance. She performed proxy baptisms in 1841 and 1843 for her parents and other family members who had passed away, thus becoming a "savior on mount zion"—another example of how Emma's ordinance work connected her to Christ.[11] In the early Church, many Saints were rebaptized for health, drawing upon the priesthood power of the ordinance for healing.[12] Emma was very ill in the fall of 1842, most likely with malaria.[13] From the end of September to the beginning of October, her health declined, and Joseph often spent the day at home with her. She was baptized twice in the Mississippi River on October 5, "which evidently did her much good." Joseph's clerk recorded the following day that Emma appeared better; "May the Lord speedily raise her to the bosom of her family that the heart of his servant may be comforted."[14] The connection of Emma's health with the ordinance of baptism for the benefit of her family indicates priesthood power in her life that allowed her to save others as well as herself.

"I speak unto you, my daughter"—
Emma's Revelation, Doctrine and Covenants 25

After her baptism, Emma returned to Harmony with Joseph before she could be confirmed. Joseph had been working on a translation of the Bible, particularly the accounts of the Creation and the Fall. Emma may have been his scribe.[15] Perhaps the narrative of the work of the Gods and of Adam and Eve inspired a question regarding Emma's own mission. In a quiet moment sometime in July 1830, Joseph voiced the words of the Lord concerning His will for Emma. The revelation was not a confirmation nor a patriarchal blessing—that practice began four years later.[16] As his scribe, Emma may have written down the words spoken by Joseph. The original copy is not extant; perhaps Emma kept it close to her through her numerous moves, or maybe it was lost in the hustle and bustle.[17] A close examination of what is now known as Doctrine and Covenants 25 provides insight into Emma and her specific covenants and instructions from the Lord. He immediately established a relationship with Emma, calling her "my daughter," based on her baptismal covenant.[18] Her sins were forgiven, and she was promised a bestowal of the Holy Ghost. The Lord cautioned her to not murmur, to be meek, to beware of pride, to not fear, to lay aside worldly things—rather, to cleave to her covenants.

In addition to *not* doing certain things, Emma was *to do* other things, personal responsibilities. The Lord specified "the office of [her] calling" was to assist her husband and she was to spend time studying, writing, and "learning much," and to select sacred hymns for the Church. An 1828 dictionary defined *office* as a duty, charge, or trust of a sacred nature, conferred by God, and *ordain* as to properly set in order; to appoint or decree.[19] With Emma having such authority, the Lord said, "Thou shalt be ordained under [Joseph's] hand to expound scriptures, and to exhort the church."[20] The Lord promised Emma He would preserve her life, give her an inheritance in Zion, and crown her in His presence. She could come to be at one with God as she developed her distinct talents and fulfilled her assignments. Emma's official assignments were given to her before the ordination of Apostles, Seventies, or Patriarchs, perhaps indicating the importance of her office as companion to Joseph before the further development of the priesthood.[21]

Emma's revelation also revealed much about the Lord. He knows His daughters and sons individually, and He recognizes the intertwining roles and needs of each as they connect in building His kingdom and achieving their own salvation. He works within a proper order, with offices and ordination. He also is a God of wisdom with a plan concerning the things Emma had not yet seen. He is a God of revelation: He reveals His will to those who seek to understand His mysteries. He finds joy and delight in music. This covenant connecting Emma to God was available to all people.

27TH COMMANDMENT[22]

> A Revelation to Emma given at Harmony Susquehan[na] County state of Pennsylvania giving her a command to select Hymns &c
>
> A Revelation I give unto you concerning my will Behold

thy sins are for given thee & thou art an Elect Lady whom I have called murmur not because of the things which thou hast not seen for they are withheld from thee & the World which is wisdom in me in a time to come & the office of thy calling shall be for a comfort unto my Servent Joseph thy husband in his afflictions with consoleing words in the spirit of meekness & thou shalt go with him at the time of his going & be unto him a Scribe that I may send Oliver [Cowdery] whithersoever I will & thou shalt be ordained under his hand to expound Scriptures & exhort the Church according as it shall be given thee by my spirit for he shall lay his hands upon the[e] & thou shalt receive the Holy Ghost & thy time shall be Given to writings & to Learning & thou needest not fear for thy husband shall support thee from the Church for unto them is ~~thy~~ his calling that all things might be revealed unto them whatsoever I will according to their faith & verily I say unto ~~you~~ thee that thou shalt lay aside the things of this world & seek for the things of a better & it shall be given thee also to make a selection of Sacred Hymns as it shall be given thee which is pleasing unto me to be had in my Church for my Soul delighteth in the song of the heart yea the song of the ~~heart~~ righteous is a prayer unto me & it shall be answered with a blessing upon their heads wherefore lift up thy heart & rejoice & cleave unto the covenants which thou hast made continue in the spirit of meekness & beware of Pride let thy soul delight in thy husband & the glory which shall come upon him keep my commandments continually & a crown of righteousness thou shalt receive & except thou do this where I am ~~thou~~ ye cannot come & verily I say unto you that this is my voice unto all even so amen[23]

Emma carried the thoughts and ideas of this counsel with her throughout her life. She learned the importance of being humble.

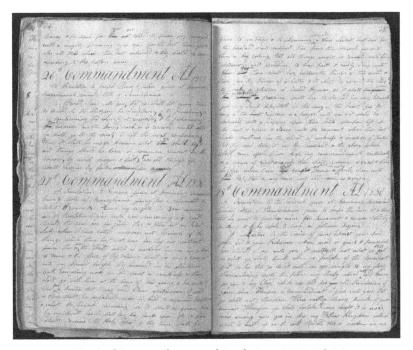

*A Book of Commandments and Revelations, 1833, 34–35.
Courtesy of Church History Library, Salt Lake City, Utah.*

"Lay aside the things of this world, and seek for the things of a better," the Lord had told her. One way for her to do this was to "continue in the spirit of meekness" and "beware of pride."[24] Seven years later, the Kirtland Saints faced a financial crisis as well as a spiritual one as the private bank led by Joseph began to fail amid a national economic depression, the Panic of 1837. In the midst of widespread apostasy, Joseph left town.[25] Emma wrote, "I verily feel that if I had no more confidence in God than some I could name, I should be in a sad case indeed," referring to those whose faith was troubled. She continued, "but I still believe that if we humble ourselves, and are <as> faithful as we can be we shall be delivered from every snare that may be laid for our feet, and our lives and property will be saved and we redeemed from all unreasonable encumbrances."[26] Emma lived what she believed.

Emma recognized her role with her prophet-husband. She was to "go with him," and to comfort him; she shared his burdens. She wrote tenderly to him while he was imprisoned in Liberty Jail: "Was it not for conscious innocence, and the direct interposition of divine mercy, I am very sure I never should have been able to have endured the scenes of suffering that I have passed through." And yet she pressed forward. "I still live and am yet willing to suffer more if it is the will of kind Heaven, that I should for your sake."[27] Her bond to Joseph was magnified because of her covenants.

"Thou shalt receive the Holy Ghost"—Emma's Confirmation

Early in August 1830, within a month of Emma receiving her revelation, Newel and Sally Knight and John Whitmer visited Harmony. Emma and Sally had been baptized at the same time on the Knight farm in June. Together they partook of the sacrament, and then Joseph confirmed the two women, according to his priesthood authority. They "spent the evening in a glorious manner," Joseph remembered. "The Spirit of the Lord was poured out upon us, we praised the Lord God, and rejoiced exceedingly."[28] All were blessed on a day that Emma probably never forgot. A couple of weeks after Emma's confirmation, she and Joseph moved to Fayette to join the body of Saints. Her revelation had taught her to "not fear, for thy husband shall support thee in the church," and to "lay aside the things of this world, and seek for the things of a better."[29] Little could she have imagined what lay ahead.

Thirty-eight years later, Emma reminded her son Joseph III to rely on God, as she had learned to do through her perilous times.

Joseph III had been baptized by his father in the Mississippi River in Nauvoo in November 1843.[30] "Keep up your courage Joseph that promise is for you, and with the resolution of good old Job, trust in God as he felt he would tho God should slay him."[31] She taught her family of her conviction based on her baptismal ordinance.

"Thou art blessed of the Lord"—Emma's Patriarchal Blessing

After a few months in Fayette, Joseph and Emma moved to Kirtland, Ohio, the first gathering place of the Saints in this dispensation. Joseph traveled, revealed, organized, and expanded Church membership and restoration; Emma raised children, studied, collected hymns, and cared for others. In May 1834, Joseph left Emma, Julia, and little Joseph III to lead Zion's Camp to western Missouri. He returned in the summer, but then left again on a mission to Michigan in October. It seemed impossible for Emma to "go with him at the time of his going," for she now had little ones to care for.[32]

Joseph had learned about the role of the patriarch and patriarchal blessings as he translated the Book of Mormon and the Bible. He read about Adam and Lehi blessing their sons and how the seed of Abraham received blessings through their lineage.[33] On December 6, 1834, Joseph ordained his father, Joseph Smith Sr., as patriarch of the Church. The ordination introduced "a more refined order into the Church."[34] Three days later, Joseph, Emma, and three-year-old Julia received blessings from patriarch Joseph Sr.[35]

PATRIARCHAL BLESSING GIVEN TO
EMMA SMITH BY JOSEPH SMITH SR[36]

> Emma, my daughter-in-law, thou are blessed of the Lord, for thy faithfulness and truth: thou shalt be blessed with thy husband

and rejoice in the glory which will come upon him: thy soul has been afflicted because of the wickedness of men in seeking the destruction of thy companion, and thy Lord thy God has heard thy supplication. Thou has grieved for the hardness of the hearts of thy father's house, and thou hast longed for their salvation. The Lord will have respect to thy cries, and by his judgements he will cause some of them to see their folly and repent of their sins; but it will be by affliction that they will be saved. Thou shalt see many days; yea, the Lord will spare thee till thou are satisfied, for thou shalt see thy redeemer. Thy heart shall rejoice in the great work of the Lord, and no one shall take thy rejoicing from thee. Thou shalt ever remember the great condescension of thy God in permitting thee to accompany my son when the angel delivered the record of the Nephites to his care. Thou has seen much sorrow because the Lord has taken from thee three of thy children: in this thou are not to be blamed, for he knows thy pure desires to raise up a family, that the name of my son might be blessed. And now, behold, I say unto thee, that thus saith the Lord, if thou will believe, thou shalt yet be blessed in this thing and thou shalt bring forth other children, to the joy and satisfaction of thy soul, and to the rejoicing of thy friends. Thou shalt be blessed with understanding, and have power to instruct thy sex. Teach thy family righteousness, and thy little ones the way of life, and the holy angels shall watch over thee, and thou shalt be saved in the kingdom of God, even so. Amen.

Again, God revealed His knowledge of Emma and her deep losses: He recognized her grief for her family, whom she had not seen or communicated with in four years. Almost as a continuation of her 1830 revelation, Emma was encouraged to work with her husband despite the efforts of people anxious to stop the progress of the

Church. He acknowledged her sorrow at losing three children and her "pure desires to raise up a family." He observed her skills and abilities and saw the future when she would "have power to instruct" women. Finally, God promised Emma that her life would be preserved and that she would see Christ.[37]

Emma took these words to heart in connection with her 1830 revelation. Nearly forty years later, the promises continued to be on her mind when she wrote her son, Joseph III: "I have seen many, yes very many trying scenes in my life, in which I could not see any good in them, neither could I see any place where any good could grow out of them." She had lived through countless difficulties. She went on, "But yet I feel a divine trust in God, that all things shall work for good, perhaps not to me, but it may be to some one else, and I am still hoping and praying trusting that you will not be hindered in the great and good work."[38] Emma was a woman of faith.

"A queen and a priestess"— Emma and Her Temple Covenants

From 1833 to 1836, the Saints worked long and hard to build a House of the Lord in Kirtland. Emma boarded construction workers in her house, often at a great sacrifice, sleeping on the floor while others slept in her bed.[39] She prepared the Church's first hymnal in time for the dedication on March 27, 1836. Emma didn't record a witness of heavenly manifestations—angels, solemn assemblies, spiritual outpourings—but her friends Eliza R. Snow, Nancy Tracy, and Mary Fielding Smith did.[40] On the evening of March 27, when Joseph met with the male priesthood quorums to instruct them about the ordinance of washing of feet, no women were allowed.[41] The ordinance was intended only for "official members," according to Joseph, and apparently only men holding the priesthood were considered official members.[42] George A. Smith reported, "That almost made the women mad, and they said, as they were not admitted into the Temple while this washing was being performed, that some mischief was going on, and some of them were right huffy about it."[43] Emma recognized the promises of the dedicatory prayer: "That thy servants may go forth from this house armed with thy power, and that thy name may be upon them, and thy glory be round about them, and thine angels have charge over them."[44]

Joseph received revelation incrementally regarding the highest covenants and ordinances we now participate in at the temple. Considering the nature of their marriage and her role as a companion or helpmeet, it is possible that Emma talked through ideas with him, causing Joseph to think about the inclusion of women and to seek revelation from the Lord.[45] The organization of the Nauvoo Relief Society in 1842 contributed to Joseph's understanding of a more complete endowment. He referred to the Relief Society as a holy order after the pattern of the priesthood or the order of heaven.[46] Men received a portion of the endowment ritual first, in May 1842, over a year before women did.[47] Even then, the ordinance wasn't complete without women. On May 27, 1842, Newel K. Whitney visited the growing Society in the grove. He spoke about his new understanding of the grand patriarchal and matriarchal salvific order leading to exaltation, including women. He proclaimed: "In the beginning God created man male and female and bestow'd upon man certain blessings peculiar to a man of God, of which woman partook." Newel continued, "Without the female all things cannot be restor'd to the earth it takes all to restore the Priesthood."[48] Women were a crucial part of the complete temple endowment. One way in which Emma assisted Joseph with the initiatory and endowment was in the creation of the original sacred garments for the initiated, with the assistance of Eliza R. Snow, even before either one of them received it for herself.⁴⁹

A year later, in May 1843, Emma and Joseph were sealed to each other in the new and everlasting covenant. The ordinance occurred on a chilly Sunday evening in the upper room of the Red Brick Store.⁵⁰ Emma did not record her experience, but her friend Mercy Thompson described her own sealing, which took place the following day and probably was very similar to Emma's. Joseph taught Mercy about a revelation concerning a new contract of marriage "for All Eternity." She joined members of the First Presidency and Quorum of the Twelve in an upper room. "Such a wedding I am quite sure never witnessed before in this generation," she wrote.⁵¹

Joseph—and perhaps Emma, as he discussed ideas and bursts of inspiration and revelation with her—came to understand the priesthood and temple ordinances incrementally. At this point, husbands and wives were sealed before women received their temple endowment. Joseph may have seen the marriage sealing as the highest order of priesthood, where men and women shared priesthood robes, symbols, and priesthood fullness. Joseph saw sealing as connecting men to women and even connecting families, such as the Whitneys to the Smiths. This bond occurred in the summer of 1842 with his sealing to Sarah Whitney, daughter of Newel and Elizabeth Ann.⁵² Perhaps Joseph and Emma initially saw sealing worthy single women or women not married to worthy men as a stepping stone of an evolving priesthood to receive a temple endowment. Sealing before endowment was a common practice in 1840s Nauvoo as Joseph continually worked out—under revelation—the details of priesthood and temple.

Finally, on September 28, 1843, Emma received her endowment—a sacred, holy event—from her prophet-husband, the first woman to do so in this dispensation.⁵³ In turn, she both officiated in and authorized other women to perform the initiatory and endowment ceremonies of other women, including Elizabeth Ann Whitney, her Relief Society second counselor and dear friend; her sister-in-law, Mary Fielding Smith; her mother-in-law Lucy Mack Smith; and the wives of men who worked closely with Joseph: Vilate Kimball, Jenetta Richards, Leonora Taylor, Sally Phelps, and Bathsheba Smith.[54] Bathsheba connected the endowment she received from Emma with plural marriage. Remembering the ritual years later, she wrote, "At the time I was anointed in Sister Emma Smith's home, she (Emma Smith) said in my presence, to me and to others who were also present upon that occasion: 'Your husbands are going to take more wives, and if you don't consent to it, you must put your foot down and keep it there.'"[55] Each of these women, except Lucy, accepted plural wives. It was a complicated connection, and Emma struggled to separate her own endowment and sealing to Joseph from those of his plural wives.

The endowment and sealing connected husbands and wives in significant ways as together they shared the highest level of patriarchal priesthood—effective only with a matriarch. Bathsheba connected the experience with Joseph's instructions to the Nauvoo Relief Society: "He wanted to make us, as the women were in Paul's day, 'A kingdom of priestesses.' We have the ceremony in our endowments as Joseph taught."[56] Women sealed by sacred ordinance to men shared their priesthood, and some gave blessings by virtue of this shared priesthood.[57] These religious rites were first reserved for a select group of people in whom Joseph had extreme trust. The "Anointed Quorum," or "Holy Order," included only husbands and their first wives, and recognized what Joseph called "Abraham's patriarchal priesthood," allowing the couples to receive the crowning ordinances of the fullness of the Melchizedek Priesthood—kings and priests, and queens and priestesses.[58] Joseph acted as president of the group and Emma as a priestess or queen with her husband.[59] The temple ordinances transformed Emma—they sanctified her and made her holy—helping her visualize earlier revelations and practice earlier covenants, seeing her through the troubles and losses of marriage and family and the work of restoration and building God's kingdom.

"The richest of heaven's blessings"—Emma's Final Blessing from Joseph

Before Joseph left for Carthage, both he and Emma sensed an imminent end. Together they had seen financial struggles, breaches of loyalty, loss of children, and separation, as well as high moments of union, joy, and powerful spiritual manifestations. Emma requested one last priesthood blessing, although the account and provenance are debated by scholars.[60] Because Joseph didn't have time to give her a blessing, as the story goes, he suggested that she write one and he would sign it. The situation empowered Emma, giving her the opportunity to discern her immediate needs and to make heartfelt requests.

EMMA SMITH BLESSING[61]

> First of all that I would crave as the richest of heaven's blessings would be wisdom from my Heavenly Father bestowed daily, so that whatever I might do or say, I could not look back at the close of the day with regret, nor neglect the performance of any act that would bring a blessing. I desire the Spirit of God to know and understand myself, that I might be able to overcome whatever of tradition or nature that would not tend to my exaltation in the eternal worlds. I desire a fruitful, active mind, that I may be able to comprehend the designs of God, when revealed

through His servants without doubting. I desire the spirit of discernment, which is one of the promised blessings of the Holy Ghost.

I particularly desire wisdom to bring up all the children that are, or may be committed to my charge, in such a manner that they will be useful ornaments in the Kingdom of God, and in a coming day arise up and call me blessed.

I desire prudence that I may not through ambition abuse my body and cause it to become prematurely old and care-worn, but that I may wear a cheerful countenance, live to perform all the work that I covenanted to perform in the spirit-world and be a blessing to all who may in any wise need aught at my hands.

I desire with all my heart to honor and respect my husband as my head, ever to live in his confidence and by acting in unison with him retain the place which God has given me by his side, and I ask my Heavenly Father that through humility, I may be enabled to overcome the curse which was pronounced upon the daughters of Eve. I desire to see that I may rejoice with them in the blessings which God has in store for all who are willing to be obedient to His requirements. Finally, I desire that whatever may be my lot through life I may be enabled to acknowledge the hand of God in all things.

Emma carried these heartfelt desires throughout the rest of her life. She wrote her son Joseph III in 1868 about her contentment through earnest prayer in her daily activities. "I can pray let me be doing what else I may have on hand. I can pray and work in the kitchen, or in the cellar or up stairs. My heart can send up fervent prayers but to be thankfull." She demonstrated a sense of humility: "I have to confess I have not learned to put in practice yet, but I live in hopes that I shall be able to learn that in time." Emma connected these thoughts to the present in her older age: "I have a promise that my last days shall be my best days, and according to the years that is allotted to mankind, those days are not very far distant, as I am now fast living out my sixty fourth year."[62] She firmly believed.

Revelations, blessings, and ordinances defined Emma and established her personal relationships with God and with her husband Joseph. They gave her a sense of the divine amid her earthly sorrows and troubles. They connected her to a higher power of holiness, which guided her through her rocky and dry places. Emma's covenants saw her through the troubles of her life and assured her compensation and blessings to come. She and Joseph learned together that the priesthood was not meant for men alone; they shared it with their wives, and women had priesthood authority in the assignments to which they were called.

Emma wrote to her son Joseph III in 1866, "How often I have been made deeply sensable that my pilgrim age has been an arduous one."[63] Perhaps at the end of her life, when Emma remained in Nauvoo, denying Joseph's practice of plural marriage and no longer participating in temple ordinances, she questioned the validity of her covenants. But her covenants enabled her to see through a vision Joseph and baby Don Carlos at the end of her life, to receive a crown of righteousness, and to enter the presence of the Lord.[64]

Notes

1. D&C 84:20.
2. Joseph Smith, History, 1839–1842 [Draft 2], 37, JSP.
3. Mark Staker, "Joseph and Emma's Susquehanna Home: Expanding Mormonism's First Headquarters," *Mormon Historical Studies* 16, no. 2 (Fall 2015): 100–101.
4. Joseph Smith III, "Last Testimony of Sister Emma," *The Saints' Herald* 26, no. 19 (1 Oct. 1879): 289–90.

5. Joseph Smith, Minute Book 2, 9 Jun. 1830, 1, JSP.
6. D&C 22:1; "The Mormon Creed," *Painesville Telegraph* 2, no. 44 (19 Apr. 1831), 4, JSP.
7. Joseph Smith, History, vol. A-1, 41–45, JSP.
8. John S. Reed, "Some of the Remarks of John S. Reed, Esq., as Delivered before the State Convention," *T&S* 5, no. 11 (1 Jun. 1844): 551.
9. Mosiah 18:8–10.
10. Joseph Smith, History, vol. A-1, 47, JSP.
11. Nauvoo Temple Baptisms for the Dead, book A, book C FHL; Joseph Smith, discourse, "Minutes of a Conference of the Church of Jesus Christ of Latter Day Saints," *T&S* 2, no. 24 (1 Oct. 1841): 577.
12. This followed biblical examples such as Elisha and Naaman. Jonathan A. Stapley and Kristine L. Wright, "'They Shall Be Made Whole': A History of Baptism for Health," *Journal of Mormon History* 34, no. 4 (Fall 2008): 69–112.
13. See Kyle M. Rollins, Richard D. Smith, M. Brett Borup, and E. James Nelson, "Transforming Swampland into Nauvoo, the City Beautiful: A Civil Engineering Perspective," *BYU Studies* 45, no. 3 (2006): 125–57.
14. Joseph Smith, Journal, 29 Sep.–6 Oct. 1842, 205–7, JSP.
15. Elizabeth Maki, "Joseph Smith's Bible Translation," *RIC*.
16. Carol Cornwall Madsen, "The 'Elect Lady' Revelation: The Historical and Doctrinal Context of Doctrine and Covenants 25," in *The Heavens are Open: The 1992 Sperry Symposium on the Doctrine and Covenants and Church History*, ed. Byron R. Merrill (Salt Lake City: Deseret Book, 1993), 210.
17. Emma told her son Joseph III that she lost her marriage certificate "many years ago, in some of the marches we were forced to make." It could be that the same thing happened with her revelation. "Last Testimony of Sister Emma," 289.
18. See D&C 25:1.
19. "Office," "Ordain," Noah Webster, *American Dictionary of the English Language* (1828).
20. D&C 25:5, 7.
21. Jonathan Stapley, "Ecclesiology, Liturgy, and Cosmology in Spring 1842," paper presented at the Joseph Smith Papers Conference, 2019, copy in author's possession.
22. The original manuscript of Emma Smith's revelation is not extant. There are four different versions of this revelation: one copied into Revelation

Book 1 circa 1831 as "commandment 27," one printed in the Book of Commandments in 1833 as "chapter 26," one printed in the 1835 Doctrine and Covenants, and section 25 in the 2013 Doctrine and Covenants. Some wording was clarified, and a few phrases were added after the first written copy.
23. Revelation, July 1830–C [D&C 25], Revelation Book 1, 34–35, JSP.
24. D&C 25:10, 14.
25. Richard Lyman Bushman, *Joseph Smith, Rough Stone Rolling: A Cultural Biography of Mormonism's Founder* (New York City: Knopf, 2005), 332–38; Mark Lyman Staker, *Hearken, O Ye People: The Historical Settings for Joseph Smith's Ohio Revelations* (Salt Lake City: Kofford, 2009), 521–23.
26. Emma Smith to Joseph Smith, 25 Apr. 1837, JSP.
27. Emma Smith to Joseph Smith, 7 Mar. 1839, JSP.
28. Joseph Smith, History, vol. A-1, 51–53, JSP.
29. D&C 25:9–10.
30. Reorganized Church of Jesus Christ of Latter Day Saints, Plano Branch, Plano, Kendall Co., IL, Church Records, 1861–1914, Membership Records, 1861–1974, microfilm, FHL.
31. Emma Smith Bidamon to Joseph Smith III, 27 Dec. 1868, CCLA.
32. D&C 25:6.
33. Moses 5:10–12, 59; 2 Nephi 2–4; Genesis 22:17–18.
34. Joseph Smith, History, 9 Dec. 1834, 20, JSP.
35. Matthew C. Godfrey, "A Season of Blessings: The Function of Blessings in Kirtland, Ohio, 1834–1835," *Mormon Historical Studies* 18, no. 1 (Spring 2017): 26–27.
36. Joseph Smith Sr., Blessing to Emma Smith, Patriarchal Blessing Book 1, 4–5, JSP.
37. Joseph Smith Sr., Blessing to Emma Smith.
38. Emma Bidamon to Joseph Smith III, 17 [no month] 1869, CCLA.
39. Lucy Mack Smith, History, bk. 14, 3, JSP.
40. See, for example, Eliza R. Snow in *The Women of Mormondom*, Edward W. Tullidge (New York: Tullidge and Crandall, 1877), 65, 95; Nancy N. Tracy, "Life History of Nancy Naomi Alexander Tracy, Written by Herself," 9–10, BYU; Mary Fielding Smith to Mercy Fielding Thompson, 8 Jul. 1837, Mary Fielding Smith Collection, CHL.
41. Joseph Smith acknowledged "the administering of angels" at the dedication ceremony. Journal, 27 Mar. 1836, 184–87, JSP.

42. Joseph Smith, Journal, 12 Nov. 1835, 33, JSP.
43. George A. Smith, "Gathering and Sanctification of the People of God," 18 Mar. 1855, in *Journal of Discourses*, ed. Brigham Young (Liverpool, England: F. D. Richards, 1855–1886), 2:215.
44. D&C 109:22.
45. See Angela Ashurst-McGee, "'Help Meet': Women's Power to Serve," *Ensign*, Sept. 2020, 29–31.
46. Nauvoo Relief Society minute book, 1842–1844, 28 Apr. 1842, 36, FFYRS, 54.
47. Joseph Smith, Journal, 4 May 1842, 94, JSP.
48. Nauvoo Relief Society, 27 May 1842, 58, FFYRS.
49. Maria Dougal, statement, in George F. Richards, diary, 11 Oct. 1922, CHL.
50. Bushman, *Joseph Smith, Rough Stone Rolling*, 494.
51. Mercy Fielding Thompson, Reminiscence, in *In Their Own Words: Women and the Story of Nauvoo*, ed. Carol Cornwall Madsen (Salt Lake City: Deseret Book, 2002), 194–95.
52. Jonathan Stapley, *The Power of Godliness: Mormon Liturgy and Cosmology* (New York City: Oxford University Press, 2018), 17–20. Joseph Smith, revelation, 27 Jul. 1842, Whitney Family Documents Collection, CHL.
53. Joseph Smith, Journal, book 3, 28 Sep. 1843, 225, JSP.
54. See Carol Cornwall Madsen, "Mormon Women and the Temple: Toward a New Understanding," in *Sisters in Spirit: Mormon Women in Historical and Cultural Perspective*, ed. Maureen Ursenbach Beecher and Lavina Fielding Anderson (Urbana, IL: University of Illinois Press, 1987), 80–110.
55. Bathsheba W. Smith, affidavit, Affidavits about Celestial Marriage, 1869–1915, CHL.
56. Clara L. Clawson, "R.S. Reports: Pioneer Stake," *WE* 34, no. 2–3 (Jul.–Aug. 1905):14; see FFYRS, xxviii.
57. Susa Young Gates, the first daughter of Brigham Young born in Utah, remembered how Eliza R. Snow "and her cohorts, when they blessed anybody, always said—'We seal this blessing upon you by virtue of the priesthood which we hold through our husbands and fathers.'" Susa Young Gates to Leah Widtsoe, 21 Feb. 1928, CHL.
58. Joseph Smith, discourse, 27 Aug. 1843, in Andrew F. Ehat and Lyndon W. Cook, eds., *The Words of Joseph Smith: The Contemporary Accounts of the Nauvoo Discourses of the Prophet Joseph* (Provo, UT: Brigham Young University Religious Studies Center, 1980), 244–47, 302–7; Glen M.

Leonard, *Nauvoo: A Place of Peace, A People of Promise* (Salt Lake City: Deseret Book, 2002), 260–61. See also "Anointed Quorum ('Holy Order')," GTE.

59. Devery A. Anderson, "The Anointed Quorum in Nauvoo, 1842–1845," *Journal of Mormon History* 29, no. 2 (Fall 2003), 146–47.
60. The original blessing Emma wrote is lost. Historian Juanita Brooks reported that she studied the original in about 1946 and verified Emma's handwriting. See Juanita Brooks to George Albert Smith, 29 Apr. 1946, Joseph K. Nicholes Collection; Joseph Fielding Smith, Papers, CHL. See *Saints: The Standard of Truth, 1815–1846* (Salt Lake City, The Church of Jesus Christ of Latter-day Saints, 2018), 653fn.24.
61. Emma Smith, blessing, Joseph L. Heywood papers, CHL.
62. Emma Smith Bidamon to Joseph Smith III, 27 Dec. 1868, CCLA.
63. Emma Hale Smith Bidamon to Joseph Smith III, 19 Aug. 1866, CCLA.
64. Alexander Hale Smith, "Sermon at Bottineau, N.D.," Jul. 1, 1903, *Zion's Ensign* 14, no. 53 (Dec. 31, 1903): 7.

Chapter 5

FIRST SCRIBE

Emma and the Scriptures

Growing up in the Susquehanna Valley, young Emma soaked in the religious culture of the Second Great Awakening. She was a woman of the Book; she studied the Bible and knew its stories and teachings. She engaged in secret prayer in the woods, a common practice among revival Methodists seeking God's spirit. She was exposed to a branch of "shouting Methodists," praising God and witnessing of their own conversions.[1]

As Emma learned of Joseph's First Vision and other divine manifestations, she was not perplexed—such encounters felt familiar to her. Emma's childhood faith and education contributed to her distinct partnership with Joseph in the Restoration and the translation of the Book of Mormon. She understood and loved the word of God: she helped Joseph retrieve and protect the plates, assisted in the translation and preservation of scripture, and expounded Restoration teachings. Near the end of her life, Emma told her sons, "I was an active participant in the scenes that transpired." She described her experience witnessing the translation of the plates. "It is marvelous to me, a 'marvel and a wonder.'"[2]

"The right person"—Emma's Assistance in Retrieving the Plates

When the angel Moroni appeared the first time to Joseph on September 21, 1823, in his Palmyra attic bedroom, he told the seventeen-year-old about the ancient record inscribed on gold plates giving an account of Christ. He instructed Joseph to find the plates, buried in a nearby hill. Once Joseph arrived at the appointed place the following day, he learned more about the sacred nature of the plates. Moroni warned Joseph that he would need to return the following year, with the "right person," perhaps as a safeguard to protect the record and preserve it for its intended purposes.[3] Joseph initially considered the "right person" to be his brother Alvin, a serious, hardworking, and trustworthy young man, seven years older than Joseph.[4] But just two months after Moroni's first visit, in November 1823, Alvin died unexpectedly of illness.[5]

For the next three years, every September 22, Joseph returned to the hill to meet Moroni. Each time he anticipated receiving the plates and beginning translation, but each year he was turned back for one reason or another. In September 1826, Moroni gave Joseph one more year to align his will with God's; the angel again emphasized bringing the right person with him the following year. Joseph prayed faithfully and found revelation in a seer stone—another "vision."[6] That person, it turns out, was Emma Hale, Joseph's future bride. Emma was not only the right person for Joseph to marry, but she was the person chosen by God to aid Joseph in bringing forth the Book of Mormon and the Restoration of the gospel. Emma was integral.

Following their marriage in Colesville, New York, in January 1827, Joseph brought Emma to his family home in Manchester. On the evening of September 22, 1827, Lucy Mack Smith recorded that Emma, dressed in riding clothes, joined her husband in Joseph

Knight's carriage and drove away. An excellent horsewoman, Emma waited in the carriage with the horses while Joseph received the plates from Moroni.[7] They came home in time for breakfast, having successfully obtained the plates.[8]

"My small sphere of labor"— Emma Protected the Scriptures

Emma realized the immense value of the ancient record. She also realized that she did not have the translation gift that Joseph had. In a letter to her son later in life, she expressed an understanding of her part in the process of bringing forth and restoring scripture: "Indeed I know what it is in my small sphere of labor."[9] She did all she could to protect the plates and preserve the space around Joseph to translate. While Joseph met with Moroni, Emma waited in the carriage, keeping the horses quiet and ready for a quick escape. One account states that she knelt to pray while Joseph obtained the plates.[10] Lucy also prayed—all night. She, too, believed fiercely in her son's mission.[11] Emma then waited while Joseph hid the plates in a hollow birch log in the woods.[12] The following day, Joseph went ten miles away to Macedon to work and earn money for a lock to secure the plates. When word of a gathering mob looking for the valuable gold came to Joseph Sr., he immediately told Emma. Thanks to the expert equine skills she had learned from her brothers as a young girl, she found a spare horse and rode bareback to warn Joseph.[13] A few months later, Emma's brother Alva, an elected Pennsylvania constable, came to Manchester to help his sister and Joseph move back to Harmony to escape increasing persecution in New York. They hid the plates in a barrel of beans for the journey, and Alva slept in the wagon at night along the way.[14]

Once in Harmony, Emma supplied a linen tablecloth to cover

the plates—similar to the way women provided protection for scriptures for centuries.[15] She also made a pouch to hold Joseph's seer stone.[16] Emma felt the plates through the cloth, moving them to clean: "They seemed to be pliable like thick paper, and would rustle with a metallic sound when the edges were moved by the thumb."[17] She never physically saw the plates, but she was, in truth, a witness of the sacred record. She validated what the official eleven male witnesses said.

Emma obtained from her carpenter brother-in-law Benjamin Wasson a sturdy "glass box"—used to protect glass panes in transport—to contain the plates, locked each night under the bed she shared with Joseph. She and Joseph went to Harpursville, New York, to procure a Moroccan leather box, probably made by Benjamin, in which to secure the manuscript pages and the Urim and Thummim.[18] Lucy Mack Smith noticed the fine trunk right away when she visited them in Harmony in February 1829.[19]

The Book of Mormon was not the only holy writ that Emma protected; the Bible translation was also significant. Joseph completed his translation and revision of the New Testament in February 1833 and his translation of the entire Bible in July, planning to publish it in Missouri. Persecution hindered the task.[20] James Mulholland, Joseph's scribe, protected the manuscript when Joseph was imprisoned. When trouble mounted, James passed it to his sister-in-law Ann Scott; he believed it would be safer in the hands of a woman, as a mob would probably not strip search a female. Ann sewed two cotton bags attached to a waistband to hide the papers under her skirt. Emma retrieved the manuscript and pouches from Ann.[21] Then, carrying two infants with the other two clinging to her skirts, loaded with precious papers underneath, Emma crossed over the frozen Mississippi River to safety in Illinois.[22]

In Nauvoo, Joseph planned to prepare the manuscripts for the press but was not able to before he died. Emma continued to fiercely protect the translation. A year after Joseph's death, John Bernhisel visited Emma on an errand from Brigham Young. Emma allowed John to borrow the transcription and the marked Bible for three months, during which he copied as much as possible.[23] Years later, she told her son that the manuscripts, like a holy relic, protected their family. "I have often thought the reason why our house did not burn down when it has been so often on fire was because of them, and I still feel there is a sacredness attached to them."[24] What she protected had protected her—a form of divine compensation.

In 1866, Emma released the manuscripts into the custody of the RLDS church, of which she was a member. She wrote to her son Joseph III, church president, in January 1867: "I am very thankful that you are getting along so well with the manuscripts."[25] In response to the preservation of the manuscripts, Joseph III published a poem extolling Emma in the RLDS *The Saints' Herald* newspaper. In part, he wrote: "Through many a changing year, these words have been / Thy constant care. . . . And thou, elect, art worthy found, to hold / These priceless treasures in a sacred trust."[26] The RLDS church published the Inspired Version of the Holy Scriptures later that year and obtained a copyright.[27]

"I frequently wrote day after day"—Emma as Scribe

Emma didn't just protect the scriptures; she also helped produce them. "Be unto him for a scribe," the Lord counseled Emma about her husband—interestingly, through Joseph's own voice.[28] The 1830 revelation spoke retroactively and proactively: she had scribed for Joseph since he had received the plates in 1827, and the Book of Mormon had been published by March 1830. She later scribed for the translation of the Bible.[29] A witness of the manuscript acknowledged Emma's "womanly handwriting."[30]

Emma was extremely invested in the Book of Mormon translation process—she both scribed herself and heard the words Joseph spoke aloud when others came to assist as she went about her daily domestic work. She did not record her impressions as Oliver Cowdery did: "These were days never to be forgotten—to sit under the sound of a voice dictated by the *inspiration* of heaven, awakened the utmost gratitude of this bosom!"[31] But two experiences illustrate her investment in the process.

Martin Harris came to Harmony to assist Joseph in translation as Emma's first pregnancy progressed. He implored Joseph to let him take the first batch of pages to show his wife when he left in June, the day before Emma's agonizing labor and delivery.[32] The birth and death of her first baby in June 1828 and her subsequent long recovery removed both her and Joseph from translation for a period, but it was always at the back of her mind. After two weeks, Emma's health improved and her concern about the manuscript increased. She implored Joseph to track down Martin while her mother cared for her postpartum. Joseph returned to Palmyra to recover the manuscript—the majority of which Emma had written out herself.[33] When he discovered that the manuscript was irretrievably lost, he proclaimed, "Oh my God! . . . all is lost! all is lost!" Lucy wrote that as he recognized the depth of the situation, "he wept and groaned, and walked the floor continually." His second thought was how he could return to Emma "with such a tale as this? I dare not do it." After all, it had been her work, too. When Moroni retrieved the plates and Urim and Thummim from Joseph, Emma lost something too—not only her baby, but also her work on the sacred manuscript. A few months later, after humble repentance, Joseph received the plates from Moroni on September 22, 1828, and Emma returned to writing for her husband until Oliver Cowdery arrived and became Joseph's next scribe.[34]

The 1830 revelation sanctioned Emma's scribal work and encouraged her to assist Joseph in his sacred work translating scriptures. When Joseph and Emma experienced tension in their relationship, Joseph could not translate. David Whitmer recalled that one morning as they prepared to translate in Fayette, Joseph was concerned about an encounter with Emma earlier that day. He retreated to the orchard to pray for about an hour, then came back to the house, asked Emma's forgiveness, and the translation continued.[35] Emma knew the Bible enough that she could answer Joseph's questions about a wall around Jerusalem while translating the plates. She was amazed at her uneducated husband's ability to pick up right where he left off after a break without any prompt. This was a man who, she recalled, "could neither write nor dictate a coherent and well-worded letter; let alone dictating a book like the Book of Mormon." Surely, she believed, this was "a marvel and a wonder."[36]

Emma was not the only one who aided Joseph with the Book of Mormon; many people stepped up and assisted in diverse and substantial ways. Martin Harris provided cash as needed; in December 1827, he gave Emma and Joseph fifty dollars for the move from New York to Pennsylvania.[37] While the Hale family was generally not supportive of the endeavor, Emma's brother Reuben helped scribe when Emma was not available.[38] Joseph Knight occasionally visited Joseph to provide needed supplies.[39] Oliver Cowdery found Joseph in Harmony after his own vision and played a remarkable role in assisting with the translation.[40] David Whitmer came to Harmony to assist the Smiths in their move to Fayette, and his family provided lodging for them, sometimes at a great cost to the Whitmers.[41] Bringing forth the Book of Mormon was not only a joint effort between Joseph and Emma, but was the work of a large group of people who all helped and supported the Smiths. And yet Emma was a constant presence throughout the process.

"Advis'd all to abide the Book of Mormon"—Emma as a Witness of the Scriptures

In addition to protection and translation assistance, Emma taught from the scriptures. Her 1830 revelation encouraged her "to expound scriptures, and to exhort the church."[42] The responsibility was weighty. In expounding, Emma was by definition tasked to "explain, to lay open the meaning, to clear of obscurity, to interpret;" in exhorting, she was to "encourage, to embolden, to cheer, to advise, to excite or to give strength, spirit, or courage."[43] These were not socially appropriate activities for women at the time.[44] The Lord told Emma, "Thy time shall be given to writing, and to learning much."[45] The scriptures informed her of vital doctrine and theology, which she included in her selection of hymns.

Both in her hymnal and in the Relief Society, Emma taught from restoration scripture (see chapters 6 and 8). On a personal note, the Book of Mormon contained additional restoration teachings that must have calmed Emma's troubled heart. The concept that infant baptism was not required soothed her grief for lost babies.[46] The seed of faith that grew within her produced delicious fruit.[47] The transformation of her weaknesses into strengths after the trial of her faith provided the will to endure.[48] The promise of Christ, who suffered everything she did, provided her hope in her own repentance, both in her immediate afflictions and in her future salvation.[49]

Toward the end of her life, Emma continued to testify of the truthfulness of the Book of Mormon. She told Edmund C. Briggs in May 1863 that "she had allwise beleaved the B of M, and the Doc & Covenants from their first being published and had never doubted them but she knew they were true."[50] Her oldest grandson, Frederick Alexander Smith, son of Alexander Smith, remembered that she was deeply religious and believed in the Book of Mormon.[51] Shortly before Emma's death, Joseph III and others interviewed her about her life. She remained convinced that the Book of Mormon was the work of God and of divine authenticity.[52]

Without Emma, Joseph could not have received the plates, protected them, or translated them. She expounded scripture in her hymns and as she conducted the Relief Society and exhorted women. In her later years in Nauvoo, Emma quoted scripture in letters to her son, Joseph III. "I am daily trying to learn St. Paul's lesson," she wrote, "to be contented without condition, to pray always and in all things give thanks."[53] She remained a firm believer in Joseph as a prophet and the Book of Mormon as holy scripture to the end of her life.[54]

Notes

1. Mark Staker, "Isaac and Elizabeth Hale in Their Endless Mountain Home," *Mormon Historical Studies* 15, no. 2 (Fall 2014): 55–70; Mark H. Forscutt, "Commemorative Discourse on the Death of Mrs. Emma Bidamon," *The Saints' Herald* 26, no. 14 (15 Jul. 1879): 209–10; Linda King Newell and Valeen Tippetts Avery, *Mormon Enigma: Emma Hale Smith* (Urbana, IL: University of Illinois Press, 1994), 3. See Candy Gunther, "The Spiritual Pilgrimage of Rachel Stearns, 1934–1937: Reinterpreting Women's Religious and Social Experiences in the Methodist Revivals of Nineteenth-Century America," *Church History* 5, no. 4 (Dec. 1996): 583–84.
2. Joseph Smith III, "Last Testimony of Sister Emma," *The Saints' Herald* 26, no. 19 (1 Oct. 1879): 289.
3. Joseph Knight, Reminiscences, 1, CHL; Joseph Smith Journal, 9–11 Nov. 1835; Joseph Smith, History, vol. A-1, JSP.
4. Joseph Smith, Journal, 23 Aug. 1842, JSP.
5. Lucy Mack Smith, History, 1844–1845, book 3, [12]; JSP.
6. According to Joseph Knight, a close acquaintance of Joseph Smith at the

time and supporter of the Restoration, Joseph received revelation by looking in a seer stone and saw Emma Hale. Joseph Knight, Sr., Reminiscences, CHL.

7. Lucy Mack Smith, History, 1845, 105, 111, JSP.
8. Lucy Mack Smith, History, 1844–1845, book 5, [6–7], JSP.
9. Emma Bidamon to Joseph Smith III, 17 [Mar.] 1869, CCLA.
10. Martin Harris, in "Mormonism—No. II," *Tiffany's Monthly* 5, no. 4 (Jul. 1859): 164–65.
11. Lucy Mack Smith, History, 1844–1845, book 5, [6–7], JSP.
12. Lucy Mack Smith, History, 1844–1845, book 5, [6–7], JSP.
13. Lucy Mack Smith, History, 1845, 108–10, JSP.
14. Lucy Mack Smith, History, 1845, 121, JSP. "Prophet Smith's Family Relations," *Salt Lake Daily Tribune,* 17 Oct. 1879, 2; see Mark Lyman Staker and Robin Scott Jenson, "David Hale's Store Ledger: New Details about Joseph and Emma Smith, the Hale Family, and the Book of Mormon," *BYU Studies Quarterly* 53, no. 3 (2014): 88–89.
15. See, for example, David Ganz and Barbara Schellewald, *Clothing Sacred Scriptures: Book Art and Book Religion in Christian, Islamic, and Jewish Cultures* (Boston, De Gruyter, 2018).
16. Franklin D. Richards, journals, vol. 30 (1882), 8 Mar. 1882, Richards Family Collection, CHL.
17. Smith III, "Last Testimony of Sister Emma," 289–90.
18. Isaac Hale, "Statement of Mr. Hale," *Susquehanna Register and Northern Pennsylvanian* 4, no, 21 (1 May 1834): [1]; Mark Staker, "Joseph and Emma Smith's Susquehanna Home: Expanding Mormonism's First Headquarters," *Mormon Historical Studies* 16, no. 2 (Fall 2015): 90–92; Nels Madsen, "Visit to Mrs. Emma Smith Bidemon, Historian's Office, Nov. 27, 1931," CHL.
19. Lucy Mack Smith, History, 1845, 136; JSP.
20. Joseph Smith, History, vol. A-1, 271, JSP.
21. F. M. Cooper, "Spiritual Reminiscences in the Life of Sister Ann Davis, of Lyons, Wisconsin," *Autumn Leaves* 4, no. 1 (Jan. 1891): 18.
22. Inez Smith Davis, *The Story of the Church: A History of the Church of Jesus Christ of Latter Day Saints, and of its Legal Successor, the Reorganized Church of Jesus Christ of Latter Day Saints* (Independence, MO: Herald Publishing House, 1938), 213–14.

23. John Bernhisel, statement, in L. John Nuttall, Diary 1, 10 Sept. 1879, 335, BYU.
24. Emma Bidamon to Joseph Smith III, 2 Dec. 1867; Edmund C. Briggs to R. J. Hawkins, 28 Mar. 1908, CCLA.
25. Emma Bidamon to Joseph Smith III, 20 Jan. 1867, CCLA.
26. Joseph Smith III, "To the Elect Lady, on Her Faithful Care of the MSS. of the New Translation," *The True Latter Day Saints' Herald* 11, no. 2 (15 Jan. 1867): 25–27.
27. Joseph Smith, Jr., *The Holy Scriptures, Translated and Corrected by the Spirit of Revelation, by Joseph Smith, Jr., the Seer* (Plano, IL: Church of Jesus Christ of Latter-day Saints, 1867).
28. D&C 25:6.
29. Mark L. Staker, "'A Comfort unto My Servant, Joseph': Emma Hale Smith (1804–1879)," in *Women of Faith in the Latter Days, Volume One, 1775–1820*, ed. Richard E. Turley Jr. and Brittany A. Chapman (Salt Lake City: Deseret Book, 2011), 353–56.
30. Forscutt, "Commemorative Discourse on the Death of Mrs. Emma Bidamon."
31. Oliver Cowdery to William W. Phelps, 7 Sep. 1834, *Latter Day Saints' Messenger and Advocate* 1, no. 14 (Oct. 1834), italics in original.
32. Joseph Smith History, vol. A-1, Feb.–Jun. 1828, 9–10, JSP.
33. Michael Hubbard MacKay and Gerrit J. Dirkmaat, *From Darkness unto Light: Joseph Smith's Translation and Publication of the Book of Mormon* (Provo, UT: Religious Studies Center, Brigham Young University), 89–92.
34. Lucy Mack Smith, History, 1845, 131, 138; History, 1844–1845, book 7, 2–3, 8–11, JSP.
35. David Whitmer to William H. Kelley, *The Saints' Herald* (1 Mar. 1882).
36. Smith III, "Last Testimony of Sister Emma," 289–90.
37. Lucy Mack Smith, History, 1844–1845, book 6, 6; History, 1845, 121, JSP.
38. Isaac Hale, "Affidavit, March 20, 1834," in Eber D. Howe, *Mormonism Unvailed* (Painesville, OH: E. D. Howe, 1834), 263; Emily C. Blackman, *History of Susquehanna County, Pennsylvania* (Philadelphia: Clayton, Remsen, & Haffelfinger, 1873), 104; Seraphine Gardner, ed., *Recollections of the Pioneers of Lee County, Pennsylvania* (Dixon, IL: Inez A. Kennedy, 1893), 141–42.
39. Knight, Sr., Reminiscences, 5.

40. Joseph Smith, History, vol. A-1, 15; History, circa Summer 1832, 6; Lucy Mack Smith, History, 1844–1845, book 8, 1, JSP. D&C 6:22–23.
41. "Testimony of David Whitmer," *The Saints' Herald* 26, no. 1 (1 Jan. 1879): 7.
42. D&C 25:7.
43. "Exhort," and "expound," in Noah Webster, *An American Dictionary of the English Language* (1828).
44. See Timothy 2:11–12; and Ann Braude, "Women's History *Is* American Religious History," in *Retelling U.S. Religious History*, ed. Thomas A. Tweed (Berkeley: University of California Press, 1997), 87–107.
45. D&C 25:8.
46. Moroni 8:5–15.
47. Alma 32:21, 28–32, 41–42.
48. Ether 12:6, 27.
49. Mosiah 3:5–11; Alma 7:11–15.
50. Edmund C. Briggs, Diary, 24 May 1863, CCLA.
51. Mary Audentia Smith Anderson, Interview with Frederick Alexander Smith, in Buddy Youngreen, *Reflections of Emma* (Orem, UT: Keepsake, 1982), 95.
52. Smith III, "Last Testimony."
53. Emma Smith Bidamon to Joseph Smith III, 17 Dec. 1868, Emma Smith Papers, CCLA.
54. Smith III, "Last Testimony."

Chapter 6

FIRST LATTER-DAY SAINT HYMNAL

Emma and the Hymns

"Know then that ev'ry soul is free, / To choose his life and what he'll be; / For this eternal truth is given, / That God will force no man to heaven."¹ So begins *A Collection of Sacred Hymns for the Church of Jesus Christ of Latter Day Saints*, Emma's first hymnal. The song had been included in an 1805 Freewill Baptists camp-meeting collection of hymns under the title "The Freedom of the Will."² The lyrics reveal the power of human agency—the ability to act independently. The hymn marked Emma's full engagement with the restored Church, not only as a believer, but also as a determined contributor.

One of Emma's significant lasting influences on the modern restored Church is her hymns. The 1830 revelation invited her to "make a selection of sacred hymns."³ She compiled three books and expanded another. Hymnals continue to play an invaluable part in the Church. Over time, songbooks have been published for Primary, Relief Society, and youth, in a wide variety of languages with modern translation. Congregational singing creates a strong sense of institutional identity and connection in a culture that shares worship and divine partnership. Family and individual singing call down the powers of heaven.

"Possessed of a fine voice"—
Emma's Musical Background

Music was an inherent part of Emma's life. Hymns permeated nineteenth-century activity, public and private, in formal church and at home. The Second Great Awakening encouraged active evangelism—the communication of personal conversion through enthusiastic expression. People gathered in camp meetings, often outdoors, led by Methodist, Baptist, and Presbyterian preachers or individuals called by the Spirit. These hymns expressed spiritual experiences and faith in a practical, understandable way.[4]

Emma was known as a natural musician in the Susquehanna Valley, "a good singer and possessed of a fine voice."[5] She was a soprano and probably attended local singing schools in private homes; she was often asked to sing at church gatherings.[6] As a "shouting" Methodist, Emma would have been very vocal in her worship at camp meetings and Sunday services. The local Harmony newspaper, *The Centinel,* regularly published religious music lyrics, including hymns written by townspeople, exposing her from an early age to worship music.[7]

"Make a selection of sacred hymns"—Emma's Divine Charge

One of Emma's roles outlined in her 1830 revelation was to "make a selection of sacred hymns," again intimating the character of the Lord. He requested music that was "pleasing" and revealed that His soul delights "in the song of the heart."[8] A year earlier, another revelation explained that "there is none else save God that knowest thy thoughts and the intents of thy heart."[9] Musical expression was a soul-filled communication, for "the song of the righteous is a prayer unto me." Singing, a form of worship, unites us with our God, a type of at-one-ment.

Hymns pedagogically taught doctrine to singers and congregations, expanding the definition of expounding scripture and exhorting the Church. Emma found lyrics and music that testified of Joseph's Restoration vision, inviting divine connection for all Saints. Emma's hymns gave her an opportunity to teach doctrine, inspire, and provide strength and courage through music.[10]

"A Collection of Sacred Hymns"— Emma's Creation of Three Hymnals

Gathering, selecting, and editing hymns was not a typical project for women in the nineteenth century. That did not stop Emma, a visionary woman in her own sense of the word.[11] She had been promised in her 1830 revelation: "Thy time shall be given to writing, and to learning much."[12] She probably gathered hymns from her hometown newspaper as well as other papers and denominational hymnals.[13] The process, like so many other endeavors in her life, would ebb and flow with loss and compensation, requiring more than five years to produce.

Two years after the 1830 revelation, on April 30, 1832, Joseph attended a council of the Literary Firm, a committee responsible for Church publications in Independence, Missouri. The Firm formally approved the hymnal as well as publication of the Book of Commandments and an almanac. William W. Phelps was appointed to edit the publications.[14] While Emma may have been taking time for "writing, and to learning much," including finding hymns according to her 1830 revelation, her time had also been filled with moving between Pennsylvania, New York, and Ohio; struggling with difficult pregnancies; grieving lost babies; and adjusting to adoption.

In Independence in June 1832, William printed the first copy of *The Evening and the Morning Star*, a monthly newspaper devoted to communication among the Saints scattered in Missouri, Ohio, and the eastern United States. The paper printed revelations, then known as "commandments," to promulgate faith and doctrine for Saints and their missionaries.[15] In addition to scripture and instruction, the *Star* included hymns, many of which may have been contributed by Emma. The first issue included six hymn lyrics under the title: "Hymns, Selected and prepared for the Church of Christ, in these last days."[16] The *Star* printed twenty-six hymns the first year, twenty of which were included in the 1835 hymnal. Unfortunately, the printing office was destroyed in July 1833, putting a halt to the hymn project. Gone was the collection Emma had sent from Kirtland to Missouri and other paperwork for the unfinished Book of Commandments. In his personally-bound copy of recovered pages from the Book of Commandments, Wilford Woodruff copied by hand eight hymns from the paper, six of which appeared in the first hymnal.[17] The loss of Emma's hymns would have been devastating—a bit like the loss of the first section of the Book of Mormon manuscript. Two heartfelt endeavors representing two sacred assignments were lost.

Emma did what she perhaps did best in opposition: waited a bit, then dug back in. After the destruction of the Independence press office and the ejection of the Saints from Jackson County, Oliver Cowdery opened a new press in Kirtland in October 1834. The first publication there was a newspaper—*The Latter Day Saints' Messenger and Advocate*—another opportunity to print Emma's collection of hymns. The *Messenger* printed seven hymns by William Phelps, Parley P. Pratt, and Frederick Williams, all of which were later included in Emma's hymnal.

The hymnal project began again in earnest in the fall of 1835 in preparation for the dedication of the Kirtland Temple. On September

14, the high council met in the unfinished temple and once more formally appointed Emma to publish her hymn book, pledging their full support, again with William Phelps as publisher.[18] Emma was not present at either this council meeting or the earlier 1832 meeting in Independence to hear their support; these meetings were generally conducted and held by men. She learned to work through increasing institutional bureaucracy, particularly with a direct connection to Joseph, who held ecclesiastical authority. At the same time as the council meeting, in another part of the edifice, Joseph Smith Sr. was holding a patriarchal blessing meeting. Emma's friend Elizabeth Ann Whitney received her blessing and was promised the gift of tongues. She immediately stood and sang a song in what was determined to be the Adamic language, interpreted by Parley P. Pratt.[19] Elizabeth Ann's song revealed the same type of divine worship that the high council wanted to encourage in the production of a Church hymnal—one specific to the Restoration and to their institution. Emma hoped to capture this type of worship by tapping into her understanding of lived religion.

Emma's hymnal was finally typeset in 1835, the date of the imprint, but the run of one thousand copies was printed in early 1836. Frederick G. Williams owned the press—the same Frederick Granger Williams for whom Emma and Joseph named their son born later that year. Emma titled the book *A Collection of Sacred Hymns for the Latter Day Saints*. The hymnal displayed the new official name of the Church, one way in which Emma contributed to the production of institutional identity. The hymnal cost one dollar.

The book contained ninety hymn texts on 127 pages. It was a small book—3½ by 4 inches—typical for contemporary hymnals, easily kept in a pocket for daily use. Also typical was the lack of printed music; instead, the book offered metrical designation,

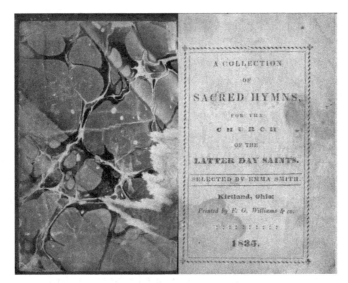

Emma Smith, comp., A Collection of Sacred Hymns for the Church of the Latter Day Saints, *Kirtland, OH: F. G. Williams & Co., 1835, Courtesy of Church History Library, Salt Lake City, Utah.*

allowing lyrics to be sung to any number of familiar tunes with the same meter.[20] Emma selected fifty hymns from various Protestant hymnals and forty from Latter-day Saint authors, including William Phelps, Parley P. Pratt, Eliza R. Snow, Edward Partridge, Thomas Marsh, and Philo Dibble.[21] The preface, most likely written by Emma, reflected both her revelation and the Church:

> In order to sing by the Spirit, and with the understanding, it is necessary that the church of the Latter Day Saints should have a collection of "Sacred Hymns," adapted to their faith and belief in the gospel, and, as far as can be, holding forth the promises made to the fathers who died in the precious faith of a glorious resurrection, and a thousand years' reign on earth with the Son of Man in his glory. Notwithstanding the church, as it were, is still

in its infancy, yet, as the song of the righteous is a prayer unto God, it is sincerely hoped that the following collection, selected with an eye single to his glory, may answer every purpose till more are composed, or till we are blessed with a copious variety of the songs of Zion.

The 1835 hymnal was an immediate success. After the temple dedication, the Literary Firm designated five hundred copies to be sent to Saints in Missouri, expanding its reach.[22] Almost immediately, the book was sold out. The Quorum of the Twelve Apostles saw the need for a second Church-approved hymnal and began selecting hymns in July 1839.[23] But without their knowledge, in 1838, David Rogers had already printed a hymnal for the growing number of Saints in New York, switching out forty songs but selling it as the one compiled and published by Emma.[24] This caused concern among the Nauvoo High Council, who brought charges against him in the April 1840 conference.[25] Meanwhile, Brigham Young and others took the 1839 list with them on missions to England, intent on printing a hymnal for the British Saints.[26] While they were away, the Nauvoo High Council again discussed the hymn book on October 27, 1839, and voted that Emma edit the second hymn book, perhaps in respect to her 1830 revelation assignment, rather than anyone in England.[27] Due to the lengthy time of overseas correspondence and the high cost of importing foreign books into England for a growing number of Church members there, Brigham had already published the Manchester hymnal before Joseph's communication of disapproval arrived.[28]

Emma moved forward with her second edition during a malaria epidemic and while caring for four young children. She continued to try to find time to study and write. She wrote Joseph, "I have many more things I could like to write but have not time and you may be astonished at my bad writing and incoherent manner, but you will pardon all when you reflect how hard it would be for you to write, when your hands were stiffened with hard work, and your heart convulsed with intense anxiety."[29] Her writing was a true labor of love. The November 1, 1840, issue of the *Times and Seasons* called for submissions: "Feeling desirous to have an extensive, and valuable book; it is requested that all those who have been endowed with a poetical genius, whose *muse* has not been altogether idle, will feel enough interest in a work of this kind, to immediately forward all *choice*, newly composed, or *revised* hymns."[30] Emma's second hymnal was ready for sale by March 15, 1841, as announced in the *Times and Seasons*.[31] The new book included 304 hymns, using seventy-eight from the 1835 hymnal's ninety hymns. Emma included seventy-seven new texts from the Manchester hymnal, then available in Nauvoo.[32] The Manchester hymnal, however, seemed to have gained more popularity and use than Emma's 1841 book, and it became the popular hymnal taken across the plains to Utah. The large number of British Saints in Nauvoo may have been partial to it, and Brigham Young's connection to the book may have been a factor. A notice in the *Times and Seasons* indicates a third effort to compile a Nauvoo hymnal in 1843, requesting hymns be sent to "Emma Smith, immediately," but the book was never published.[33]

Emma's membership and participation in the RLDS church allowed her to utilize her musical talents thirty years after her initial assignment. In October 1860, the church commissioned a hymnal from Emma, her third such publication. *The Latter Day Saints' Selection of Hymns* was published in Cincinnati in 1861, with an expanded version of the same book printed in 1864, including eight texts by David Hyrum Smith, Emma's youngest son. He had been raised with his mother's appreciation for music and the arts. These two hymnals formed the foundation of sacred music for the RLDS church.[34]

"Hosanna to God and the Lamb!"—Influence of Emma's Hymns

Emma's assignment to select hymns for a new church was a significant task. The hymnal needed to unite converts from a variety of religious backgrounds with diverse educational and cultural experience. Hymns allowed otherwise inarticulate or illiterate people to voice their faith and to increase their efforts to commune with God.[35] Emma drew from Congregational, Methodist, Baptist, Latter-day Saint, and other religious traditions, inclusively incorporating the diverse congregations of the early Saints into one united body to sing of Christ and restoration. The hymns Emma selected for the 1835 hymnal provided words of praise, doctrine, worship, and community to the new Church. They also reflected the fulfillment of prophecy and an invigorating effort to build Zion in preparation for the millennial reign of Christ at His Second Coming.[36] Her second hymnal reflected a shift in theme. After the expulsion from Missouri and the decline of hope and practicality in building an immediate Zion, the 1841 hymnal featured songs of grace and the private redemption of the soul through Christ.[37] Thus Emma's hymn selections define and mirror contemporary Church experiences, theology, and belief.

Joseph planned for music to be a significant part of the Kirtland Temple. As early as 1833, he designed the floor plan to include corner pews for a choir.[38] A choir school was organized on January 4, 1836, under the direction of Marvel Davis, in preparation for the dedication.[39] They met twice a week, from adolescent to adult, practicing six hymns from Emma's hymnal.[40] Joseph visited a rehearsal before the dedication and recorded, "They performed admirably, considering the advantages they have had."[41] After Joseph dedicated the house of the Lord and the final "amen," the choir sang "The Spirit of God."

The congregation then shouted "Hosanna! Hosanna! Hosanna to God and the Lamb!"[42] Together they raised their voices in music and worship, embodying Joseph's vision. Then, and throughout the next few weeks and months, manifestations of heavenly fire and angels—a season of Pentecost—encircled the Saints.[43] Emma's hymns facilitated unity among the Saints.

Hymns were an important part of the Nauvoo Relief Society (see chapter 8). Of the thirty-four meetings recorded in the minute book, twenty-five opened with either congregational or choir music. The minutes note titles of fifteen hymns, all from Emma's 1841 hymnal, printed a year before the Relief Society was organized. From those listed, there was not a repeat song; each meeting had a new hymn. On July 7, 1842, the women opened singing Isaac Watts's hymn "When I Survey the Wondrous Cross," from the 1841 hymnal. Emma was not present, so regular business was deferred, "and the time spent in exhortation and speaking, singing and prayer, much to the comfort and edification of those present."[44] Emma taught her sisters to use music both as a means to unite them in their sisterhood and to worship the Lord they served.

In addition to congregational worship, Emma's hymns became significant in family and individual worship. William Holmes Walker remembered arriving at the Smith home one evening just as the family was singing, as was customary before their family prayer. Emma led the music. William remembered, "I thought I had never heard such a sweet, heavenly music before."[45] Nauvoo artist Sutcliffe Maudsley painted a portrait of Julia Murdock Smith sometime between 1842 and 1844; he included an organ and music in the background, something that would have largely enhanced the music and entertainment in the Mansion House.[46] When Joseph was in Carthage, he asked John Taylor to sing one of his favorite hymns, "A Poor Wayfaring Man of Grief," included in the 1840 Manchester hymnal.[47] Using familiar songs to calm his anxiety may have been something he learned from his wife. In this manner, he could bring Emma with him in his last moments of life.

There are many of Emma's contemporaries who could have selected hymns and edited the first Church hymnals. William Phelps was both an editor and a hymn writer, and he adapted many popular songs of the time to fit the Restoration.[48] Eliza R. Snow wrote hymns expounding important Church doctrine, such as "O My Father" and other sacrament hymns still used today; years later she compiled song books for Primary children.[49] But none of these talented people had received the charge the Lord gave specifically to Emma in 1830. This was Emma's assignment, and she did the best she could with the resources she had. Her best attempt has become an endearing legacy, influencing Saints all over the world.

The hymn "Asleep in Jesus" was sung at Emma's funeral in 1879: "Asleep in Jesus! blessed sleep! / From which none ever wake to weep; / A calm and undisturbed repose, / Unbroken by the last of foes." The hymn came from the 1871 *Saints' Harp: A Collection of Hymns and Spiritual Songs for Public and Private Devotion*, edited by a group that included two of Emma's sons: Joseph III and David.[50] It seems appropriate that the public commemoration of Emma's life at her death would include a song of the righteous, a prayer. She would have approved.

Notes

1. Hymn 1, *A Collection of Sacred Hymns, for the Church of the Latter Day Saints*, ed. Emma Smith (Kirtland, OH: F. G. Williams, 1835), 5–6.
2. Elias Smith and Abner Jones, *Hymns, Original and Selected, for the Use of*

Christians (Boston: Manning and Laring, 1805), 231; Mary D. Poulter, "Doctrines of Faith and Hope Found in Emma Smith's 1835 Hymnbook," *BYU Studies* 37, no. 2 (Spring 1997): 37–38.
3. D&C 25:11.
4. Mary De Jong, "Textual Editing and the 'Making' of Hymns in Nineteenth-Century America," in *Sing Them Over Again to Me: Hymns and Hymnbooks in America*, ed. Mark A. Noll and Edith L. Blumhofer (Tuscaloosa, AL: University of Alabama Press, 2006), 77–78, 85.
5. Seraphina Gardner, ed., *Recollections of the Pioneers of Lee County* (Dixon, IL: Inez A. Kennedy, 1893), 96.
6. Vesta Crawford and Fay Olloerton, "The Elect Lady: A Yankee Woman Who Married the Prophet Joseph Smith," typescript manuscript, 5, 7, Vesta Crawford Collection, UofU.
7. Mark Staker, "Isaac and Elizabeth Hale in Their Endless Mountain Home," *Mormon Historical Studies* 15, no. 2 (Fall 2014): 61, 66–67.
8. D&C 25:11–12.
9. D&C 6:16.
10. D&C 25:7. See "exhort" and "expound" Noah Webster, *American Dictionary of the English Language* (1828).
11. Rachel Cope, "A Sacred Space for Women: Hymnody in Emma Hale Smith's Theology," *Journal of Religious History* 42, no. 2 (Jun. 2018): 242.
12. D&C 25:8.
13. Staker, "Isaac and Elizabeth Hale in Their Endless Mountain Home," 61, 66–67.
14. Literary Firm, Minutes, "Zion," Independence, MO, 30 Apr. 1832, Minute Book 2, 25-26, JSP.
15. Ron Romig and John H. Siebert, "First Impressions: The Independence, Missouri, Printing Operation, 1832–33," *The John Whitmer Historical Association Journal* 10 (1990): 56–57; Bruce A. Van Orden, *We'll Sing and We'll Shout: The Life and Times of W. W. Phelps* (Provo, UT: Religious Studies Center, Brigham Young University, 2018), 79.
16. "Hymns," *The Evening and the Morning Star* 1, no. 1 (June 1832): 8. Printed hymns include "What fair one is this, in the wilderness trav'ling," "Glorious things of thee are spoken," "The time is nigh, that happy time," "Redeemer of Israel," "On mountain tops the mount of God," "The body is but chaff," and "He died! the great Redeemer died!"
17. *Book of Commandments*, 1833, incomplete copy owned by Wilford

Woodruff, 167–82, CHL. Woodruff included, under the title, "Songs of Zion," "Age after age has rolled away," "The great and glorious gospel light," "Ere long the vail will rend in twain," "Come ye children of the kingdom," "My soul is full of peace and love," "The happy day has rolled on," "Beyond these earthly scenes in sight," and "There is a land the Lord will bless."
18. Minutes, Minute Book 1, 14 Sep. 1835, 108, JSP.
19. Elizabeth Ann Whitney, "A Leaf from an Autobiography," *WE* 7, no. 11 (1 Nov. 1878): 83; see *At the Pulpit: 185 Years of Discourses by Latter-day Saint Women*, ed. Jennifer Reeder and Kate Holbrook (Salt Lake City: Church Historian's Press, 2017), 7–9; churchhistorianspress.org.
20. Poulter, "Doctrines of Faith and Hope," 33–34.
21. Nancy Andersen, "The Song of the Righteous," Museum Gallery Talk, 2015, CHL.
22. Literary Firm, Minute Book 1, 2 Apr. 1836, 199, JSP.
23. Joseph Smith, Journal, 1839, 8–20 Jul. 1839, 9, JSP. See "David Rogers," bio, JSP.
24. David W. Rogers, *A Collection of Sacred Hymns for the Church of the Latter Day Saints* (New York City: Vinten, 1838). See Hicks, "Emma Smith's 1841 Hymnbook," 14–15; Naida R. Williamson, "David White Rogers of New York," *BYU Studies* 35, no. 2 (1995): 73–90.
25. Joseph Smith, Minutes and Discourses, 6–8 Apr. 1840, *T&S* 1, no. 6 (Apr. 1840): 92; JSP.
26. Michael Hicks, *Mormonism and Music: A History* (Urbana, IL: University of Illinois Press, 1989), 23–27.
27. Joseph Smith, Minutes, 27 Oct. 1839, JSP.
28. Hyrum Smith to Parley P. Pratt, 22 Dec. 1839, JS Collection, CHL; Parley P. Pratt, Brigham Young, John Taylor, eds., *A Collection of Sacred Hymns for The Church of Jesus Christ of Latter Day Saints, in Europe* (Manchester, England: 1840); Michael Hicks, "Emma Smith's 1841 Hymnbook," *Journal of Book of Mormon Studies* 21, no. 1 (2012): 14–18.
29. Emma Smith to Joseph Smith, 7 Mar. 1839, JSP.
30. "Hymns!! Hymns!!" *T&S* 2, no. 1 (1 Nov. 1839): 204, emphasis in original.
31. "Books," *T&S* 2, no. 10 (15 Marc 1841): 355.
32. Nancy J. Andersen, "Mormon Hymnody: Kirtland Roots and Evolutionary Branches," *Journal of Mormon History* 32, no. 1 (Spring 2006): 154.
33. "Sacred Hymns," *T&S* 6, no. 6 (1 Feb. 1843): 95.
34. Richard Clothier, "'Cultivate the Gifts of Music and Song': The Hymnals

of the Reorganization," *The John Whitmer Historical Association Journal* 23 (2003): 138–40.
35. Noll and Blumhoffer, *Sing Them Over to Me*, vii.
36. Cope, "A Sacred Space for Women," 242.
37. Hicks, "Emma Smith's 1841 Hymnbook," 13.
38. Plan of the House of the Lord in Kirtland, Ohio, fragments, circa June 1833, JSP.
39. Joseph Smith, History, vol. B-1, 4 Jan. 1836, 679, JSP.
40. Caroline Barnes Crosby, Journal, in *Women's Voices: An Untold History of the Latter-day Saints, 1830–1900*, ed. Kenneth W. Godfrey, Audrey M. Godfrey, and Jill Mulvay Derr (Salt Lake City: Deseret Book, 1982), 48; Hicks, *Mormonism and Music*, 39.
41. Joseph Smith, Journal, 16 Mar. 1835, 170, JSP.
42. *Collection of Sacred Hymns*, 120–21; Joseph Smith, Journal, 27 Mar. 1836, 172–84, JSP.
43. See, for example, Eliza R. Snow in Edward W. Tullidge, *The Women of Mormondom* (New York: Tullidge and Crandall, 1877), 95; and, Mary Fielding [Smith] to Mercy Fielding Thompson, 8 Jul. 1837, 1–2, CHL.
44. NRS, 7 July 1842, 73, CHL; FFYRS, 87.
45. William Holmes Walker, *The Life Incidents and Travels of Elder William Holmes Walker and His Association with Joseph Smith, the Prophet* (Elizabeth Jane Walker Piepgrass, 1943), 8.
46. S. Reed Murdock, *Julia, the "Other" Twin: A Biography* (Salt Lake City, Eborn, 2004), 52–54.
47. Willard Richards, Journal Excerpt, 23–27 Jun. 1844, 36, JSP.
48. "William Wines Phelps," JSP; Hicks, *Mormonism and Music,* 12–14, 19, 28.
49. Eliza R. Snow, *Hymns and Songs: Selected from Various Authors for the Primary Associations of the Children of Zion* (Salt Lake City: Deseret News Press, 1880); Eliza R. Snow, *Tune Book for the Primary Associations of the Children of Zion* (Salt Lake City: Juvenile Instructor, 1880). See Jill Mulvay Derr, "The Significance of 'O My Father' in the Personal Journey of Eliza R. Snow," *BYU Studies* 36, no. 1 (Winter 1996): 84–126.
50. Mrs. Mackay, in *Saints' Harp: A Collection of Hymns and Spiritual Songs for Public and Private Devotion*, ed. Joseph Smith, Mark H. Forscutt, David H. Smith, and Norman W. Smith (Lamoni, IA: Reorganized Church of Jesus Christ of Latter Day Saints, 1871); lyrics by William B. Bradbury, *Saints' Harmony* (Lamoni, IA: 1889).

Chapter 7

FIRST LADY

Emma as Wife of the President

In January 1844, Emma prepared a meal for Joseph and William W. Phelps. Joseph remarked on his "kind, provident wife," explaining that "when I wanted a little bread and milk, she would load the table with so many good things, it would destroy my appetite." When William remarked that the Smiths should have a smaller table so Joseph could restrict his portions, Emma responded, "He can never eat without his friends." Joseph concluded, "That is the wisest thing I ever heard you say."[1] He knew that Emma, an impeccable hostess, expanded his capacity in many ways.

Emma's situation as wife of the prophet Joseph Smith put her in a pivotal position, blending private with public. Her 1830 revelation taught her that "the office of thy calling shall be for a comfort unto my servant, Joseph Smith," and that "thy husband shall support thee in the church; for unto them is his calling."[2] When Emma married Joseph, he had not yet begun his work as the Prophet of the Restoration. But as the Book of Mormon was translated and published and the Church organized, she quickly learned that her marriage to a man who would soon become the Church President required her to act as the president's wife—a First Lady. The transition from their private marriage to a public role was gradual over the years, but increasingly consumed her time and energy. Emma opened her home, shared her skills, cared for the poor and sick, and demonstrated the same kind of refinement for the Church that she had learned from her family in Harmony. Most importantly, Emma expanded the delineation of her immediate family to include a community of Saints.

"The office of thy calling"—Relief from Persecution

Immediately following her baptism on June 28, 1830, when Colesville neighbors charged Joseph with misconduct, Emma gathered with a group of women to pray for his release.[3] By October, she had organized the efforts of women to prepare clothing for missionaries traveling west.[4] Lucy Mack Smith observed that sewing "was no easy task, as most of it had to be manufactured out of the raw material." Emma used her resources at hand, often overexerting herself to the point of extended illness. Lucy described Emma's public activity in Kirtland in 1831 as ambitious; Emma's whole heart was occupied in the work of the Lord with no interest except the Church.[5] The precarious balance between their private and public lives was one that Joseph and Emma struggled with throughout their marriage.

Emma experienced Joseph's persecution early on and used her resources to protect him and the Church. Within the first three years of their marriage, she defended him to her family, she warned him of impending trouble with the plates in Manchester, and she prayed for him to be released from jail after her baptism. Then, in March 1832, she witnessed firsthand mob violence when Joseph was forcibly removed from their bedroom—a front room in the Johnson home in Hiram, Ohio—by a group that took him to a field to tar and feather him. Joseph wrangled away from his captors and crawled, naked, back home. Emma found him in the dark, and thinking the tar was blood and that Joseph was "mashed to pieces," fainted. Neighbor women gathered at the Johnson home came to the rescue; they spent the night attending to Emma and helping her scrape the tar off of Joseph's body in preparation for his sermon the following morning.[6] She helped him publicly present a persona of strength, endurance, and authority on the very steps from which he had been dragged, while she struggled to maintain her own composure and security.

Emma's 1834 patriarchal blessing recognized the calamities she had seen and would see, reminding her of promised divine comfort. Joseph Sr., as voice, said, "Thy soul has been afflicted because of the wickedness of men in seeking the destruction of thy companion, and thy Lord thy God has heard thy supplication." He continued, "The Lord will have respect to thy cries."[7] When Joseph was imprisoned in Liberty Jail, Emma's correspondence kept him linked to the Saints. She visited him twice in December 1838 and once in January 1839, bringing with her other wives whose husbands were with Joseph, as well as news about Church members in Far West.[8] Joseph dictated a letter to the Saints a week after Emma's first visit, based on her report.[9] He addressed another epistle to the Church to her "because I wanted you to have the first reading of it." He asked her to keep the original and make a copy for his parents.[10]

On March 7, 1839, Emma wrote a letter from Quincy, Illinois, to Joseph, who was still in prison in Missouri. She acknowledged Joseph's personal trials as well as the trouble of countless Saints, including their own family. "No one but God knows the reflections of my mind and the feelings of my heart when I left our house and home," she wrote, "and almost all of everything that we possessed excepting our little children." She also wrote of the afflictions of other Saints. "The daily sufferings of our brethren in travelling and camping out nights, and those on the other side of the river would beggar the most lively description." Emma continued, "The recollection is more than human nature ought to bear, and if God does not record our sufferings and avenge our wrongs on them that are guilty, I shall be sadly mistaken."[11] Her words must have struck his heart, for a short time later, on March 20, he wrote another letter to the Church. He pleaded with God to reveal Himself with compassion to the Saints and to exact justice on those who persecuted them. His prayer to God mirrored the words he had recently read from Emma: "Let thine anger be kindled against our enemies and in the fury of thine heart with thy sword avenge us of our wrongs. Remember thy suffering saints, oh our God."[12] Joseph's pleas were the act of an intercessor for his people, based on Emma's intercession between them.

Emma rallied the Saints to provide protection for Joseph in times of trouble. In August 1842, he faced renewed threats of extradition back to Missouri for the attempted murder of previous governor Lilburn Boggs. He went into hiding, and for a while, Emma passed messages to him from Nauvoo. On August 16, she wrote to him, "I shall make the best arrangements I can and be as well prepared as possible. But still I feel good confidence that you can be protected without leaving this country." She recognized the influence of his immediate leadership to the Saints. "There is more ways than one to take care of you."[13] Joseph and Emma shared persecution and, while sometimes living in fear-ravaged faith, led the Saints through trouble.

"Ever ready to alleviate the distress of the afflicted"—Care for the Saints

While Emma would have naturally extended healing and hospitality to all in need, her position as wife of the prophet gave her extraordinary opportunities to widen the number of people to whom she could minister. Her experience in moving from place to place and living off the generosity of others led her to always open her doors to those in need. Her relationship with the Whitney family illustrates a transaction of care over time. Elizabeth Ann welcomed Emma and Joseph into her Kirtland home several times. She wrote, "Joseph and Emma were very dear to me, and with my own hands I ministered to them, feeling it a privilege and an honor to do so," for this was the presidential First Family.[14] Years later, when Emma was in a better situation in Nauvoo, the roles were reversed. The Whitneys, having lost all their possessions upon leaving Ohio, arrived in town and became sick with malaria, a common ailment in the swampy area. Joseph visited the family in the spring of 1840 and, seeing their condition, brought them to the Smith homestead. Elizabeth Ann remembered, "One day while coming out of the house into the yard the remembrance of a prophecy Joseph Smith had made to me, while living in our house in Kirtland, flashed through my mind like an electric shock." She continued, "It was this: that even as we had done by him, in opening our doors to him and his family when he was without a home; even so should we in the future be received by him into his house."[15]

Emma's nursing of the Whitneys demonstrated a natural healing skill, perhaps learned from her mother, Elizabeth Hale, and mother-in-law, Lucy Mack Smith—both true frontier women. In December 1835, Samuel Brannan, a new convert, came to the Smith home with a swollen arm from a bruise on his elbow. Emma prepared "a poultice of herbs." She knew how to be resourceful with the plants around her. Joseph recognized her ability to heal: "Sister Emma is ever ready to alleviate the distress of the afflicted, . . . through the blessings of God."[16]

Emma demonstrated her healing capacity in the summer of 1839 when swarms of mosquitos came to the swampy marshlands of Commerce (later Nauvoo), causing a malaria epidemic. Emma rode with Joseph on horseback throughout the settlement; together, the couple visited the sick, anointing and blessing them, and brought many to their home.[17] Joseph III helped his mother nurse the sick in their yard. Emma instructed him to carry a small bucket and get cool water for the patients.[18] She nursed the Whitneys, the Huntingtons, and her in-laws, the Smiths, among others.[19] Lucy Mack Smith remembered, "I was taken very sick and brought nigh unto death." She continued, "For five nights Emma never left me, but stood at my bedside all the night long, at the end of which time she was overcome with fatigue and taken sick herself."[20]

Emma warmly welcomed orphans, the homeless, and the sick into her home, providing lodging and often work. Joseph III remembered with fondness the way his mother created an open home: "Our house was a convenient place of gathering and was always more or less crowded with those who came from a distance and those employed in household affairs."[21] Jane Manning was one. She arrived in Nauvoo in 1843 after being denied passage on a steamship because of her race and subsequently losing all her belongings. She remembered Emma welcoming her and her family from the front door of the Mansion House. Emma's racially inclusive perspective began when she was young; her aunt married a free Black man, so she grew up with biracial cousins.[22] Emma offered Jane a job and lodging and became her friend.[23] Jane is just one example of many others who benefited from Emma's hospitality and grace.

After Joseph's death and Emma's subsequent marriage to Lewis Bidamon, Emma continued to provide assistance to her community based on her experience as First Lady. Her adult children and grandchildren, as well as neighbors in Nauvoo, often came to her for herbal remedies. Granddaughter Emma Smith McCallum remembered, "Every body knew of Mother Bidamon's salves for cuts—bruises—fever—rheumatism—for every kind of ache & pain." She knew how to make salves of herbs, lobelia, sage, sassafras, ginseng, saffron, spearmint, and catnip.[24] She lovingly sent detailed instructions to Joseph III on how to make a special salve. The recipe was complicated, and she offered possible substitutions if some ingredients weren't available at different times of the year. "Now if you did not save any gymson [gypsum] last fall you can make it with the elder alone." She then described her own first salve and offered help: "If you have not the gymson and elder let me know it and I will send You the salve ready made."[25] She remained eager to help however she could.

"Seated around her table"—Presidential Entertainment

Emma welcomed people to her table, both friend and foe, a skill that she honed in the Hale home in Harmony as she cooked meals shared with travelers, farm hands, and neighbors.[26] On October 28, 1835, Newel and Elizabeth Ann Whitney, Newel's parents, and others stopped by the Smith home to discuss the ongoing establishment of Zion in Missouri. Emma expressed a fervent desire that all "might be seated around her table in the land of promise." Joseph appreciated his wife's efforts: "My heart responded Amen God grant it, I ask in the name of Jesus Christ."[27] He loved sharing a celebration and a meal with fellow Saints, often prepared by and shared with Emma. On January 17, 1836, Joseph attended a dinner party at William Cahoon's home. "It is good for brethren to dwell together in unity," he commented. "It is like the dew upon the mountains of Israel where the Lord commanded blessings even life forever more."[28] Emma even served a banquet of "the best which my house afforded," according to Joseph, to a group of officers who had attempted to extradite Joseph to Missouri in June 1843.[29] Emma could support a lifestyle of refinement and provide fine meals for others.

As the First Family, the Smiths often invited a host of friends to family celebrations; these became community parties. The year 1843 illustrates just a few of these events. On January 18, Joseph and Emma marked their sixteenth wedding anniversary with a "jubilee" and fifty guests in their home. Eliza R. Snow and Wilson Law wrote songs for the event. The "governor and governess"—Joseph and Emma—served guests, including children, at large tables.[30] When the small homestead could no longer contain the Smiths' entertainment, and to provide more lodging for guests, the family moved into the Mansion House on August 31, 1843. They celebrated with an open house dinner for one hundred people on October 3.[31] Later that year, Joseph spent his birthday, December 23, preparing for a party for "young ladies and gentlemen" at the Mansion House held on Christmas day. Before the party, though, the Smiths hosted fifty guests for Christmas lunch. They then fed dinner to the large party and "spent the evening in Music and Danci[n]g &c. in a most cheerful and frie[n]dly mannr during the festivities."[32] Anniversaries, housewarmings, even holiday celebrations were not private, but public affairs.

In June 1843, Joseph purchased half-ownership of the steamboat *Maid of Iowa*.[33] The boat had been used to transport British emigrants, as well as departing and returning missionaries, from the New Orleans harbor up the Mississippi River to Nauvoo, but it soon became a form of entertainment. Joseph and Emma hosted day trips on the river for Church and civic leaders and young people. The excursions often included food, bands, speeches, and cannon salutes.[34] Helen Mar Whitney remembered one trip in June of 1843. William Pitt's brass band played, and "every heart was made glad, and everything looked bright and hopeful." The fifteen-year-old relished being in the company of Joseph, Emma, and a "score" of friends.[35]

"Harmony and decorum that existed among the brothers and sisters"—Church Events

In her public role as Joseph's wife, Emma accompanied him on ministry visits and to ecclesiastical events, increasing feelings of fellowship among the Saints. The last months of 1835 in Kirtland demonstrate a busy time in Emma's life: she was also compiling the hymnal and caring for two young children while she supported Joseph in his duties. On October 31, 1835, Emma and the children accompanied Joseph to call on his brother Don Carlos, his friend Shadrach Roundy, and their families. On November 18, she attended the funeral of Nathan Harris, father of Martin Harris, and heard Joseph preach on the topic of resurrection to an attentive congregation. She attended weddings: Newel Knight married Lydia Goldthwaite in a ceremony performed by Joseph on November 24, followed by the wedding of Warren Parrish and Martha H. Raymond on December 5. On December 2, the Smith family took a sleigh ride to Painesville about ten miles away, where Joseph attended to business and the family dined with Sister Harriet Howe, sister of journalist Eber D. Howe—one of Joseph's major critics at the time. Joseph recorded that they "had a fine ride, and agreeable visit; the sleighing is good and weather pleasant."[36] Each occasion allowed Emma to witness Joseph developing his ecclesiastical authority and expounding theological doctrine, and for the family to be seen publicly. Such public interactions increased a sense of community, expanded their family, and extended Church doctrine. Emma and Joseph were partners in his ministry.

Following a busy season of visits, the winter of 1835 through early spring of 1836 was a season of feasts in Kirtland, representative of biblical events. In November and December 1835, Joseph attended patriarchal blessing meetings directed by his father, often including lavish meals; one of the events had sixty in attendance.[37] At these dinners, Emma assisted in creating an atmosphere of "harmony and decorum that existed among the brothers and sisters," for which Joseph was extremely grateful.[38] In early January 1836, Bishop Newel and Elizabeth Ann Whitney held a three-day "love feast" for the poor, attended by Joseph and Emma. The Whitneys considered this as a part of their ecclesiastical responsibilities. Joseph described the first day as a "sumptuous feast . . . after the order of the Son of God the lame the halt and blind were invited according to the instruction of the Saviour."[39] Such events were reminiscent of charity or *agape* banquets held by New Testament Saints.[40] After the solemn assembly and dedication of the temple on March 27, 1836, feasts were held to break bread "from house to house," giving Saints opportunities to "rejoice, pray, bless, and prophecy" together, Joseph recorded. "The spirit of God was abundantly poured out upon us, the poor were bountifully regaled—and one universal scene of love, joy and hilarity prevailed this happy season continued from day to day and week to week to the entire satisfaction of all."[41] Nancy A. Tracy remembered, "The elders went from house to house, blessing the Saints and administering the sacrament. Feasts were given. Three families joined together and held one at our house. We baked a lot of bread."[42] Emma must have done the same; it was an exciting time to be a Latter-day Saint, and she was in the thick of it.

Emma's home space often became Church headquarters, temple, meeting house, and family home, all wrapped together, even when she and Joseph were living with other people. When they lived in the Johnson home in Hiram, Ohio, in 1832, Joseph received numerous revelations and worked with Sidney Rigdon and John Whitmer on the revision of the Bible.[43] When the Smiths lived in the Whitney store in Kirtland in early 1833, Joseph convened the School of the Prophets, where Emma struggled to clean the remains of the men's tobacco use. As a result of her concern about the smoky air and stained floor in the same room used to translate scripture and receive revelation, Joseph, a non-tobacco user himself, inquired of the Lord and received revelation known today as the Word of Wisdom.[44] Church councils and courts, interviews, lectures, and meetings were held in the Nauvoo Mansion House.[45] Before the temple was completed, ordinances were held in the Red Brick Store, the old homestead, and in an upper room of the Mansion House.[46] Emma often participated, going from the kitchen and nursery as a mother to a temple matron—all within different rooms of her home. Only walls, doors, and staircases separated public from private.

First Lady Emma must have felt an incumbent responsibility to set both a personal example and a model marriage and family. Joseph's naturally charismatic behavior attracted many to the Church, but it also attracted gossip from naysayers. As early as Harmony, Emma's cousin accused Joseph of attempting to seduce her friend, Elizabeth Winters. In Kirtland, Oliver Cowdery expressed concern over Joseph's relationship with Fanny Alger, a hired girl in the Smith home, with a court held in Far West in April 1838.[47] Contemporary records do not detail Emma's reactions—she knew her husband as a kind, trustworthy man.[48] In Nauvoo, the gossip surrounding John C. Bennett and his practice of spiritual wifery—he appropriated the doctrine he had heard about as an alibi for seducing women—cast a dark shadow on the First Family. The scandal augmented when Joseph's behavior, particularly toward women, seemed to reveal relationships extended beyond friendships, perhaps corroborating some of the talk.

As time went on and misunderstanding, speculation, and accusations increased, the separation between public and private decreased. Emma reached a boiling point. By 1843, she had become aware of Joseph's sealings to several of her friends in Relief Society without consulting her. These were not proper behaviors for a marriage and family in the spotlight, and she felt personally betrayed and publicly scandalized. Emma took matters into her own hands at Relief Society meetings in March 1844—a desperate attempt to restore order and refinement to the public role she held and to set an example of moral purity. She warned women against seduction, which consequently exacerbated confusion. Emotion overtook reason and chaos ensued, leading to the eventual end of the Nauvoo Relief Society and to the breakup of the First Family. This experience influenced Emma and her family after Joseph's death; she did not tell her children about plural marriage, perhaps to avoid embarrassment and maintain appropriate decorum.

First Lady in Civic Affairs

Joseph's role as prophet and Church President often included the temporal affairs of his people. The Lord instructed him to call the Saints to "the Ohio," to Zion in Missouri, and to Nauvoo.[49] In these places, Joseph did the best with what he had to make things work, including the United Firm, the Kirtland Safety Society, and land purchases in Illinois.[50] He helped to create a powerful city charter and a militia, a means of protection the Saints never had in Missouri.[51] He became the mayor of Nauvoo on May 19, 1842.[52] And through this all, Emma stood at his side, doing her best to assist him.

Joseph was appointed Lieutenant General of the Nauvoo Legion in February 1841.[53] As First Lady, Emma bore a majestic presence with Joseph and the Legion in their parades and public appearances. Emmeline B. Wells wrote, "Many recall seeing her mounted on horseback beside her husband in military parade and a grander couple could nowhere be seen. She always dressed becomingly, and a riding costume showed off her shapely figure to the best advantage. She was a woman of commanding presence."[54] Eunice Billings Snow remembered, "Some of the most impressive moments of my life were, when I saw the 'Nauvoo Legion' on parade with the Prophet, then Gen. Joseph Smith, with his wife, Emma Hale Smith, on horseback at the head of the troops. It was indeed, an imposing sight, and one that I shall always remember. He so fair, and she so dark, in their beautiful riding habits. He in full military suit, and she with her habit trimmed with gold buttons, a neat cap on her head, with a black plume in it."[55] Nancy J. Tharpe described Emma's riding dress as "black with a bonnet of a sort of poke style with which she wore a vale which could be pulled to expose [her] face. Her riding whip had an ivory handle and her side-saddle was also very elegant."[56] It must have been a delight for Emma to participate.

Joseph Smith, gouache and ink on paper, Sutcliffe Maudsley, circa 1842. Courtesy Church History Museum, Salt Lake City, Utah.

Emma Smith, gouache and ink on paper, Sutcliffe Maudsley, circa 1842. Courtesy Church History Museum, Salt Lake City, Utah.

With the First Family's public entertainment, care for the Saints, Church events, and civic duties, Emma and Joseph struggled through their private relationship regarding the Lord's requirement of plural marriage. While civic and Church counsels and mayor's court were all held in the Nauvoo Mansion, the couple talked behind closed doors, rode their horses, or took the carriage outside the city to find time and place for private conversation. Emma's public role of First Lady always intersected and even at times conflicted with her private relationship as wife.

With Joseph's death on June 27, 1844, Emma's role as First Lady suddenly ended. She hosted approximately ten thousand Saints in her home as they filed in to pay their respects to Joseph and Hyrum.[57] While she had dealt privately with continuous financial hardship, gossip and scandal, and intrusions into her marriage, she simultaneously shouldered public roles as partner, agent, and spokesperson for her husband. As First Lady, Emma's family expanded to include the body of Saints. She had seen Joseph and the Saints through persecution and parties, sickness and ceremony, starvation and fine meals, celebration and mourning. With the death of the president, Emma's function as First Lady came to a close, and she shifted her focus to caring for her immediate family.

Notes

1. Joseph Smith, History, vol. E-1, 4 Jan. 1844, 223, JSP.
2. D&C 25:5, 9.
3. John S. Reed, "Some of the Remarks of John S. Reed, Esq., as Delivered before the State Convention," *T&S* 5, no. 11 (1 Jun. 1844): 551.
4. See "Oliver Cowdery and Others Covenanted to Preach to Indians," 17 Oct. 1830, Events, JSP.
5. Lucy Mack Smith, History, 1844–1845, book 13, 7–8, JSP.
6. Joseph Smith History, vol. A-1, 207–8, JSP; "History of Luke Johnson," *Millennial Star* 26, no. 53 (31 Dec. 1884): 835.

7. Joseph Smith Sr., Blessing to Emma Smith, Patriarchal Blessing Book 1, 4–5, JSP.
8. Emma visited Liberty on 8–9 and 20–22 Dec. 1838 and on 21 Jan. 1839. *History of the Reorganized Church of Jesus Christ of Latter Day Saints*, vol. 2 (Independence, MO: Herald Publishing House, 1896–1976), 309, 315.
9. Joseph Smith to the Church in Caldwell County, Missouri, 16 Dec. 1838, JSP.
10. Joseph Smith to Emma Smith, 21 Mar. 1839, JSP.
11. Emma Smith to Joseph Smith, 7 Mar. 1839, Letterbook 2, 37, JSP.
12. D&C 121:5–6; Joseph Smith to the Church and Edward Partridge, 20 Mar. 1839, JSP.
13. Emma Hale Smith to Joseph Smith, 16 Aug. 1842, JSP.
14. Elizabeth Ann Whitney, "A Leaf from an Autobiography," *WE* 7, no. 7 (1 Sep. 1878): 51.
15. Elizabeth Ann Whitney, "A Leaf from an Autobiography," *WE* 7, no. 12 (15 Nov. 1878): 91.
16. Joseph Smith, Journal, 14 Dec. 1835, 66–67; Joseph Smith, History, 14 Dec. 1835, 147–48, JSP.
17. Wandle Mace, autobiography, circa 1890, 41, CHL.
18. Mary Audentia Smith Anderson, ed., "The Memoirs of President Joseph Smith (1832–1914)," *The Saints' Herald* (13 Nov. 1934): 1454.
19. Whitney, "A Leaf from an Autobiography," *WE* 7, no. 12 (15 Nov. 1878): 91; "Our Beloved President, Zina D.H. Young," *WE* 30, no. 4 (Sep. 1901): 29.
20. Lucy Mack Smith, History, 1845, 306, JSP.
21. Anderson, "The Memoirs of President Joseph Smith," *The Saints' Herald* (6 Nov. 1934): 1614.
22. Mark Staker, "Isaac and Elizabeth Hale in Their Endless Mountain Home," *Mormon Historical Studies* 15, no. 2 (Fall 2014): 12 fn23.
23. Jane Manning James, autobiography, circa 1902, CHL. See Quincy D. Newell, *Your Sister in the Gospel: The Life of Jane Manning James, A Nineteenth-Century Black Mormon* (New York City: Oxford University Press, 2019).
24. Emma Smith McCallum, reminiscences; Frederick Alexander Smith, reminiscences, in Buddy Youngreen, *Reflections of Emma* (Orem, UT: Keepsake, 1982), 61, 97–99.
25. Emma Smith Bidamon to Joseph Smith III, 20 Jan. 1867, CCLA.

26. Mark Staker surmised Emma Hale's role as a cook in a BYU Education Week class on 20 Aug. 2019. His careful research in an unpublished manuscript places Emma serving breakfast. Mark Staker, "Murder on the Susquehanna: The Execution of Jason Treadwell," 2012, copy in author's possession.
27. Joseph Smith, "Sketch Book for the Use of Joseph Smith, Jr," Sep. 1835–Apr. 1836, 12, JSP.
28. Joseph Smith, History, 17 Jan. 1836, 185, JSP.
29. Joseph Smith, History, vol. D-1, 30 June 1843, 1598, JSP.
30. Joseph Smith, Journal, Book 1, 135–38, JSP.
31. Joseph Smith, Journal, Book 3, 3 Oct. 1843, 115, JSP; "Pleasure Party, and Dinner at 'Nauvoo Mansion,'" *Nauvoo Neighbor*, 4 Oct. 1843.
32. Joseph Smith, Journal, Book 3, 23 Dec. 1843, 25 Dec. 1843, 209, 211, JSP; "Dinner Party," *Nauvoo Neighbor*, 13 Dec. 1843.
33. Joseph Smith, Journal, Book 2, 2 June 1843, 231, JSP.
34. Donald L. Enders, "The Steamboat *Maid of Iowa*: Mormon Mistress of the Mississippi," *BYU Studies* 19, no. 3 (Spring 1979): 321–35.
35. Helen Mar Whitney, "Scenes and Incidents in Nauvoo," *WE* 11, no. 8 (15 Sep. 1882): 58.
36. Joseph Smith, History, 21 Oct.–2 December 1835, 110–39, JSP.
37. Matthew C. Godfrey, "A Season of Blessings: The Function of Blessings in Kirtland, Ohio, 1834–1835," *Mormon Historical Studies* 18, no. 1 (Spring 2017): 40–41.
38. Joseph Smith, "Sketch Book for the Use of Joseph Smith, Jr," 92, JSP.
39. Joseph Smith, Journal, 7 Jan., 9 Jan. 1836, 101–3, JSP.
40. See Robert L. Millet, *Studies in Scripture: Acts to Revelation* (Salt Lake City: Deseret Book, 1987), 248; John W. Welch, lecture, in *Teachings of the Book of Mormon Semester 4*, ed. Hugh W. Nibley (Provo, UT: Foundation for Ancient Research and Mormon Studies, 1993), 147.
41. Joseph Smith, History, vol. B-1, addenda, Apr. 1836, JSP.
42. Nancy A. Tracy, "Diary of Nancy Naomi Alexander Tracy," typescript, 7–8, CHL.
43. Joseph Smith, History, vol. A-1, 153, 209, JSP; Steven C. Harper, *Making Sense of the Doctrine and Covenants: A Guided Tour through Modern Revelations* (Salt Lake City: Deseret Book, 2008), xii–xiii, xvi; Scott H. Faulring, Kent P. Jackson, and Robert J. Matthews, eds., *Joseph Smith's New*

Translations of the Bible: Original Manuscripts (Provo, UT: Religious Studies Center, BYU, 2004), 57–59.

44. D&C 89; Jed Woodsworth, "The Word of Wisdom," *RIC*.
45. See "Nauvoo Mansion, Nauvoo, Illinois," josephsmithpapers.org.
46. See Joseph Smith, Journal, book 3, 28 Sep. 1843, 110, 22 Oct. 1843, 142, 1 Nov. 1843, 152, JSP.
47. Richard Lyman Bushman, *Joseph Smith—Rough Stone Rolling: A Cultural Biography of Mormonism's Founder* (New York: Knopf, 2005), 323–26.
48. In 1872, William E. McLellin, a member of the Twelve Apostles, wrote about an incident related to him by Frederick G. Williams in 1838, stating that Emma caught Joseph in a compromised position with Fanny Alger near the time of Joseph III's birth. The length of time and trustworthiness of secondhand information present problems. William McLellin to Joseph Smith III, n.d. Jul. 1872, CCLA. In 1875, McLellin told a newspaper reporter from the *Salt Lake Tribune* that Emma witnessed Joseph's interaction with Fanny through a crack in the barn door. *Salt Lake Tribune*, 6 Oct. 1875. See Linda King Newell and Valeen Tippets Avery, *Mormon Enigma: Emma Hale Smith* (Urbana, IL: University of Illinois Press, 1994), 65–66.
49. Joseph Smith, Revelation, 30 Dec. 1830, 20 Jul. 1831, Revelation Book 1, 49, 93, JSP; D&C 37, 57; "Kirtland, Ohio," "Zion/New Jerusalem," "Nauvoo (Commerce), Illinois," *CHTE*.
50. See "The Kirtland Safety Society," "United Firm ('United Order')," "Nauvoo (Commerce), Illinois," *CHTE*.
51. Alex D. Smith, "Organizing the Church in Nauvoo: D&C 124, 125," *RIC*.
52. Joseph Smith, Journal, 19 May 1842, 122, JSP.
53. Joseph Smith, History, vol. C-1, 4 Feb. 1841, 1162, JSP.
54. Emmeline B. Wells, "L. D. S. Women of the Past; Personal Impressions," *WE* 36, no. 7 (Feb. 1908): 49.
55. "A Sketch of the Life of Eunice Billings Snow," *WE* 39, no. 3 (Sep. 1910): 22.
56. Nancy J. Tharpe, "Reminiscence of Sister N. J. Tharpe," *Journal of History* 11 (Jan. 1918): 120.
57. Joseph Smith, History, vol. F-1, 29 Jun. 1844, 189, JSP.

Chapter 8

FIRST PRESIDENTESS OF THE RELIEF SOCIETY

Emma as Elect Lady

Emma gathered women to pray for Joseph when he was imprisoned in 1830.[1] She organized women to sew clothing for missionaries.[2] She and other women housed and fed men working on the Kirtland Temple.[3] And in March 1842, she led a group of women who had initially gathered to sew shirts for men working on the Nauvoo Temple as their Elect Lady, or "presidentess" of the Relief Society. The transition illustrated a shift from building Zion to building the temple and receiving the full temple endowment. Emma's 1830 revelation named her "an elect lady, whom I have called," and stated that she would be "ordained . . . to expound scriptures, and to exhort the church."[4] In her 1834 patriarchal blessing, Joseph Sr. told her that she would "have power to instruct thy sex."[5] Emma was foreordained to work with women to provide relief to the Saints and to prepare for the temple.

Emma's title and position as Elect Lady developed over time, like many of Joseph's visionary ideas for the restored Church. The meanings of the 1830 revelation expanded as Emma addressed current needs. She had expounded scripture and exhorted the Church through her hymns and community service; she had protected the plates and manuscripts and aided Joseph in the coming forth of scripture; she had comforted and supported her husband; and she had borne, lost, and parented her children—but the Relief Society provided an entirely new locus of authority and autonomy for women and for Emma herself.

"Thou art an elect lady"—Historical Context

The term *elect lady* comes from the second New Testament epistle of John: "The elder unto the elect lady and her children, whom I love in the truth." The last verse of the chapter concludes the letter: "The children of thy elect sister greet thee."[6] Not much is known about the specific reference, but in Hebrew, *elect* means chosen out by God for the rendering of distinct service, and *lady* suggests a female lord or queen, someone strong or mighty.[7] Some early American religious traditions used the term as a title of respect for notable women, such as Shaker Ann Lee and Quaker Jemima Wilkinson. Both women lived in upstate New York, and both were strong female leaders.[8] Emma's title, though, was seen differently by Latter-day Saints—a restoration of a biblical organization. Eliza R. Snow, the second presidentess, taught that the Relief Society "existed in the church anciently."[9]

The Nauvoo Relief Society was not the first female association organized to address social needs. As early as the 1790s, women began charitable associations in New York City, Philadelphia, and Boston. The rise of urban areas led to women's evangelical groups that organized and promoted religious and social causes to meet growing local needs.[10] In 1839, the town of Commerce expanded as large groups of impoverished Saints came from Missouri with very few material possessions. By 1842, Nauvoo had grown into a bustling city with an influx of Latter-day Saints from England and from across the United States.[11] Emma and the other nineteen founders of the Relief Society followed what many other women of their generation did in organizing to meet local needs.

Emma's life had not—and would not—slow down. Her fourteen-month-old son, Don Carlos, died on August 15, 1841.[12] On February 6, 1842, she delivered a stillborn son, and her mother died in Harmony, Pennsylvania, two weeks later. So much of Emma's life revolved around family and home, yet she yearned for the companionship of female peers. This became a pattern for women of the Relief Society. They provided relief; in so doing they found relief. It must have been a relief for Emma to find divinely appointed space with other women in these prolonged weeks of mourning.

And yet, Emma was not perfect; she was human. She did not attend every single meeting of the Relief Society, nor did she devote her life entirely to its service. She, her children, or Joseph were ill for much of the fall of 1843. She had business to attend to with the Red Brick Store and other properties owned by Joseph while he attended to Church business.[13] She led a very public life as First Lady and as Presidentess, and she often needed space to work through the sticky issue of plural marriage, both with her husband and with some of her friends in Relief Society. She had to balance many competing needs in her life and relationships; at the same time, Emma was the lynchpin in the creation of the Relief Society, a companion organization to the priesthood. The Elect Lady was also the First Lady, and a wife, mother, and friend.

"Elected to a certain work"—Emma and Female Authority

The founding of Relief Society started with conversations among women with specific experience or abilities and led to a significant part of the Restoration. Margaret Cook, a seamstress, and Sarah M.

Kimball, her employer, recognized a need for financial and material support for construction workers building the Nauvoo Temple and their families.[14] Sarah invited friends and neighbors to her home to discuss organizing a ladies' sewing society.[15] The women intended to produce a constitution and bylaws to gain credence as other women's organizations did at the time, and they invited Eliza R. Snow to compose the documents.[16]

Eliza produced a draft, then sought approval from Joseph Smith. According to Sarah, Joseph "pronounced it the best constitution he had ever read," then proclaimed he had "something better" for the women. He wanted to organize them officially in the same way other early Latter-day Saint councils and quorums had been organized—after the order of the priesthood, with a president and two counselors, and with ecclesiastical sanction and authority. Joseph invited the women to the room over his Red Brick Store the following Thursday afternoon.[17]

On March 17, 1842, Joseph taught twenty women from 2 John chapter 1 in the New Testament and from section 25 in the Doctrine and Covenants. He encouraged the women to use parliamentary procedure to ensure proper order. Elizabeth Ann Whitney nominated Emma to be president; the nomination was seconded, and the motion passed unanimously. The "Presidentess Elect" then proposed Sarah M. Cleveland and Elizabeth Ann to be her counselors. Joseph said, "Let this Presidency serve as a constitution—all their decisions be considered law; and acted upon as such." The women were ordained—set apart or set in order; they appointed additional officers: Eliza R. Snow, secretary; Phebe M. Wheeler, assistant secretary; and Elvira Cowles, treasurer. Joseph explained Emma's title: "Elect meant to be Elected to a certain work &c, & that the revelation was then fulfilled by Sister Emma's Election to the Presidency of the Society, she having previously been ordained to expound the Scriptures."

John Taylor, attending as a member of the Quorum of Twelve, suggested that Emma "preside and dignify her new office."[18]

The next order of business was to name the association. Counselors Sarah and Elizabeth Ann suggested "Nauvoo Female Relief Society," after which John Taylor recommended "Nauvoo Benevolent Society." A discussion followed; *benevolent* was a popular name for other societies, and *relief* could be misconstrued to include criminals and other trouble not wanted by the women. With presidential authority, Emma spoke up: "She would like an argument with Elder Taylor on the words Relief and Benevolence." Her concern was that "the popularity of the word benevolent is one great objection—no person can think of the word as associated with public Institutions." She did not want their society to be "call'd after other Societies in the world." After listening to the opinions of Sarah Cleveland and Eliza R. Snow, the women voted and accepted the name Relief Society.[19] This was a society that allowed for

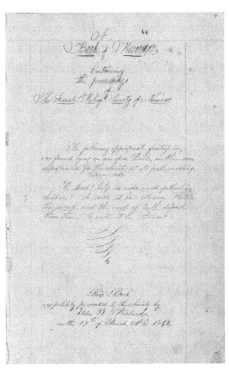

"A Book of Records, Containing the proceedings of the Female Relief Society of Nauvoo," Nauvoo Relief Society Minute Book, 17 March 1842–16 March 1844, handwriting of Eliza R. Snow. Courtesy of the Church History Library, Salt Lake City, Utah.

democratic discussion and expression, but also followed hierarchical direction.

The Relief Society was officially organized. At the sixth meeting, on April 28, 1842, Joseph told the women, "I now turn the key to you in the name of God and this Society shall rejoice and knowledge and intelligence shall flow down from this time."[20] The women held keys of authority in their work in a distinct and separate order of ecclesiastical Priesthood quorums. At this same meeting, Joseph taught them that they had the authority to perform rituals associated with spiritual gifts, including healing and speaking in tongues. In fact, Emma had administered to Elizabeth Durfee at an earlier meeting with her counselors. Elizabeth "said she never realized more benefit thro' any administration—that she was heal'd, and thought the sisters had more faith than the brethren."[21] As Relief Society president, Emma recognized her role of authority to provide relief to her sisters both spiritually and physically.

One of Emma's responsibilities as the president of the Relief Society was to teach. Her 1830 revelation recognized that she would be "ordained" to "expound scriptures, and to exhort the church, according as it shall be given thee by my Spirit."[22] Her 1834 patriarchal blessing promised that she would "be blessed with understanding, and have power to instruct thy sex."[23] The office of teacher was key to her authority. On March 16, 1844, she "advised all to abide the Book of Mormon—Dr Coven'ts."[24] From the first day of the Relief Society's organization, Emma taught the purpose of the Relief Society was to provide "extraordinary" relief, and to "seek out and relieve the distressed"—a concept littered throughout the Bible and the Book of Mormon—relief for the widows, poor, hungry, orphaned, sick, and afflicted.[25] Several times she spoke about unity and "full fellowship."[26] She taught the women about charity, a doctrine treated in the New Testament but more fully defined in the Book of Mormon.[27]

Even in an established role, Emma relied on others when she had family or business obligations. The Relief Society only met in the warmer months of the year because there was no adequate space large enough to accommodate their growing numbers. When Emma was not in attendance, one of her counselors presided.[28] First counselor Sarah Cleveland moved with her husband away from Nauvoo in May 1843, and her position was never filled.[29] On June 16, 1843, the first meeting of that year, second counselor Elizabeth Ann Whitney presided, but gave instructions from Emma, who was absent.[30] Eliza R. Snow filled the role of secretary until July 1843, when she abruptly left Nauvoo, perhaps due to a falling out with Emma over Eliza's plural marriage to Joseph.[31] Phebe Wheeler, assistant secretary, kept minutes until she married in October of that year and also left. Hanna M. Ells acted as temporary secretary in March 1844, when Emma returned to Relief Society.[32]

Even with its disruptions and gaps, the Nauvoo Relief Society presidency maintained its authority. Sarah Kimball remembered Joseph teaching the women that "the organisation of the Church of Christ was never perfect until the women were organised."[33] The Relief Society was an integral part of the complete Restoration, and Emma played a central role as Elect Lady or Presidentess. One man remembered that Emma was a natural leader, "gifted by nature with a logical mind, and inspiration in her genius."[34] As Emmeline B. Wells, a young woman in Nauvoo, noted years later, "Sister Emma was benevolent and hospitable; she drew around her a large circle of friends, who were like good comrades."[35] Emma was, indeed, chosen—selected or *elected*—by the Lord and by others.

"A loud call for relief"—Emma's Relief Society

At the first Relief Society meeting, once the women discussed the name *relief*, Emma said, "We are going to do something extraordinary." She referred to a boat stuck on rapids, such as on the Mississippi River, a stone's throw from the Red Brick Store where they were meeting. "We shall consider that a loud call for relief—we expect extraordinary occasions and pressing calls."[36] She understood both the need and value of providing relief, as she had received and given.

In 1830s Kirtland, Emma had watched her friend (and future second counselor) Elizabeth Ann provide relief. She and Newel K. welcomed Emma and Joseph into their home a couple of times. When Newel was called as bishop in December 1831, his wife assisted him in this position.[37] One of his responsibilities was to care for the poor. Emma and Joseph attended the three-day "Feast for the Poor" he and Elizabeth Ann prepared in January 1836. Elizabeth Ann described it as a means to share their abundance according to "our Savior's pattern." She remembered how Joseph considered the opportunity to "comfort the poor" and provide "genuine satisfaction."[38]

The 1836 feast for the poor served as training for Elizabeth Ann and Emma in providing relief to the poor in 1840s Nauvoo. Later, they partnered with the brethren in an official capacity. Just as Elizabeth Ann assisted her bishop-husband, and Emma partnered with her prophet-husband—as noted in the 1830 revelation, ordained to her office—the Relief Society worked with the Priesthood to extend relief.[39] Joseph illustrated the object of the Society—that the women "might provoke the brethren to good works in looking to the wants of the poor—searching after objects of charity, and administering to their wants."[40] Office. Ordination. Administration. Ministry. All words associated with leadership in the Nauvoo Relief Society, and all sacred callings.

Both of Emma's counselors, Elizabeth Ann and Sarah, had welcomed the Smith family into their homes in times of great need, and in Nauvoo, Emma was able to return the favor. When she and Joseph had settled on their homestead in Commerce (Nauvoo), they welcomed the destitute Whitneys into their home. The Smith home expanded to include so many others, including many of the women in the early Relief Society. The cycle of need and relief, both providing and receiving, rolled on. The Nauvoo minutes show an exchange of services: on March 24, 1842, for example, two Relief Society members matched each other's needs. Agnes Smith needed someone who had millinery and seamstress skills. Salome Chapman needed sewing work, and the two were matched up.[41] Emma adeptly facilitated these exchanges.

Nauvoo welcomed an influx of convert immigrants from the British Isles, adding to the prolonged poverty of Saints from Missouri who had lost most of their possessions. Under Emma's instructions, Relief Society members caught the vision of providing relief. She directed that the treasurer, Elvira A. Coles, collect funds donated "for the poor."[42] Emma would often open the meeting, calling "on those, if present who knew of cases of the poor to be represented." Phebe Ann Hawkes responded with concern about the Drury family, "still sick needing our prayers—if nothing more."[43] On March 31, 1843, Mercy Thompson mentioned a single mother from England with no friends, and Sarah Brown offered to welcome them into her home. At the same meeting, Sarah Cleveland "remark'd that they had put their shoulder to the wheel and exhorted to do with their might—we have entered into this work in the name of the Lord let us boldly go forward."[44] Emma taught them to expand their hearts and prayers, open their homes, and consecrate their possessions to the poor. These women built their own Zion.

Another important part of providing relief was unity within the group, something Emma preached often.[45] Also at the meeting on March 24, Lucy Mack Smith recognized the need for unity among her sisters. She called upon the Lord to "bless and aid the Society in feeding the hungry, clothing the naked," that the "blessings of heaven might rest upon the Society." Later in the meeting she commented, "we must watch over ourselves . . . to do good—to get good." Lucy continued, "We must cherish one another, watch over one another, comfort one another and gain instruction, that we may all sit down in heaven together."[46] In a united cause to provide relief, the women partnered with Christ, and in so doing, they found His relief.

"To save souls"—Relief Society as Temple Preparation

On June 9, 1842, Joseph visited the Relief Society and spoke again of their purpose: "The Society is not only to relieve the poor, but to save souls."[47] The practice of service taught the women more than temporal assistance, such as sewing shirts for men working on the temple. It also prepared the women for their own temple endowment. Learning the salvific practice of holiness occurred as women lifted each other and others. Eliza R. Snow wrote poetically of the Nauvoo Relief Society, "It is an *Order*, fitted and design'd / To meet the wants of body, and of mind— / To seek the wretched, in their long abode— / Supply their wants, and raise their hearts to God."[48]

Joseph watched Emma as she cared for the sick, the orphans, and the widows and welcomed them into her home; he recognized her sacred nature. He taught women of the Relief Society, "As you increase in goodness, let your hearts expand—let them be enlarged towards others." This magnification came only through partnering with Christ. Joseph also knew what the Lord taught Emma in the 1830 revelation, that by keeping His commandments, she could come to where the Lord is, and that this applied to all.[49] Joseph said in a meeting on April 28, 1842, "You are now plac'd in a situation where you can act according to those sympathies which God has planted in your bosoms." He continued, "If you live up to these principles how great and glorious!—if you live up to your privilege, the angels cannot be restrain'd from being your associates." Then, a step beyond angels, Joseph added, "Females, if they are pure and innocent can come into the presence of God."[50] As the women provided relief, they could assist Christ and find their own salvation.

At one meeting, Emma spoke about the "increasing union of the Society" based on their good works. Later, a Mrs. Chase "prophesied that henceforth, if the sisters are faithful, the gifts of the gospel shall be with us, especially the gift of healing."[51] Even when Emma was not in attendance, women recognized her example. Elizabeth Durfee "bore testimony to the great blessing she received when administered to, after the close of the last meeting, by Prest. E. Smith & Councillors Cleveland and Whitney." Elizabeth considered this blessing as a significant faith-promoting experience.[52] The following year, Dorothy Meacham commented that "our Salvation depended on our Liberality to the poor," to which counselor Elizabeth Ann responded, "By this shall ye know ye are my disciples."[53] And a week later, another Sister Chase "stood a living witness for Jesus of Nazareth knew he had poured his Spirit upon her. Inasmuch as we visit the sick we shall be blest I mean to do all that I can to relieve their necessities."[54] They learned from Emma's example and teachings, and they testified of their experiences.

Perhaps the most valuable way that Emma and Relief Society women saved souls was through the temple. Joseph visited the women's meeting on March 31, 1842, and explained "that the Society should move according to the ancient Priesthood." He said that this "select Society" must be separate from the world, "choice, virtuous and Holy." He wanted "to make of this Society a kingdom of priests as in Enoch's day—as in Paul's day."[55] Joseph hoped the women would realize "the privileges and blessings and gifts of the priesthood."[56]

Emma, as Presidentess of the Relief Society and the Elect Lady, was the first to receive her temple endowment in September 1843. She then became the first female officiator of temple rites and passed them on to other women in the Relief Society. Following her precedent, Eliza R. Snow, Zina D. H. Young, and Bathsheba Smith each served concurrently as Relief Society General President and temple matron. The sacred connection between Relief Society and the temple was significant in preparing women to understand priesthood in the temple ordinances.

Part of temple preparation for Nauvoo Relief Society women was worthiness. The Lord taught Emma in her 1830 revelation to "walk in the paths of virtue."[57] She, Joseph, and John Taylor discussed this concept in the Relief Society's opening meeting. Joseph suggested the importance of "correcting the morals and strengthening the virtues of the female community," and John spoke of Emma as a "pattern of virtue."[58] Emma enforced stringent requirements to gain membership, similar to contemporary organizations concerned with moral purity.[59] She wanted every member to "divest themselves of every jealousy and evil feeling toward each other, if any such existed—that we should bring our conduct into respectability."[60] She taught the women "to eradicate all evil from our own hearts."[61] Emma took her role seriously to determine whether certain women acted appropriately.[62] Some were not allowed to join.[63] At the last meeting, Emma "exhorted them to cleanse their hearts and ears."[64] Relief Society required repentance, which led to salvation.

"Strong-minded Women"—Troubles and the End of the Nauvoo Relief Society

News of the women's organization spread through Nauvoo quickly, and even with strict membership requirements, the Relief

Society experienced rapid growth. On May 26, 1842, two months after its founding, Joseph recorded in his journal that the meeting was "so full that many could get no admittance."[65] By 1843, Relief Society meetings were divided into four wards in order to accommodate all who wished to participate.[66] Unfortunately, the sometimes unmanageable number of members was not the only problem the women—and Emma—faced.

At the same time the women engaged in relief and salvation, rumors swirled around Nauvoo about the secret practice of spiritual wifery, or plural marriage. As early as 1841, Joseph discovered that John C. Bennett, a recent convert, mayor of Nauvoo, and an assistant president in the First Presidency, had seduced various Nauvoo women, married and single.[67] John told the women that illicit sexual intercourse was acceptable and approved by the prophet if kept secret; soon other men followed his lead. The plural marriage crisis included Emma's personal concerns. At the first meeting on March 17, 1842, she addressed the need for female purity, calling members "to watch over the morals—and be very careful of the character and reputation—of the members of the Institution."[68] Later she exhorted the sisters to be virtuous and morally pure, and to be "united among ourselves—said we shall have sufficient difficulty from abroad without stirring up strife among ourselves and hardness and evil fee[l]ings, one towards another."[69] On March 31, 1842, she had an epistle read from Joseph and others, warning the women of those falsely speaking for Joseph and distorting true authority.[70] All of this Relief Society meeting discussion occurred as polygamy gossip swirled through Nauvoo.

After John Bennett's misbehavior became public and Joseph disavowed him of public office and Church leadership, John publicly accused Joseph of adultery and published exposés referring to clandestine and secret wives in the *Sangamo Journal*, a Springfield,

Illinois, newspaper, in July 1842.[71] Under Emma's direction, the Relief Society acted accordingly. Even before John's published accusations of Joseph, Emma proposed that the Relief Society issue a statement "expressive of our feelings in reference to Dr. Bennett's character." She "requested all who could wield the pen, to write," that "the true situati[on] of matters be represented—said we had nothing to do but fear God and keep the commandments, and in doing so we shall prosper."[72] On October 1, Emma and eighteen other prominent members published a statement in the *Times and Seasons*, Nauvoo's newspaper. Their proclamation reiterated an 1835 statement defining marriage between one man and one wife, and condemned the practices of any "secret wife system."[73] At least three of the nineteen women included in the publication had firsthand experience with plural marriage, including Eliza R. Snow and Sarah Cleveland, both sealed to Joseph, and Elizabeth Ann Whitney, whose daughter was sealed to Joseph. In July, approximately one thousand women signed a petition for Illinois governor Thomas Carlin to issue an official complaint of the sordid behavior of John Bennett.[74] The tension in the Smith home must have been thick: Joseph was privately teaching and expanding plural marriage, and Emma was publicly refuting it, often in meetings with Joseph's plural wives, often unbeknownst to her—her own friends and Relief Society sisters.

Emma did not attend any Relief Society meetings in 1843—she traveled for business with the Red Brick Store, and she suffered from physical illness and emotional trouble. Personal tension heightened with Joseph as she discovered his plural marriage to many of her Relief Society sisters.[75] Suddenly, for Emma, the idea of celestial sociality within sealed networks of friends and family turned to include the possibility of sexual activity, sharply dividing her from her husband, rather than expanding their family network.

In March 1844, Emma conducted four Relief Society meetings,

each one denouncing licentiousness—and, surreptitiously, plural marriage. By this time, she knew that plural wives of her husband and others were in the congregation. At each meeting she read a speech written by William W. Phelps titled "Voice of Innocence"—calling for a "reformation in boath men & woman." In the name of female virtue and the "sanctity of Society," she furtively called out the men who spurned mothers and children to seduce women. The text suggested the need to protect the purity and chastity of girls and women and to prevent extramarital affairs. The underlying message, however, condemned the practice of plural marriage. Little did Emma know that Hannah Ells—the woman who kept the minutes for those meetings since secretary Eliza R. Snow had moved out of town and assistant secretary Phebe Wheeler got married—sealed to Joseph.[76]

The minutes are sparse, but contention was evident, and it extended beyond the crowd of women to bolster men eager to cause trouble for Joseph and ecclesiastical and civil authority.[77] Women in attendance included the small circle of women who had received the temple endowment through Emma's administration and joined with her in the Anointed Quorum. They respected her temple and Relief Society authority, and they certainly had influence with their husbands. Joseph said he "never had any fuss with these men until that Female Relief Society brought out the paper against adulterers and adulteresses."[78] Years later, in 1880, then-President John Taylor spoke of these final Nauvoo Relief Society meetings: "Sister Emma . . . made use of the position she held to try to pervert the minds of the sisters" and taught the women that plural marriage "as taught and practiced by Joseph Smith the prophet was not of God."[79] Emma did use her public role as Relief Society president to express her concerns from her own marriage. Those were the last meetings recorded of the Nauvoo Relief Society.

After Joseph's death on June 27, 1844, Nauvoo continued to experience chaos. Questions over Church leadership, finances, and doctrine roiled the Saints as they worked to complete the temple while outsiders continued to persecute and produce fear and chaos in the city. Women proceeded to relieve the poor and save souls in the spirit of their charge. Zina Jacobs [Young] recorded in her diary personal visits to female friends in 1844 and 1845 Nauvoo, most of whom were members of the Relief Society.[80] By 1845, tensions between Brigham Young and Emma had escalated over Joseph's properties and authority. Brigham maintained Church leadership while Emma protected her family, whose finances had become inexorably intertwined with Church ecclesiology and finances. Emma's opposition to the practice of plural marriage also presented a schism between her, Brigham, and the Apostles. In meetings with the Nauvoo High Priests and the First Council of the Seventy, both on March 9, Brigham expressed his opposition to Relief Society, publicly shutting down the organization. To the High Priests Quorum, he said, "I will curse ev[e]ry man that lets his wife or daughters meet again—until I tell them." He continued, placing an extraordinary amount of blame on the women: "What are relief societies for? To relieve us of our best men—They relieved us of Joseph and Hyrum." To the Seventies Quorum, he said, "Many of our Sister[s] have been engaged they have no right to meddle in the affairs of the kingdom of God."[81] Emotions escalated in a very personal way as the President of the Quorum of the Twelve discounted the work of the Elect Lady.

Even after the disbandment of Relief Society, Latter-day Saint women continued to care for one another in the same spirit of Relief Society, through Winter Quarters and across the plains. The organization was permanently reinstituted by Brigham Young and Eliza R. Snow in Utah in 1868.[82] Joseph Smith III visited Utah in 1868–69, around the time of Relief Society starting up again. Emma wrote her son: "I think you must have had an interesting time in the excitement among the strong minded women. Well I am not one of those strong minded ones." She continued, claiming that she had no time to clamor "for some unenjoyed privilege which if granted would be decidedly a damage to me and mine."[83] No matter what she thought then, Emma had been a strong and capable Elect Lady, despite how things ended with her Relief Society. She planted a seed of female community and partnership with priesthood in the hearts of those who had worked with her, then prepared them and even participated in their temple endowments. Emma was, indeed, a woman chosen or elected by God for a select purpose.

Notes

1. John S. Reed, "Some of the Remarks of John S. Reed, Esq., as Delivered before the State Convention," *T&S* 5, no. 11 (1 Jun. 1844): 551.
2. Lucy Mack Smith, History, 1845, 190, JSP.
3. Lucy Mack Smith, History, 1844–1845, book 14, 3, JSP.
4. D&C 25:3, 7.
5. Joseph Smith Sr., Blessing to Emma Smith, Patriarchal Blessing Book 1, 4–5, JSP. See chapter 4.
6. 2 John 1:1, 13.
7. Francis Brown, S. R. Driver, and Charles A. Briggs, *The Brown-Driver-Briggs Hebrew and English Lexicon* (Peabody, MA: Hendrickson, 1997), 103, 149–50.
8. Adam Jortner, "The Political Threat of a Female Christ: Ann Lee, Morality, and Religious Freedom in the United States, 1780–1819," *Early American Studies: An Interdisciplinary Journal* 7, no. 1 (Spring 2009): 179–204.
9. Eliza R. Snow, "Female Relief Society," *Deseret Evening News* 1, no. 127 (18 Apr. 1868): 2.
10. Anne M. Boylan, *The Origins of Women's Activism: New York and Boston, 1797–1840* (Chapel Hill, NC: University of North Carolina Press, 2002); Nancy A. Hardesty, *Women Called to Witness: Evangelical Feminism in the Nineteenth Century* (Nashville, TN: Abingdon Press, 1984), 113; Nancy F. Cott, *The Bonds of Womanhood: "Woman's Sphere" in New England,*

1780–1835 (New Haven, CT: Yale University Press, 1997), 126–59; Lori D. Ginzberg, *Women and the Work of Benevolence: Morality, Politics, and Class in the Nineteenth-Century United States* (New Haven, CT: Yale University Press, 1990).

11. "Nauvoo (Commerce), Illinois," *CHTE*.
12. Joseph Smith Family Bible, ca. 1831–1866, private possession, copy of genealogical information, CHL; "Obituary," *T&S* 2, no. 21 (1 Sep. 1841): 533.
13. See Linda King Newell and Valeen Tippets Avery, *Mormon Enigma: Emma Hale Smith* (Urbana, IL: University of Illinois Press, 1994), 155–68.
14. See Willard Richards, "Tithings and Consecrations for the Temple of the Lord," *T&S* 3, no. 7 (1 Feb. 1842): 677; Joseph Smith, "To the Brethren in Nauvoo City, Greeting," *T&S* 3, no. 9 (1 Mar. 1842): 715.
15. Sarah M. Kimball, "Early Relief Society Reminiscence," 17 Mar. 1882, Relief Society Record, 1880–1892, 29–30, CHL; *FFYRS*, 493–96.
16. Eliza R. Snow, "Sketch of My Life," in Maureen Ursenbach Beecher, ed., *The Personal Writings of Eliza Roxcy Snow* (Logan: Utah State University Press, 2000), 6, 9.
17. Relief Society Record, "First Organisation," ca June 1880, 5, Relief Society Record, 1880–1892, CHL; Sarah M. Kimball, "Early Relief Society Reminiscence," 17 Mar. 1882, Relief Society Record, 29–30, CHL; *FFYRS*, 493–96.
18. Joseph Smith, Journal, 17 Mar. 1842, 91, JSP; *NRSM*, 17 Mar. 1842, 7–13; *FFYRS*, 31–33.
19. *NRSM*, 17 Mar. 1842, 10–12; *FFYRS*, 34–35.
20. *NRSM*, 28 Apr. 1842, 40; *FFYRS*, 59.
21. Elizabeth Davis Durfee received her "great blessing" after the Relief Society meeting held on 14 Apr. 1842, and spoke about it at the meeting on 19 Apr. *NRSM*, 19 Apr. 1842, 31; *FFYRS*, 50–51.
22. D&C 25:7.
23. Joseph Smith Sr., Blessing to Emma Smith. See chapter 4.
24. *NRSM*, 14 Mar. 1844, 125; *FFYRS*, 130.
25. *NRSM*, 17 Mar. 1842, 12–13; *FFYRS*, 34–36. Exodus 22:22; Deuteronomy 10:18; 26:13; Isaiah 1:17, 23; Jeremiah 7:6–7; Zechariah 7:10, James 1:27; Jacob 2:19; Mosiah 4:26.
26. *NRSM*, 24 Mar. 1842, 15; *FFYRS*, 37. Mosiah 18:21; 4 Nephi 1:2–3; Moses 7:18.

27. *NRSM*, 24 Mar. 1842, 18; *FFYRS*, 39. 1 Corinthians 13; 2 Nephi 26:30; Ether 12:28, 34–37; Moroni 7:44–47.
28. On September 28, 1842, Emma was sick, and Sarah Cleveland and Elizabeth Ann Whitney presided. Joseph Smith, Journal, 29 Sep.–7 Oct. 1842, 205–7, JSP; *NRSM*, 28 Oct. 1842, 85, *FFYRS*, 96.
29. Sarah M. Cleveland, "To the Presidency, and Ladies of the Female Relief Society of Nauvoo," *T&S* 4, no. 12 (1 May 1843): 187; *FFYRS*, 145–46.
30. *NRSM*, 16 Jun. 1843, 90; *FFYR*, 100.
31. Eliza R. Snow, Nauvoo Journal and Notebook, 20–21 Jul. 1843, in Beecher, *Personal Writings*, 80–81.
32. See Jennifer Reeder, "The Textual Culture of the Nauvoo Female Relief Society Leadership and Minute Book," in *Foundational Texts of Mormonism: Examining Major Early Sources*, ed. Mark Ashurst-McGee, Robin Scott Jensen, and Sharalyn D. Howcroft (New York City: Oxford University Press, 2017), 167–70, 183–84.
33. Kimball, "Early Relief Society Reminesence," 29–30.
34. Mark Forscutt, "Commemorative Discourse on the Death of Mrs. Emma Bidamon," *The Saints' Herald* 26, no. 14 (15 Jul. 1879).
35. Emmeline B. Wells, "L. D. S. Women of the Past; Personal Impressions," *WE* 36, no. 7 (Feb. 1908): 49.
36. *NRSM*, 17 Mar. 1842, 12; *FFYRS*, 35.
37. Andrew Jenson, *Latter-day Saint Biographical Encyclopedia: A Compilation of Biographical Sketches of Prominent Men and Women in the Church of Jesus Christ of Latter-day Saints* vol. 1 (Salt Lake City: Deseret News, 1901), 224–25. D&C 72:1–8.
38. Elizabeth Ann Whitney, "Leaves from an Autobiography," *WE* 7, no. 9 (1 Oct. 1878): 71; 7, no. 11 (1 Nov. 1878): 83.
39. See D&C 25:5, 7.
40. *NRSM*, 17 Mar. 1842, 7; *FFYRS*, 31.
41. *NRSM*, 24 Mar. 1842, 20; *FFYRS*, 41.
42. *NRSM*, 23 Jun. 1842, 68; *FFYRS*, 84.
43. *NRSM*, 14 Apr. 1842, 28; *FFYRS*, 48.
44. *NRSM*, 31 Mar. 1842, 24–25; *FFYRS*, 44–45.
45. See *NRSM*, 24 Mar. 1842, 14; 27 May 1842, 58; *FFYRS*, 37, 75.
46. *NRSM*, 24 Mar. 1842, 17–19; *FFYRS*, 38–40.
47. *NRSM*, 9 Jun. 1842, 63; *FFYRS*, 79.

48. Eliza R. Snow, "The Female Relief Society of Nauvoo. What Is It?" *T&S* 3, no. 17 (1 Jul. 1842): 846; *FFYRS*, 134–35.
49. D&C 25:15–16.
50. *NRSM*, 28 Apr. 1842, 38; *FFYRS*, 57.
51. *NRSM*, 23 Jun. 1842, 69; *FFYRS*, 84–85.
52. *NRSM*, 19 Apr. 1842, 30; *FFYRS*, 50–51.
53. *NRSM*, 28 Jul. 1843, 101; *FFYRS*, 109.
54. *NRSM*, 5 Aug. 1843, 105; *FFYRS*, 113.
55. *NRSM*, 31 Mar. 1842, 22; *FFYRS*, 43.
56. Joseph Smith, Journal, 28 Apr. 1842, 94, JSP; see *NRSM*, 28 Apr. 1842, 34, *FFYRS*, 53.
57. D&C 25:2.
58. *NRSM*, 17 Mar. 1842, 8–9; *FFYRS*, 32–33.
59. Mary P. Ryan, "The Power of Women's Networks: A Case Study of Female Moral Reform in Antebellum America," *Feminist Studies* 5, no. 1 (Spring 1979): 66–85; Lori D. Ginzberg, *Women and the Work of Benevolence: Morality, Politics, and Class in Nineteenth-Century United States* (New Haven, CT: Yale University Press, 1990), 113–14.
60. *NRSM*, 24 Mar. 1842, 14; *FFYRS*, 37.
61. *NRSM*, 14 Apr. 1842, 27; *FFYRS*, 47.
62. See, for example, the case of Clarissa Marvel, *NRSM*, 24 Mar. 1842, 17, 31 Mar. 1842, 23, 2 Apr. 1842, 26, 14 Apr. 1842, 89; *FFYRS*, 38–39, 43–44, 46, 99.
63. See, for example, Jane Neyman, *NRSM*, 28 Apr. 1842, 61, 14 July 1842, 76; *FFYRS*, 61, 89.
64. *NRSM*, 16 Mar. 1844, 125; *FFYRS*, 129.
65. Joseph Smith, Journal, 26 May 1842, 124, JSP.
66. *NRSM*, 7 Jul. 1843, 93; *FFYRS*, 102.
67. "John Cook Bennett," bio, JSP.
68. *NRSM*, 17 Mar. 1842, 13; *FFYRS*, 36.
69. *NRSM*, 4 Aug. 1842, 77; *FFYRS*, 91.
70. *NRSM*, copied documents, 31 Mar. 1842, 86–88; *FFYRS*, 97–99.
71. "Astounding Mormon Disclosures! Letter from Gen. Bennett," *Sangamo Journal* (8 Jul. 1842): 2; "Further Mormon Developments! 2d Letter from Gen. Bennett," and Gen. Bennett's Third Letter," *Sangamo Journal* (15 Jul. 1842): 2; "Gen. Bennett's 4th Letter," *Sangamo Journal* (22 Jul. 1842): 2.
72. *NRSM*, 23 Jun. 1842, 69; *FFYRS*, 84–85.

73. Statement on Marriage, ca. Aug. 1835, Doctrine and Covenants 1835 edition, 251–52, JSP; Emma Smith, Elizabeth Ann Whitney, Sarah M. Cleveland, Eliza R. Snow, Mary C. Miller, Lois Cutler, Thirza Cahoon, Ann Hunter, Jane Law, Sophia R. Marks, Polly Z. Johnson, Abigail Works, Catherine Petty, Sarah Higbee, Phebe Woodruff, Leonora Taylor, Sarah Hillman, Rosannah Marks, and Angeline Robison, Statement, *T&S* 3, no. 23 (1 Oct. 1842): 940; *FFYRS* 142–44.
74. Nauvoo Female Relief Society, Petition, to Thomas Carlin, [ca. 22 Jul. 1842], CHL; *FFYRS*, 136–41.
75. See "Plural Marriage in the Church of Jesus Christ of Latter-day Saints," and "Plural Marriage in Kirtland and Nauvoo," *GTE*. See also chapter 2.
76. Reeder, "The Textual Culture of the Nauvoo Female Relief Society," 170, 175–78, 182–83.
77. *NRSM*, 9 Mar. 1844, 123–24, 16 Mar. 1844, 125–27; *FFYRS*, 126–31. William W. Phelps, "The Voice of Innocence from Nauvoo," ca. Feb. 1844, revisions by Emma Smith, Mar. 1844, CHL; *FFYRS*, 126–31, 151–56.
78. Joseph Smith, discourse, 26 May 1844, comp. Leo Hawkins, JSP.
79. "Relief Society Report, Seting Apart Officers, &c.," 17 Jul. 1880, Relief Society Record, 1880–1892, 11, CHL; *FFYRS*, 476.
80. Zina Jacobs, diary, in "'All Things Move in Order in the City': The Nauvoo Diary of Zina Diantha Huntington Jacobs," *BYU Studies* 19, no. 3 (Spring 1979): 285–320.
81. Brigham Young, discourse, 9 Mar. 1845, Nauvoo High Priests Quorum Record, CHL; Brigham Young, discourse, 9 Mar. 1845, Record of Seventies, Book B, 77–78, CHL; *FFYRS*, 168–71.
82. See Laurel Thatcher Ulrich, *A House Full of Females: Plural Marriage and Women's Rights in Early Mormonism, 1835–1870* (New York City: Knopf, 2017), 135–83.
83. Emma Smith Bidamon to Joseph Smith III, 13 Aug. [1868 or 1869], CCLA.

Chapter 9

FIRST PARTNER

Emma as a Woman of Property, Business, and Political Activism

As a young woman, Emma raised cows and managed a dairy from her home in Harmony, Pennsylvania.[1] As an adult, she again kept cows in Nauvoo, and she also ran a hotel.[2] In many cases, Emma defied social norms for her time, namely the idea of Victorian separate spheres and the older law and tradition of coverture—both restricting women from full public economic and political participation. Much of her sharp sense of business acuity and political activism came from experience; when Joseph was out of town, in hiding or on Church business, Emma literally took care of business. Her motivation for her economic and political activity was to protect and provide for her family.

The word *coverture* means simply "covered." Specifically, according to eighteenth-century English common law, *feme covert* asserted that a married woman's legal rights and obligations were covered by her husband, that only he had the right to own property and make contracts for her. Before marriage, *feme sole* allowed a woman to own property.[3] This legal tradition required a woman to depend upon her husband for protection in every sense of the word. As the American economy shifted from the home to the marketplace, the idea of separate spheres emerged as men's work became more public and women's more private or domestic.[4] Earlier they worked together to farm and provide for the family. Emma stood on the cusp of these economic and cultural changes, and she acted progressively in economic and political efforts.

Emma came from a more "refined" or genteel family than did Joseph at a time when the American middle class was just emerging.[5] The Hales had become more financially viable than the Smiths, indicated in part by their stability in Pennsylvania compared to the Smiths' movement across Vermont, New Hampshire, and New York. Emma's father Isaac had been a hunter, shipping his meat downriver to the Philadelphia market, while Joseph Sr. experienced financial ruin.[6] Emma's husband Joseph had great visionary and religious development and leadership, but she had more business acuity. Together, Emma and Joseph complemented each other and made a strong partnership, each with different skills.

A Woman of Property—Emma's Defiance of Coverture

The summer after Emma married Joseph and moved to Manchester, New York, she wrote to ask her father if she could retrieve her property left in Harmony—cows, furniture, and clothing purchased as a *feme sole*. Isaac Hale agreed: her property was at her disposal. She and Joseph, with the assistance of neighbor Peter Ingersoll, arrived in the Susquehanna Valley in August 1827. Isaac offered to help Joseph procure land and a job if they wanted to return to Harmony. Emma's brother Alva helped them relocate from New York later that fall. As promised, Isaac aided Joseph in purchasing a valuable piece of property on his farm previously owned by Emma's brother, Jesse Hale. Isaac wanted to help his daughter, hoping that Joseph would give up his religious inclination and work as others in the area—farming, hunting, or shipping commerce on the river.⁷ When Joseph continued working on the translation of the Book of Mormon, Isaac threatened to evict them, causing a precarious financial situation.⁸ Joseph paid Isaac a deposit for the land and home, then expanded the home Jesse had built.⁹ The extension most likely facilitated Emma's dairy and allowed her to ship milk products down the Susquehanna River. They paid off the property in 1830 then left for Fayette, New York.¹⁰ Three years later, they sold the property to a Hale neighbor in Harmony.¹¹

Joseph and Emma lived on the benefit of others for the next three years—including the Whitmers, the Whitneys, the Morleys, and the Johnsons—moving from New York to Ohio. In Kirtland in 1834, they and Julia and Joseph III moved into their own home near the temple lot.¹² Many people boarded there as they ran the new printing office and worked on temple construction.¹³ Once they did have their own homes in Kirtland, Far West, and Nauvoo, Emma often shouldered the burden of domestic work. Years later, she wrote to her adult son Joseph III, describing some of that difficulty: "I never wanted [Joseph] to go into the garden to work for if he did it would not be fifteen minutes before there would be three or four or some times a half dozen men around him and they would tramp the garden down faster than he could have it up."¹⁴

Emma became much more involved in Nauvoo property as lines blurred between what the Smiths owned and what the Church owned. The Smith family lived first in the homestead, then in the Mansion House when it was completed in August 1843. Joseph spent the day on July 13, 1843, in conversation with Emma, and deeded sixty city lots to her and their children as well as his half of ownership rights to the steamboat *Maid of Iowa*.¹⁵ As this was immediately after Emma learned about Joseph's revelation on plural marriage, the transaction was probably executed as a term of agreement between the two, assuring that she would be able to provide for herself and the children if anything happened, including a potential prelude to divorce.[16] The following month, the Smiths moved into the Mansion House. Initially Joseph had allowed guests to stay for no cost, but due to financial need, they began requesting payment in September 1843.

After Joseph's death, Emma maintained the properties of the Smith homestead, the Mansion House, and the uncompleted Nauvoo House. On August 25, 1844, she signed a rental agreement with William Marks on the Mansion House and barn.[17] Then in November 1844, Emma moved her children, mother-in-law, and niece from the Mansion House back to the smaller, older Smith homestead, where she could find more privacy before her baby was born. They moved back into the Mansion House by May 1845.[18]

When persecution of the Saints in Nauvoo came to a head in 1846, after the majority had crossed the river into Iowa, Emma felt unsafe. She rented the Mansion House to Abram Van Tuyl in September 1846 and took her family 150 miles upriver to Fulton, near her brother Jesse Hale and Rosannah and William Marks, old friends who had opposed plural marriage and with whom Emma felt comfortable.[19] The hiatus north didn't last long; word came that Abram planned to abscond with the furniture and household items, so Emma quickly returned and staked her claim.[20] Emma and her family lived in the Mansion House until 1871, when her second husband, Lewis Bidamon, completed construction on the Riverside Mansion, using bricks from the unfinished walls of the Nauvoo House.[21] Emma spent the last years of her life there.

"I have a great deal of business"—Emma's Economic Activity

Emma's business experience helped Joseph with his lack of financial expertise. She witnessed the failure of the Kirtland Safety Society in 1837, an almost inevitable event due to the American economic downturn and the complexity of involved individuals.[22] And she was aware of the way that Joseph both relied on support from Church members and in turn committed his own resources to the Church. She likewise knew that Smith family finances had easily become intertwined with the Church. She understood the laws of coverture, revealing her legal limits, and realized that many of the current Church leaders were not necessarily loyal to Joseph.

Joseph went into business in Kirtland to help provide for the Saints, many of whom had very little money. It was difficult to sort out private enterprises from Church-owned endeavors, some of which were owned by various combinations of Joseph, Sidney Rigdon, Hyrum Smith, and Oliver Cowdery. For example, the mercantile firm of Rigdon, Smith & Co. (in which Joseph was a partner) owned and operated a store in Chester, Ohio, on the southern end of Kirtland township.[23] Emma was somewhat involved; in October 1835, she accompanied Joseph to purchase goods in nearby Willoughby for the Chester store.[24] These partnerships created financial problems for the Smith family as Joseph faced litigation for outstanding debts owed to the wholesale merchants from whom he and his partners had bought the goods. The Chester store gave Emma experience in mercantile business.

When Joseph was absent, because of enemies seeking his life or his money, Emma was left to deal with immediate needs; as a result, Emma became a practiced manager. Their correspondence during this period demonstrates her natural business acuity as she navigated business in his absence. On August 19, 1836, Joseph wrote to her: "I can think of many things concerning our business but can only pray that you may have wisdom to manage the concerns that involve upon you."[25] He trusted her implicitly to make decisions and maintain business relationships for him. In the spring of 1837, Joseph faced litigation for outstanding debts owed to various merchants and land speculators. One of them, anti-Mormon banker Grandison Newell, threatened to have Joseph killed.[26] Joseph and Sidney left Kirtland for much of April and May because of such threats. On April 25, 1837, Emma wrote, "I have a great deal of business to see to." She referred to different properties, the store in Chester, and the constant surveillance of enemies. "Be assured," she wrote, "I shall do the best I can in all things." By this point, Emma recognized the religious implications in such ventures: "I hope that we shall be so humble and pure before God that he will set us at liberty to be our own masters in a few things at least."[27] She combined temporal matters with spiritual.

Financial circumstances grew worse. "I do not know what to tell you," Emma wrote to Joseph on May 3. "The situation of your business is such as is very difficult for me to do any thing of any consequence." She grew frustrated with so many different people claiming so many different things without careful documentation and that others wouldn't honor their agreements when she came to them for the food, money, or resources they had promised her or Joseph. "I have been so treated that I have come to the determination not to let any man or woman have anything whatsoever without being well assured, that it does to your own advantage." She requested additional details, "that if possible I can benefit by the information." And she suggested that Joseph assign power of attorney to Vinson Knight, a clerk in the Chester store and a trusted counselor in the Kirtland bishopric working with Newel K. Whitney. Emma wanted to protect Joseph, but it seemed impossible to untangle ownership claims.[28]

A few years later after settling in Nauvoo, Emma continued to assist Joseph with his business opportunities. In the late fall of 1839, Joseph and other Church delegates traveled to Washington, DC, to seek federal financial assistance for the Saints' property losses in Missouri. While he was gone, she wrote, expressing concern about his long absence: "Buisness in this place does not go on quite as well as when you was here."[29] Three years later when Joseph went into hiding in August 1842 due to extradition efforts to bring him back to Missouri for trial, Emma wrote him, "I believe that you can still direct in your business concerns if we are all of us prudent in the matter."[30] She made every effort to allow him to maintain a voice in what was going on in Nauvoo.

Emma assisted Joseph with business for the Red Brick Store and the Mansion House. She traveled to St. Louis, Missouri, to purchase supplies for the store and for the Mansion House when it was unsafe for Joseph to go due to an extradition request from the state of Missouri in May and August of 1843 and in April 1844.[31] She also facilitated the exchange of services within the Relief Society, overseeing the secretary and treasurer, who carefully kept records of each donation and each recipient. After Joseph's death, she offered the Red Brick Store for rent to Joseph Heywood—it was too much for her to keep everything up.[32] Even through her later years, Emma continued to manage the Mansion House and the Riverside Mansion as a hotel, producing a small but consistent income.[33]

"Better days to come to us yet"—Political Activism

Emma's life experiences educated her in matters of politics, including local and federal laws, city charters, and the Constitution.

This knowledge helped her as she worked to improve circumstances, mostly through petitions and letter-writing campaigns. She learned from watching her husband and others seek state and federal protections as well as witnessing countless trials and legal proceedings. She was personally aware of the loss of land and property in Missouri. The 1838–39 expulsion from Missouri caused the Saints to be careful and wary of politicians promising assistance and incited Emma to take political action to protect her husband. She expressed her hard work and anxiety in March 1839 when she wrote to Joseph, who was in Liberty Jail, looking to the future: "I hope there is better days to come to us yet."[34] She wrote to Joseph on December 6, 1839, while he was in Washington with a report of Missouri Governor Lilburn Boggs's efforts to retain ammunition belonging to Latter-day Saint merchants—yet another cause of concern for those seeking redress for their losses.[35] In 1841, the state of Missouri renewed charges of violence at Far West in 1838 and issued a writ of extradition to Illinois governor Thomas Carlin, asking him to return Joseph Smith to Missouri for trial. Joseph was arrested on June 5, and he obtained a writ of *habeas corpus*, protecting him in the state of Illinois from extradition to Missouri.[36]

In May 1842, the attempted murder of former governor Boggs in Missouri prompted additional charges against Joseph Smith, claiming that he committed the act, even though he was in Illinois at the time. Then, in July, Relief Society women rallied to create a petition for Governor Carlin, seeking his protection as chief magistrate. Under Emma's direction, the petition was signed by every member of the Relief Society—about one thousand women.[37] "It may be considered irrelevant for Ladies to petition," the second paragraph stated, "and that it would be more becoming for our husbands, fathers, brothers and sons to engage in this work." But this was an extraordinary occasion. The women referred to the "scenes of great misery and woe that we had to experience from the hands of ruthless and bloodthirsty mobs" in Missouri. "Let the blood of our fathers, our brothers, our sons and daughters speak. Let the tears of the widows, the orphans, the maimed, the impoverished speak." They asked for protection for Joseph and for their community.[38]

A week later, Eliza R. Snow and Amanda Barnes Smith accompanied Emma to personally deliver the petition to the Illinois governor's residence in Quincy, fifty miles south of Nauvoo. These women had all suffered from violence in Missouri: Eliza as a purported victim of sexual violence, Amanda as a widow who lost her husband and son at Hawn's Mill, and Emma as the wife of a man unjustly imprisoned for four months in squalid conditions in Liberty Jail.[39] They were women with a firm political purpose. Governor Carlin received the women with great cordiality, assuring them of the protection guaranteed them by the US Constitution. Eliza recorded in her journal that Carlin "manifested much friendship, and it remains for time and circumstance to prove the sincerity of his professions."[40] Despite his affability, however, Carlin issued a writ for Joseph's arrest on August 2, and Joseph went into hiding until January 1843.[41]

Emma did all she could to persuade local and state leaders to assist in the matter and to coordinate with her absent husband.[42] Joseph wrote Emma in mid-August: "I take the liberty to tender you my sincere thanks for the two interesting and consoling visits that you have made me during my almost exiled situation. Tongue cannot express the gratitude of my heart, for the warm and true-hearted friendship you have manifested in these things toward me." He asked Emma to continue correspondence with the governor, although he had little faith it would help.[43]

Emma's letters to Governor Carlin on August 16 and August 27, 1842, demonstrate her political acumen, something that had increased over time and experience. In her first letter, she wrote, "Was my cause the interest of an individual or a number of individuals; then, perhaps I might be justified in remaining silent. But it is not!" Emma was adamant about seeking protection for the Saints and their prophet; she could not remain silent. She requested that Joseph receive "the privilege of the laws of this State," making reference to the "consequent suffering of myself and family; and the incalculable losses and suffering of many hundreds who survived, and the many precious lives that were lost; all, the effect of unjust prejudice and misguided ambition, produced by misrepresentation and calumny." She claimed to speak for "fathers and mothers, of brothers and sisters, widows and orphans."[44] Emma was a spitfire!

Governor Carlin politely responded a week later, claiming he had no legal obligation to protect Joseph and attempting to excuse himself of the matter entirely. Emma promptly responded, drawing on her city, state, and Constitutional rights: "We do believe that it is your duty to allow us in this place the privileges and advantages guaranteed to us by the laws of this State and the United States." She made specific reference to the Nauvoo city charter, specifically the eleventh section, claiming the right of *habeas corpus* to protect her husband, mayor of the city. "These powers are positively granted in the charter over your own signature," she asserted. "It only requires a knowledge of the Constitution of the United States, and statutes of the State of Missouri, and a knowledge of the outrages committed by some of the inhabitants of that State," she wrote.[45] However, requisitions from political equals in Missouri issued to Governor Carlin in September spoke stronger than Emma's letters, and he refused to protect Joseph.[46] She was adept enough to maintain political conversation in an admirable manner, even though her efforts were not successful.

Emma witnessed other political endeavors secondhand. After realizing that none of the 1844 US presidential candidates would offer support to the Saints seeking redress from Missouri losses and protect their religious freedoms, Joseph joined the campaign and involved many of his close friends and family.[47] Emma entertained candidates. Grandson Frederick Alexander Smith remembered that many would come to the Mansion House in Nauvoo during a political campaign, even years after Joseph's death. On one occasion, Emma made fritters, served with honey and syrup. One politician asked her what she called the food placed before them. She said, "It all depends. A year like this we call them candidates, all puffed up and air in them."[48] By this point in her life, she realized the reality of politicians' empty promises.

"All that is for your good, temporal and spiritual"—Emma's Work after Joseph's Death

Joseph died without a will. He also died in debt, leaving Emma to worry about finances for years.[49] Soon after his death and before the Quorum of the Twelve had arrived in Nauvoo, Emma called for a meeting with Nauvoo stake president William Marks, a friend she trusted as a loyal Smith family ally. She nominated him as trustee in trust, hoping that he could immediately protect her family. Others protested the nomination, requesting time for the absent Quorum of the Twelve to meet.[50] Emma rode to Carthage to file the necessary paperwork designating her as the legal administrator of the Smith estate.[51] She met with William Clayton in an unsuccessful attempt to untangle family and Church accounts in August 1844.[52] She struggled to maintain possession of Joseph's papers, but between William and Brigham Young, she learned that they belonged to the Church.[53] In despair, she realized she would have to fend for herself.

In the years after Joseph's death, Emma continued to maintain her properties and business to provide for her children. With the

*Emma Hale Smith Bidamon, photograph, Charles Carter.
Courtesy Church History Library, Salt Lake City, Utah.*

chaos and commotion in Nauvoo, including the Church leadership succession crisis, Emma remained out of the public eye, seeking legal recourse only upon matters involving family. In later years, she persisted in her high work ethic to support her household, with the additional concern of her adult children and their families. She wrote to Joseph III in 1869 that she wanted "all that is for your good, temporal and spiritual."[54] She continued to maintain a hotel and to harvest grapes to sell wine. She wrote Joseph III in 1872, "I only wish we may have a little, just to keep us living."[55]

Over time and through experience, Emma became a very astute property owner, businesswoman, and political activist, transcending the legal concept of coverture. Oliver Cowdery believed she had "a decidedly correct mind and uncommon ability of talent and judgment," with a well-developed sense of morality and virtue.[56] Mark Forscutt, a contemporary of Emma's in the Reorganized Church, stated: "When wrongs were perpetrated against her family, her sex, her friends, or her faith, she was bold, intrepid and public spirited."[57] In her roles as First Lady and president of the Nauvoo Relief Society, Emma had gained the vital experience she needed to act as a strong, independent woman with a keen mind and loud voice. These were her efforts to seek for the things of a better world.[58]

Notes

1. Mark Staker, "Joseph and Emma Smith's Susquehanna Home: Expanding Mormonism's First Headquarters," *Mormon Historical Studies* 16, no. 2 (Fall 2015): 100–103.
2. Emma Smith McCallum, reminiscences, in Buddy Youngreen, *Reflections of Emma* (Orem, UT: Keepsake, 1982), 53.
3. William Blackstone, *Commentaries on the Laws of England*, 2 vols. (New York: W. E. Dean, 1840), 1:355.
4. Ellen Carol DuBois, *Woman Suffrage and Women's Rights* (New York City: New York University Press, 1998), 32–33.
5. Richard L. Bushman, *The Refinement of America: Persons, Houses, Cities* (New York: Vintage Books, 1993), xii–xiii; see Mark Staker, "Isaac and Elizabeth Hale in Their Endless Mountain Home," *Mormon Historical Studies* 15, no. 2 (Fall 2014): 7–8.

6. Staker, "Isaac and Elizabeth Hale," 41; Richard Lyman Bushman, *Joseph Smith—Rough Stone Rolling: A Cultural Biography of Mormonism's Founder* (New York: Knopf, 2005), 18–19, 42.
7. Isaac Hale, "Affidavit;" Peter Ingersoll, "Affidavit," in E. D. Howe, *Mormonism Unvailed* (Painesville, NY: E. D. Howe, 1834), 18–19, 234–35, 263; Staker, "Joseph and Emma Smith's Susquehanna Home," 89.
8. Joseph Smith, History, circa Summer 1832, 6, JSP.
9. Joseph Smith, Agreement with Isaac Hale, 6 Apr. 1829, Harmony, PA, JSP.
10. Isaac Hale and Elizabeth Lewis Hale, Deed, Harmony, PA, 25 Aug. 1830, JSP; Staker, "Joseph and Emma Smith's Susquehanna Home," 94–108, 113–16.
11. Joseph Smith and Emma Hale Smith, deed, to Joseph McKune, Jr., Harmony PA, 28 Jun. 1833, JSP.
12. Mark Lyman Staker, *Hearken, O Ye People: The Historical Settings for Joseph Smith's Ohio Revelations* (Salt Lake City: Greg Kofford, 2009), 249–52.
13. Lucy Mack Smith, History, 1844–1845, book 14, p. JSP.
14. Emma Smith Bidamon to Joseph Smith III, 1 Aug. 1868, CCLA.
15. Joseph Smith, Journal, 13 Jul. 1843, 308, JSP; Joseph Smith, deed, to Emma Smith, Julia M. Smith, Joseph Smith III, Frederick Smith, and Alexander Smith, 12 Jul. 1843, Deed Book M, 400–401, Hancock County Recorder's Office; JSP. William Clayton, journal, 12–15 Jul. 1843, in *An Intimate Chronicle: The Journals of William Clayton*, ed. George D. Smith (Salt Lake City: Signature, 1995), 110.
16. See Clayton, Journal, 16 Aug. 1843, 117.
17. Emma Smith to William Marks, 25 Aug. 1844, CCLA.
18. *Nauvoo Neighbor* 2, no. 20 (13 Nov. 1844): [3]; 3, no. 1 (7 May 1845): [3].
19. See Linda King Newell and Valeen Tippets Avery, *Mormon Enigma: Emma Hale Smith* (Urbana: University of Illinois Press, 1994), 158.
20. Roger D. Launius, *Joseph Smith III: Pragmatic Prophet* (Urbana, IL: University of Illinois Press, 1995), 53–54.
21. Newel and Avery, *Mormon Enigma*, 286–87.
22. "Kirtland Safety Society," *CHTE*.
23. Staker, *Hearken, O Ye People*, 442–43.
24. Joseph Smith, Journal, 12 Oct. 1835, 8, JSP.
25. Joseph Smith to Emma Smith, 19 Aug. 1836, Charles Alrich Autograph Collection, State Historical Society of Iowa, Des Moines; JSP.
26. See "Grandison Newell," Biography, JSP.

27. Emma Smith to Joseph Smith, 25 Apr. 1837, in Letterbook 2, 35, JSP.
28. Emma Smith to Joseph Smith, 3 May 1837, in Letter Book 2, 35, JSP. See Joseph Smith, Minute Book 1, 13 Jan. 1836, 200, JSP.
29. Emma Hale Smith to Joseph Smith, 6 Dec. 1839, Charles Aldrich Autograph Collection, JSP.
30. Emma Hale Smith to Joseph Smith, 16 Aug. 1842, Book of the Law of the Lord, 175, JSP.
31. Emma went to St. Louis in Apr. 1843, 6–12 Aug. 1843, and 20–25 Apr. 1844. See Joseph Smith, Journal, Books 2–4, JSP.
32. Emma Smith to Joseph Heywood, 18 Oct. 1845, CCLA.
33. Newell and Avery, *Mormon Enigma*, 262.
34. Emma Hale Smith to Joseph Smith, 7 Mar. 1839, Letterbook 2, JSP.
35. Emma Smith to Joseph Smith, 6 Dec. 1839, Charles Aldrich Autograph Collection, JSP.
36. "The Late Proceedings," *T&S* 2, no. 16 (15 Jun. 1841): 447.
37. Eliza R. Snow, "The Female Relief Society: A Brief Sketch of its Organization and Workings in the City of Nauvoo, Hancock Co., ILL," *WE* 1, no. 3 (1 Jul. 1872): 10; "Amanda Smith," *WE* 10, no. 2 (15 Jun. 1881): 13.
38. Nauvoo Female Relief Society, petition to Thomas Carlin, ca. 22 Jul. 1842, CHL; *FFYRS*, 136–41.
39. See Andrea Radke Moss, "Silent Memories of Missouri: Mormon Women and Men and Sexual Assault in Group Memory and Religious Identity," in *Mormon Women's History: Beyond Biography,* ed. Rachel Cope, Amy Easton-Flake, Keith A. Erekson, and Lisa Olsen Tait (Vancouver, BC: Fairleigh Dickinson University Press, 2017), 69–72; "Amanda Barnes Smith," *CHTE*.
40. Eliza R. Snow, Nauvoo Journal, 29 Jul. 1842, in *Personal Writings of Eliza Roxcy Snow*, ed. Maureen Ursenbach Beecher (Logan, UT: Utah State University Press, 2000, 52–53.
41. *FFYRS*, 137.
42. See Joseph Smith, Journal, 12–15 Aug. 1842, 130–31, JSP.
43. Joseph Smith to Emma Smith, 16 Aug. 1842, Book of the Law of the Lord, 173, JSP.
44. Emma Smith to Thomas Carlin, 16 [17] Aug. 1842, CCLA.
45. Emma Smith to Thomas Carlin, 27 Aug. 1842, CCLA.
46. Thomas Carlin to Emma Smith, 3, 7 Sep. 1842, Joseph Smith, Journal, 185–86, 201–3, JSP.
47. Benjamin E. Park, *Kingdom of Nauvoo: The Rise and Fall of a Religions*

Empire on the American Frontier (New York City: Liverwright, 2020), 183–90, 208–19.
48. Frederick Alexander Smith, in Youngreen, *Reflections of Emma*, 103–5.
49. See Newell and Avery, *Mormon Enigma*, 200.
50. Parley P. Pratt, *Autobiography of Parley Parker Pratt*, ed. Parley P. Pratt Jr. (Salt Lake City: Deseret Book, 1950), 335.
51. Newell and Avery, *Mormon Enigma*, 202.
52. William Clayton, Journal 2, 15 Aug. 1844, in *An Intimate Chronicle*, 145–47.
53. William Smith to Brigham Young, 24 Aug. 1844, Brigham Young Collection, CHL.
54. Emma Smith Bidamon to Joseph Smith III, 17 [no month] 1869, CCLA.
55. Emma Smith Bidamon to Joseph Smith III, 5 Dec. 1871, CCLA.
56. Oliver Cowdery to W. W. Phelps, *Latter Day Saints Messenger and Advocate* 2, no. 1 (Oct. 1835): 201.
57. Mark H. Forscutt, "Commemorative Discourse, on the Death of Mrs. Emma Bidamon," *The Saints' Herald* 26, no. 14 (15 July 1879): 209.
58. D&C 25:10.

Chapter 10

FIRST WIDOW

Emma After Joseph

Things came to a head for Emma in June 1844. Over her forty years of life, she had lived both in relative comfort and abject poverty, in a powerful marital partnership and in tension with plural marriage, and with grief and rejoicing for her children. She had been integral in the development of Latter-day Saint community, doctrine, and practice. She found her own female space and authority with the Relief Society and in her public activity at the same time that she struggled with a broken body and a broken heart. With the death of Joseph, Emma lost her center. No longer was she the Elect Lady or the First Lady.

Now Emma was simply the widow of the prophet and the mother of his children. Her troubles certainly did not end with the death of her husband. She continued to work hard to care for her family—children, grandchildren, and, as always, others' children. She witnessed the transition of leadership in the church she had helped to found. She married another man, Lewis Bidamon, in 1847. She denied Joseph's practice of plural marriage but maintained her firm belief in his role as a prophet and in the Book of Mormon. She supported her sons in their activity in the Reorganized Church. She was known throughout the community and beyond as intelligent, kindhearted, and business-savvy. And she remembered her patriarchal blessing, given by her father-in-law Joseph Smith Sr. in 1834: "Thou shalt see many days; yea, the Lord will spare thee till thou are satisfied, for thou shalt see thy redeemer."[1]

And yet Emma's legacy was often tarnished by Latter-day Saints in Utah. It seemed people both loved and hated her. Her mother-in-law Lucy Mack Smith wrote of Emma in 1845:

> I have never seen a woman in my life, who would endure every species of fatigue and hardship, from month to month, and from year to year, with that unflinching courage, zeal and patience, which she has always done; for I know that which she has had to endure; that she has been tossed upon the ocean of uncertainty; that she has breasted the storm of persecution, and buffeted the rage of men and devils, until she has been swallowed up in a sea of trouble which have borne down almost any other woman.[2]

Emma's life both with Joseph and after Joseph was complicated, but like always, she did the best she could with what she had.

"Have they taken you from me at last!"—Death of Joseph

Emma had seen trouble for a good portion of her life, but June 1844 Nauvoo swarmed with an ever-increasing unrest. Allegiances shifted as those previously close to Emma and Joseph sought authority in ecclesiastical, municipal, economic, and domestic activity. The publication, then destruction, of the *Nauvoo Expositor* in June 1844 demonstrated breaches of trust, continuing gossip, and competing factions.³ As tensions in Nauvoo escalated, Joseph requested men to stand guard at the Mansion House to protect Emma and the children before he and Hyrum crossed the Mississippi River to escape death threats, considering flight to a different part of the country. He left Emma written instructions about family finances and property, then pled, "May God Almighty bless you and the children, and mother & all my friends."⁴ With great anxiety, Emma requested her husband return. He did on June 23, and upon arrival at the Mansion House, she and the children embraced him.⁵ Joseph left his family again to go to Carthage to respond to charges on the morning of June 24, returning one more time to say goodbye and imploring Emma to come with him. She remained to care for the children and family.⁶ Before he left, though, Emma asked him for a blessing, but with no time to spare, Joseph asked her to write down what she desired and he would sign it upon his return.⁷ This was the last time she saw Joseph alive.

Joseph's death was of course extremely traumatic, and Emma was in the middle of her last pregnancy. Before sunrise on June 28, Lorenzo Wasson, Emma's nephew, came with word of Joseph's death. While Willard Richards made a public announcement to a large crowd outside, Emma and her children—fourteen-year-old Julia, eleven-year-old Joseph III, seven-year-old Frederick, and six-year-old Alexander—remained secluded inside the Mansion House, grieving in what privacy they could find.⁸

Later that day, Willard Richards brought the bodies of Joseph and Hyrum back to the Mansion House, where they were washed and dressed in white burial clothing. Seeing her husband was traumatic; Emma was carried back to her room. She soon returned to Joseph's body, where she knelt beside him and touched his cheek: "Oh, Joseph, Joseph! Have they taken you from me at last!"⁹ She cut a lock of his hair, which she wore until her own death.¹⁰ The next day, the bodies laid in state in her dining room while thousands of people passed by and mourned the deaths.[11] "Every heart is filled with sorrow," Vilate Kimball, a friend of Emma's, wrote to her missionary husband Heber in Boston, "and the very streets of Nauvoo seem to mourn."[12]

William W. Phelps preached a funeral sermon, and then, in fear of threats to steal the bodies of Joseph and Hyrum, the outer coffins were filled with sandbags and buried in the city cemetery. The actual coffins containing the bodies were temporally buried across the street from the Mansion House in the basement of the unfinished Nauvoo House. A few months later, on a dark fall night, Emma gathered a close group of friends to remove the bodies of Joseph and Hyrum and bury them near the Homestead.[13] For unknown reasons, Emma didn't include Mary Fielding Smith, her sister-in-law and widow of Hyrum—a wedge that widened the distance in their relationship.[14] While the graves were not marked, years later Emma showed her grandson Frederick Alexander Smith the lilac bush that noted the exact location.[15]

Many Saints cared for Emma and her family in the year following the death. Wilford Woodruff, of the Quorum of the Twelve, and his wife Phebe paid a visit of respect in August 1844. Emma recognized the grief that so many shared with her at the loss of Joseph and Hyrum. She gave them a few memory pieces: oak from the original coffin, a pair of white cotton gloves, and a white handkerchief from Joseph.[16] Emily Partridge visited—one of the plural wives of whom Emma was aware. Emily came to see Emma's new baby boy born in November 1844, after Joseph's death, and found Emma to be very gracious.[17] Eliza R. Snow, an estranged friend, also came to see David Hyrum and wrote a poem to the baby published in the local newspaper.[18] On July 9, 1845, Bishops Newel K. Whitney and James Miller provided a meal for the Smiths at the Mansion House, served to them by Apostles and bishops.[19]

There was certainly an emotional toll. In July 1847, Joseph T. Buckingham, editor of the *Boston Courier*, traveled through town and met Emma. "She is an intelligent woman, apparently about fifty years of age, rather large and good looking with bright sparkling eyes," he reported, "but a countenance of sadnesss when she is not talking."[20] Emma's granddaughter, Emma Smith Kennedy, remembered that "her eyes were brown and sad. She would smile with her lips to me, as small as I was, I never saw her brown eyes smile. I asked my mother one day, why don't Grandma laugh with her eyes like you do and my mother said because she has a deep sorrow in her heart."[21] Emma's heart continued to break throughout the rest of her life.

"A certain degree of hostility"—Succession and Separation

Without a clear succession plan in place at the time of Joseph's death, many people claimed authority as immediately as a week later. Emma initially favored William Marks, the Nauvoo stake president.[22] Sidney Rigdon returned to Nauvoo in August 1844 and based his claim on his position in the First Presidency. As President of the Quorum of the Twelve Apostles, Brigham Young asserted that Joseph had given him the keys.[23] Others alleged young Joseph III had been ordained by his father before his death.[24] Joseph's brother William also claimed leadership over the Church, as he had been sustained as patriarch after the death of Hyrum.[25] Even after the body of Saints left Nauvoo with Brigham Young, James J. Strang approached Emma in Fulton, Illinois, enlisting her support for his leadership over those who did not follow Brigham. Emma initially refused to join any splinter group.[26] She remained a central historical figure for many factions who shared the legacy of Joseph Smith and the Book of Mormon.

Both Emma and Brigham Young were fiercely dedicated to

Joseph for different reasons: he was committed to seeing the future success of the Church, while she was devoted to preserving her fatherless family. Even when Joseph was alive, there seemed to be a triangulation between the three, each vying for Joseph's ear. Brigham and other Apostles took most of Joseph's papers, considering them valuable documentation of history and doctrine of the Church they now led. Emma saw that as a loss of her family history. Young Joseph III remembered how Brigham requested Joseph's horse to ride in a parade of the Nauvoo Legion when he assumed Joseph's role as Lieutenant General in August 1844. The horse came back in poor condition, and it appeared to young Joseph that Brigham had little regard for the Smith family.[27] Joseph III also remembered that Brigham ordered police surveillance around the Mansion House, contributing to tension with Emma. "She spoke openly against them," he wrote, "with the result that a certain degree of hostility grew up against her." These "petty annoyances," together with more significant differences, contributed to an aggressive enmity between Emma and Brigham, the biggest of which was plural marriage.[28]

Brigham and Joseph had very different marital relationships and social perspectives in general, including on race and coverture. Joseph was ahead of his time, welcoming Black people into the Church and deeding land to his wife, while Brigham was steeped in New England tradition. After Brigham's first wife died quite young, he married Mary Ann Angell, a young convert, in Kirtland. Brigham and Mary Ann both grew up in strictly gendered New England families with the man as the head of the house. Mary Ann's father had been abusive, and she had a generally introverted nature.[29] She never joined the Nauvoo Relief Society, but she and Brigham were members of the Anointed Quorum. Their relationship was quite different than that of Emma and Joseph, whose marriage presented a more progressive, equal relationship. While Joseph encouraged women to practice spiritual gifts, Brigham later discouraged it.[30] Perhaps he felt threatened by the assertive Emma, who was so different from Mary Ann.

Brigham practiced plural marriage in secret under Joseph's direction in Nauvoo. After Joseph's death, he and some Apostles married some of Joseph's plural wives for time. While Mary Ann accepted the practice, Emma struggled. Emma believed that Brigham and Orson Pratt blemished the reputation of the Church with the public announcement of the practice of polygamy in 1852.[31] The personal embarrassment continued in 1876, when Orson Hyde compiled a revised version of the Doctrine and Covenants in Utah and included the revelation perhaps intended to be personal for Emma and Joseph (now section 132).[32] When one tourist to Nauvoo asked if Emma would consider moving to Utah, she responded, "I was a devout believer in the faith as disclosed by Joseph Smith; but I would not follow false prophets."[33] And yet, despite their differences, Emma and Brigham, committed to Joseph in their own ways; both died calling his name.[34]

Regardless of the hostility between Brigham and Emma, other Saints remained close to her. In 1845, Benjamin F. Johnson was appointed with Newel K. Whitney to visit Emma and try to persuade her to come West with the Saints. "Nearly all night we labored with her," Johnson remembered.[35] Emma determined to remain in Nauvoo. Her 1830 revelation had told her to "go with [Joseph] at the time of his going," which she may have interpreted as staying with his body after his death.[36] She later wrote to Joseph III about Nauvoo: "It is my home, and my Childrens home, and I shall not cease to pray that they may all live to enjoy it."[37] When the majority of Saints left Nauvoo in 1846, John M. Bernhisel remained to settle financial and temporal affairs.[38] He had previously lived with the Smiths, and before he left for the Salt Lake Valley, he thanked Emma for her hospitality to him. "The bond of obligation shall ever remain binding on my heart and life," he wrote. "I fervently pray that

God may reward you in this world with a thousand fold, and in the world to come with life everlasting."[39]

Latter-day Saints from Utah often visited Emma in Nauvoo as they traveled to and from missions. In the summer of 1860, her nephews Joseph F. Smith and Samuel H. B. Smith came; they hadn't seen their aunt in fourteen years.[40] Another nephew, John Smith, son of Hyrum and Jerusha Smith, wrote in December 1866, anxious to maintain family relationships. He asked Emma for details about his birth that only she would have remembered.[41] Nels Madsen stopped in 1877 with Parley P. Pratt Jr., when Emma was seventy-three years old. They asked the typical questions about Joseph's role as prophet and the translation of the Book of Mormon, which she confirmed; then they asked about plural marriage, which she denied. She told them, "You may think I was not a very good Saint not to go West but I had a home here and did not go because I did not know what I should have there."[42] When people's questions probed too deeply for her comfort, Emma replied, "Thank you—those things are personal."[43] Security for her family continued to be her highest concern.

"A source of anxiety"—Hard Work

Almost immediately following Joseph's death, Emma struggled to find ways to provide for her family against the bleak reality that she now held his outstanding debts—approximately seventy thousand dollars. He had pledged his personal credit to purchase most of the land for Nauvoo, legally considered his property.[44] Remaining assets were used to pay for the funeral, leaving Emma with two cows, two horses, her spinning wheels, and other household goods, and an annual rent payment of $124. Before his death, Joseph had transferred several properties to Emma and the children. Brigham Young, who was in desperate financial need to move the Saints west, speculated

Emma Hale Smith Bidamon, photograph. Courtesy Community of Christ Library-Archive, Independence, Missouri.

Emma owned around fifty thousand dollars in real estate, when in reality, her 1847 tax bill indicated holdings of just over eight thousand dollars, then dropping to half of that just two years later.[45] The misperception added to their tense relationship.

Emma worked hard to provide for herself and her family for the rest of her life. She attempted to rent out the Red Brick Store in 1845 without success.[46] Years later, she and Lewis spent a thousand dollars for renovations and supplies, hoping that Joseph III could revive the store. The enterprise, unfortunately, failed.[47] Emma wrote her son in 1869, "Joseph I cannot be thankful that those old debts trouble you, I know that you done the very best you know how, they have been a sourse of anxiety to me for years, yet I am hoping that they will never be permitted to distress you." She continued, searching to teach her son something of her own life experiences: "I have often turned those hard matters over, and over in my mind, and wondered why such hard blows should have been dealt on you and have never been able to come to a satisfactory conclusion, and have had to rest on the blessed promice, that all things shall work to gether for good, to those that love God and keep his commandments."[48]

Emma continued to care for her home, family, and community. One neighbor remembered that Emma stayed close to home, "tended to her own business, and never gossiped." Another recalled her notable reputation: "She was a very exceptional woman. No one ever said an unkind word against her while she lived." Emma kept chickens and a garden—one acquaintance noted that "she always plucked a thistle and planted a flower." A granddaughter remembered Emma's garden with flowers, potatoes, onions, turnips, and cabbage.[49] Emma also harvested grapes. In 1867, she wrote Joseph III about that year's crop: "I think we had some of the largest clusters and the largest berys on them that I ever saw." She made good use of them: "We eat all we wanted and made pies by the section, caned a few made some jelly." She shared generously: "[I] put up a box to be opened when you come from Conference, put up an other box to keep till Alex come home sold one or two hundred and them made over three hundred gallons of wine and a cask of vinegar."[50] She hired local girls to help when needed. Always a hostess, she and Lewis held parties for young people and baked delicious cookies.[51]

Years of hard work wore Emma down. In her last decade, she finally felt she had achieved the fruits of her labors. She wrote to Joseph III: "I never lived a winter with so little hard work to do as I have so far this winter and we have a plenty of meat, and potatoes and crout in abundance, flour, and corn meal, milk, and butter of our own make, apples, and apple butter, marmalade and jellies and dried cherries, and hominy, and beans dried sweet corn." She commented on this new rarity: "I am blessed with a good appetite, and eat more and sleep more than I ever did before, one trouble I have, that is I often go to bed without being either tired or sleepy and find it hard to rest when not weary, and sleep without being sleepy, but I think I shall be in good condition when the spring comes to work at what ever comes to hand."⁵² Life was never easy, but Emma was consistent in her hard work.

"I am as ever yours wholly"—Lewis Bidamon

In early 1847, Lewis Bidamon wrote to Emma, hoping to rent the Mansion House from her.⁵³ He was no stranger to Emma; before Joseph's death, the Smiths had ordered a carriage from Lewis, owner of a carriage factory in nearby Canton, Illinois.⁵⁴ "Major" Bidamon was a lieutenant colonel of the 32nd regiment of the Illinois Infantry.⁵⁵ He was a tall, dark-haired man with dark eyes, very different from Joseph's light hair and blue eyes. They differed in other ways, as well. Lewis was an alcoholic, a gambler, and decidedly not interested in organized religion. Maybe it was because he was so unlike Joseph that Emma trusted her later years to this man, yearning for a sense of security. Lewis and Emma were married by a Methodist preacher on December 23, 1847, Joseph Smith's birthday.⁵⁶ Word quickly traveled across the river to her old friends that Emma had married.⁵⁷ Almon Babbitt, who had remained in Nauvoo under Brigham Young's direction, confronted Emma, telling her that she had no right to marry Lewis, especially by a Methodist preacher, and had therefore absolved herself from the Mormon faith.⁵⁸

Lewis had a colorful background. His first wife died, leaving him with two daughters. His second wife apparently took his money and did not treat his daughters well, so they separated. Along the way he had an affair with another woman, who raised their child alone. Some say that he wanted Emma's money. She did not have much, but she loved him, graciously looking beyond his reputation. That much is clear in the letters she wrote him while he was in California in 1849 seeking gold. "Some may think I am content, but I am not, neither can I be until you are within my grasp." She worried about his safety the same way she had for Joseph. She concluded the letter, "I am as ever yours wholly."[59] She wanted to give herself to him entirely.

Emma and Lewis lived in the Mansion House until 1871, when he took matters into his own hands. He attempted to establish his own legacy of brick—a home for Emma—by completing a project Joseph had started. In 1841, Joseph had received revelation to construct a temple boarding house: the Nauvoo House.[60] The brick L-shaped building was built up to the windows on the second floor, when all hands were called to complete the temple, and the property was left to Emma. The bodies of Joseph and Hyrum had initially been buried in the basement of the unfinished structure but had since been moved to the Smith family graveyard. Lewis tore down the unfinished walls of one side of the Nauvoo House, leaving the stone foundation as part of a barn, and used the bricks to complete a smaller home and hotel on the other length of its foundation, known as the Riverside Mansion.[61] One tourist on the Mississippi River saw the red brick building on the riverbank as a symbol of a robust river town, then discovered it was the only hotel in the area with a rocking chair on the porch for Emma to watch the river.[62] She and Lewis lived there until their deaths.[63]

"Olive Branch"—Reorganized Church of Jesus Christ of Latter Day Saints

In December 1856, Edmund C. Briggs and Samuel H. Gurley visited Emma and Lewis Bidamon in Nauvoo regarding the organization of a new church. They claimed that Joseph III, by right of his lineage, should lead the church. Emma confessed that she had avoided talking to her children about the church because of the stress it had caused. She expressed her deep love for her husband Joseph, with tears running down her cheeks.[64] She and Joseph III both refused to be involved with the new church.

Four years later, when friend and former Nauvoo stake president William Marks came to town, both Emma and Joseph III relented. They traveled to Amboy, Illinois, for an RLDS conference. Joseph III was ordained as the prophet. Neither Emma nor her son was baptized, as they had already received the ordinance.[65] While Joseph III spoke firmly to the congregation, disassociating the group from Brigham Young and plural marriage, he spoke somewhat ignorantly, as Emma had never explained the polygamy situation to him. In reality, she had been Joseph's only legal wife, and she had covenanted to never speak of it—she did not want to tarnish her children's understanding of their father or worry about half-siblings.[66] The truth of Emma's knowledge of Joseph's other wives, then, remained with her alone while the anti-polygamy sentiment perpetuated in the RLDS church over the years. While on RLDS proselytizing missions to Utah, Emma's sons encountered plural marriage affidavits concerning their father. After interviewing some of his father's plural wives, Joseph III developed an opinion: "I was convinced that wherever the word *married* or *sealed* occurred in such testimonials regarding my father it meant nothing more than that possibly those women had gone through some ceremony or covenant which they intended as an arrangement for association in the world to come."[67] He concluded the women spoke in metaphors.

Just a few months before Emma's death, Joseph III conducted an interview with his mother, who was not in the best of health. Lewis Bidamon was in the room, and his presence may have affected Emma's responses. Joseph III asked his mother directly, "What about the revelation on Polygamy? Did Joseph Smith have anything like it? What of spiritual wifery?" Emma responded, "There was no revelation on either polygamy, or spiritual wives. There were some rumors or something of the sort. . . . No such thing as polygamy, or spiritual wivery, was taught, publicly or privately, before my husband's death, that I have now, or ever had any knowledge of." Maybe Emma had gone too far in not telling the truth to correct any false assumptions and she wanted to maintain the peace of her family and new church.

Emma conferred Joseph's carefully preserved Bible translation to the RLDS church in 1866.[68] She supported the missions of her sons as they traveled to Utah to proselytize their former colleagues, expressing concern for potential abuse from Brigham Young and others, and praying for their discernment.[69] She wrote to Joseph III about his brothers Alex and David, who were on a mission in Salt Lake City. "I tried before they left to give them an idea of what they might expect of Brigham." The Utah prophet had spoken poorly of Emma, and she tenderly wanted the best for her sons in an environment where the Smith family was not necessarily looked upon with favor. "I hope they will be able to bear with patience all the abuses they will have to meet," perhaps speaking from her own experiences. "I do not like to have my Childrens feelings abused."[70] While the mountain Saints in Utah shared the history of the prophet Joseph and the Book of Mormon with their prairie Saints in the Midwest, the prairie Saints firmly denied the practice of plural marriage and did not continue the practice of temple ordinances. As Emma supported her sons in the RLDS church, she more staunchly refuted the Nauvoo practice of plural marriage. Over time, she may have felt divided in remembering her own experience of heartache over polygamy, love for her husband, shame from gossip, and testimony of truth.

Emma participated in the local Nauvoo RLDS congregation known as the "Olive Branch." The group met in the Red Brick Store—the same place the Relief Society had been organized. Prayer meetings were often held in Emma's dining room.[71] She became known as the "Mother of the Reorganization" and provided needed finances. She wrote Joseph III in 1868, "I would like to straighten out all indebtedness, and put the Bishop in possession of means to send out all on missions that are fit to go, then I feel I would willingly continue to keep tavern a long time yet."[72] Even in her senior years, she was willing to work to provide for the church.

"I'm coming"—Emma's Death

Emma's life began on the banks of the Susquehanna River in Harmony, Pennsylvania. She crossed to and from Missouri on frozen rivers. Her life ended on the banks of the Mississippi River in Nauvoo, Illinois. During the dark space after her husband's death and her children becoming adults, she wrote to Joseph III: "I have seen many, yes very many trying scenes in my life, in which I could not see any good in them, neither could I see any place where good could grow out of them but I feel a divine trust in God, that all things shall work for good."[73] Emma thought often of her own end. She wrote Joseph III about the "the neglected condition" of the family graveyard, requesting that, after her death, he "extend that fence so as to enclose the graves of your two little brothers."[74] She wanted to be near them physically when she died—her sons, her husband, and her in-laws.

Emma's health ebbed and flowed through her last years of life. "I could not write in daylight and my old spectacles has been broke and I could not see to write by lamp light," she wrote Joseph III, "but I have just got a new pair today and I am now trying them."[75] In another letter, Emma mentioned, "I am very thankful that I am able to write," but she continued to have sight problems. "My eyes has been very sore for the last ten days, and they are yet, I think they might have been well by this time." Despite this condition, she continued to work. "I had some sewing to do, and I taxed them a little too much, and they have rebeled, but still I am making all I can out of them." The next morning after rereading the letter, she tagged on, "Joseph when I come to look at my writing by day light I can hardly read it myself."[76] At one point, Emma fell on the stairs to the cellar as she carried milk; she broke her arm and it healed crooked.[77] Crookedness—not quite perfectly straight—seemed to be a pattern in some form or another in Emma's life.

Emma's children gathered around her bedside in Nauvoo at the end of April 1879. Joseph III recorded her condition daily in his journal. "Found Alex here at Nauvoo and Julia in care of mother." Three days later, he wrote, "Mother fails more rapidly. Has taken no nourishment for some hours, her pulse grows feeble constantly." He added, "Her breath labored." On April 27, he did not think she would survive the night.[78] She persisted, as she always did. Then, in the middle of the night a few days later, Alexander heard Emma speak, "Joseph, Joseph, Joseph," and wakened his brother, who hurried to her bed. Emma raised herself up and extended her left arm. "Yes, yes, I'm coming," she said, then slumped back on her pillow.[79]

Emma died on April 30, 1879, the anniversary of the birth and death of her twins in 1831 in Kirtland. She was buried on May 2, 1879, a few hundred feet from the river, on the southern end of a peninsula that had been the bustling heart of Nauvoo, next to Joseph.[80] Emma's obituary in the *Deseret News* said: "To the old members of this Church the deceased was well known, as a lady of more than ordinary intelligence and force of character." The author then concluded that her denial of plural marriage and remaining in Nauvoo "in consequence lost the honor and glory that might have crowned her brow as 'the elect lady.'"[81] The *Woman's Exponent* stated: "She was considered rather a remarkable woman, possessing great influence and unusually strong characteristics, which if properly directed, as in the early days of the Church, would have made her name illustrious in the history of the Latter-day Saints down to the end of time."[82]

A Devil and an Elect Lady— Conflicted Memories of Emma

During her life, Emma planted seeds whose harvest she would not see. The separation of the Latter-day Saints in Utah and the Reorganized Saints in the Midwest contributed to differing perspectives of Emma, perpetuated by time and distance and foggy memories influenced by current events, especially with anti-polygamy legislation in Utah. A few things have become apparent with succeeding generations who escaped the high emotions of betrayal on both sides. Emma did not catch Eliza in the arms of Joseph and throw her down the stairs, making it impossible for Eliza to bear children.[83] She did not poison Joseph in a fit of anger, nor was she the cause of Joseph's death, begging him to come back to Nauvoo and go to Carthage—all unfortunate myths that have gathered momentum in their retellings.[84]

It is true that Brigham Young maintained complicated feelings for Emma. On October 1, 1866, he preached in conference in Salt Lake City, both complimenting her and harshly criticizing her, calling her both a saint and a devil. "Emma is naturally a very smart woman, she is subtle and ingenious." He then condemned her for her denial of plural marriage, "And yet there is no good thing I would refuse to do for her, if she only would be a righteous woman."[85] Perhaps he felt threatened by her intimate partnership with Joseph and her assertive voice and leadership of women. Yet a short time later, he recognized the value and importance of women's contributions and called for a reorganization of Relief Society.[86] Perhaps without realizing it, he relied upon Emma's foundational work.

Brigham Young's successor, John Taylor, also expressed concerns about Emma. In a meeting on June 19, 1880, he spoke of being present at the organization of the Relief Society. "Sister Emma got severely tried in her mind about the doctrine of Plural marriage and she made use of the position she held to try to pervert the minds of the sisters in relation to that doctrine." President Taylor then cited his memory of something Joseph may or may not have said about his wife: "Sister Emma would dethrone Jehovah to accomplish her purpose if she could."[87] Not only did President Taylor make this claim in the midst of intense anti-polygamy legislation in Utah, but he was also at the same time calling Eliza R. Snow to be the second Relief Society General President, following Emma's tradition.

Eliza R. Snow also had complex feelings about Emma, her sister wife. When she read the 1879 interview of Emma conducted by her sons in which she denied Joseph's practice of plural marriage, Eliza compiled a letter published in the newspaper. "I once dearly loved 'sister Emma,' and now, for me to believe that she, a once honored woman, should have sunk so low, even in her own estimation as to deny what she knew to be true, seems a palpable absurdity." She continued, "So far as Sister Emma personally is concerned, I would gladly have been silent and let her memory rest in peace."[88]

Eliza also recognized Emma's good work. She told the West Jordan Relief Society on September 7, 1868, that "she wished to Correct one error it has been said that the Society in Nauvoo did more harm than good but it was not so Emma Smith was Presidentess." She continued, "The society did a great deal of good saved a great many lives."[89] In her travels around Utah and Idaho Territories, organizing and visiting Relief Societies, she often read from the Nauvoo Relief Society minute book and testified of Emma's role as the first president.⁹⁰ She recounted with pride going to Quincy with Emma Smith to deliver a petition to Illinois governor Thomas Carlin.⁹¹ Eliza exhorted young women of the Weber Stake "to read carefully the revelation given to Emma Smith and notice at the close of this revelation that what the Lord said unto her, He said unto all."⁹²

Zina Young, another sister wife, also often read Emma's 1830 revelation in Relief Society meetings and paid loving tributes to Emma.⁹³ Zina, a member of the Nauvoo Relief Society, became the third Relief Society General President after Eliza died in 1887. By the fifty-year jubilee anniversary of the Relief Society in 1892, public awareness had shifted. Zina and her board held a celebration in the tabernacle in Salt Lake City. The women decorated the tabernacle pipes with a floral representation of the key "turned to women" in Nauvoo by Joseph Smith and life-sized portraits of Eliza and Zina. They wondered about including a portrait of Emma, considering the current views of her disassociation. When Emmeline B. Wells (who later became fifth Relief Society General President) asked Church President Wilford Woodruff, also a contemporary of Emma, what he thought, he responded that "any one who opposed it must be very narrow minded indeed."⁹⁴ Emma's portrait was included. Bathsheba W. Smith, another member of the Nauvoo Relief Society, who later became the fourth Relief Society General President, said that "Emma, was much beloved."⁹⁵

Emma Hale Smith Bidamon was, indeed, a complicated figure. She was not perfect by any means, but her tenacity is noteworthy. She worked hard to fill the divine assignments she had received in 1830: to scribe for the Book of Mormon and the Bible translation, to create a hymnbook, to stand by her husband as First Lady, to lead the Relief Society as the Elect Lady, and to maintain necessary business and properties. She prioritized her family, protecting her husband

and her children above all else. And yet she was a real woman, a devoted wife, a single mother, torn by love and persecution, anxiety and confidence. She was, indeed, our First.

Notes

1. Joseph Smith Sr., Blessing to Emma Smith, Patriarchal Blessing Book 1, 4–5, JSP.
2. Lucy Mack Smith, History, 1845, 190, JSP.
3. *Nauvoo Expositor*, 7 Jun. 1844. Joseph Smith, Journal, 10–18 Jun. 1844, JSP.
4. Joseph Smith, History, 22 Jun. 1844, 147, JSP; Joseph Smith to Emma Smith, 23 Jun. 1844, JSP.
5. Joseph Smith History, vol. F-1, 148–49, JSP.
6. Leonora C. Taylor, statement, circa 1856, CHL.
7. Emma Smith, blessing, 1844, typescript, CHL. See *Saints: The Standard of Truth, 1815–1846*, vol. 1 (Salt Lake City: The Church of Jesus Christ of Latter-day Saints, 2018), 544 fn24. See also chapter 4.
8. Mary Audentia Smith Anderson, "The Memoirs of President Joseph Smith," *The Saints' Herald*, 29 Jan. 1935, 143.
9. Lucy Mack Smith, History, 1845, 312–13, JSP.
10. Joseph Smith III, *Joseph Smith III and the Restoration*, ed. Mary Audentia Smith Anderson and Bertha Audentia Anderson Hulmes (Independence, MO: Herald House, 1952), 85.
11. "Awful Assassination of Joseph and Hyrum Smith," *T&S* 5, no. 12 (1 Jul. 1844): 601; Joseph Smith, History, 29 Jun. 1844, JSP.
12. Vilate Kimball to Heber C. Kimball, 30 Jun. 1844, CHL.
13. Richard L. Bushman, *Joseph Smith—Rough Stone Rolling: A Cultural Biography of Mormonism's Founder* (New York City: Knopf, 2005), 553; Glen M. Leonard, *Nauvoo: A Place of Peace, A People of Promise* (Salt Lake City: Deseret Book and Provo, UT: Brigham Young University Press, 2002), 403–4.
14. Linda King Newell and Valeen Tippetts Avery, *Mormon Enigma: Emma Hale Smith* (Champaign: University of Illinois Press, 1994), 213; Lori E. Woodland, *Beloved Emma: The Illustrated Life Story of Emma Smith* (Salt Lake City: Deseret Book, 2008), 153.
15. Frederick Alexander Smith, reminiscences, in Buddy Youngreen, *Reflections of Emma* (Orem, UT: Keepsake, 1982), 93.

16. Wilford Woodruff, Journal, 23 Aug. 1844, CHL.
17. Emily Partridge Dow Young, Diary and Reminiscences, Feb. 1874–Nov. 1899, 3, CHL.
18. Eliza R. Snow, "Lines, Written on the Birth of the Infant Son of Mrs. Emma, Widow of the Late General Joseph Smith," *T&S* 5, no. 22 (1 Dec. 1844): 735.
19. "Dinner to the Smith Family," *Nauvoo Neighbor* 3, no. 11 (16 Jul. 1845): [2].
20. J. T. Buckingham, *Boston Courier* (Jul. and Aug. 1847).
21. See Gracia N. Jones, "My Great-Great-Grandmother, Emma Hale Smith," *Ensign*, Aug. 1992.
22. William Clayton, Journal, 4–8 Jul. 1844, in *An Intimate Chronicle: The Journals of William Clayton,* ed. George D. Smith (Salt Lake City: Signature, 1995), 137–38.
23. Joseph Smith, History, vol. F-1, 7 Aug. 1844, 293, 295–96, JSP.
24. "A blessing, given to Joseph Smith, 3rd, by his father, Joseph Smith, Junr. on Jany. 17, 1844," CCLA. See Andrew F. Ehat, "Joseph Smith's Introduction of Temple Ordinances and the 1844 Mormon Succession Question," thesis, Brigham Young University, 1982; D. Michael Quinn, "Joseph Smith III's 1844 Blessing and the Mormons of Utah," *The John Whitmer Historical Association Journal* 1 (1981): 12–14.
25. William Smith, "Patriarch and Prophet of the Most High God," 28 Aug. 1847, broadside, CHL.
26. Linda King Newell, "Emma's Legacy: Life After Joseph: 2010 Sterling M. McMurrin Lecture," *The John Whitmer Historical Association Journal* 31, no. 2 (Fall/Winter 2011): 7–8.
27. Mary Audentia Smith Anderson, "The Memoirs of President Joseph Smith (1832–1914)," *The Saints' Herald* (8 Jan. 1935): 47–48.
28. Anderson and Hulmes, *Joseph Smith III and the Restoration*, 87.
29. Truman O. Angell, "Autobiography," 1884, 3, 6, CHL; Emmeline B. Wells, "In Memoriam," *WE* 11, no. 4 (15 Jul. 1882): 28–29.
30. Susa Young Gates, a daughter of Brigham Young, recalled her father putting an end to women performing blessings in the name of the priesthood which they held with their husbands and fathers. Susa Young Gates to Leah Widtsoe, 21 Feb. 1928, CHL.
31. Orson Pratt, discourse, 29 Aug. 1852, *Deseret News*, Extra, 14–20.
32. Danel W. Bachman, "A Study of the Mormon Practice of Plural Marriage

Before the Death of Joseph Smith," thesis, Purdue University, 1975, 204–5; Robert J. Woodford, "The Story of the Doctrine and Covenants," *Ensign*, Dec. 1984, 35.
33. Julius Chambers, *The Mississippi River and Its Wonderful Valley* (New York: G. P. Putnam's Sons, 1910), 188.
34. See Alexander H. Smith, "Second Coming of Christ, the Home of the Redeemed," *Zion's Ensign* 19 (31 Dec. 1903): 6–7; and Susa Young Gates and Leah D. Widtsoe, *The Life Story of Brigham Young* (New York: Macmillan, 1930), 362. See Valeen Tippetts Avery and Linda King Newell, "The Lion and the Lady: Brigham Young and Emma Smith," *Utah Historical Quarterly* 48, no. 1 (Winter 1980): 97.
35. Benjamin F. Johnson, *My Life's Review* (Grantsville, UT: Archive Publishers, 1982), 107.
36. D&C 25:6.
37. Emma Smith Bidamon to Joseph Smith III, 27 Dec. 1868, CCLA.
38. Council of Fifty, "Record of the Council of Fifty or Kingdom of God," 11 Jan. 1846, JSP.
39. John M. Bernhisel to Emma Smith, 9 Oct. 1847, CCLA.
40. Joseph Fielding Smith to Levira Smith, 28 June 1860, CHL.
41. John Smith to Emma Bidamon, 2 Dec. 1866, Joseph Smith Sr. Family Collection, BYU.
42. Nels Madsen, "Visit to Mrs. Emma Smith Bidamon," 27 Nov. 1931, CHL.
43. Frederick Alexander Smith, reminiscences, in Youngreen, *Reflections of Emma*, 99–101.
44. See Dallin H. Oaks and Joseph I. Bentley, "Joseph Smith and the Legal Process: In the Wake of the Steamship Nauvoo," *BYU Studies* 19, no. 2 (Winter 1979): 167–99.
45. Newell, "Emma's Legacy," 5–6.
46. Emma Smith to Joseph Heywood, 18 Oct. 1845, CCLA.
47. Newell, "Emma's Legacy," 10.
48. Emma Smith Bidamon to Joseph Smith III, 27 Dec. 1869, CCLA. Romans 8:28.
49. Emma Smith McCallum, reminiscences, in Youngreen, *Reflections of Emma*, 59–61.
50. Emma Smith Bidamon to Joseph Smith III, 2 Dec. 1867, CCLA.
51. See statements by Charlotte J. Stevenson, Albert Jemison, Charles Mulch,

Emile J. Baxter, Joseph B. Jemison, and Edward Argast, Jul.–Sep. 1940, CCLA.
52. Emma Smith Bidamon to Joseph Smith III, 2 Feb. 1867, CCLA.
53. Lewis Bidamon to Emma Smith, 11 Jan. 1847, CCLA.
54. Newell, "Emma's Legacy," 9.
55. Lewis Crum Bidamon, obituary, *Nauvoo Independent* (13 Feb. 1891).
56. Hancock Co., IL, Marriage Register, 1829–1915, vol. A-1, 105, U.S. and Canada Record Collection, FHL.
57. Sarah M. Kimball to Sarepta Heywood, Nauvoo, n.d., Joseph L. Heywood letters, CHL.
58. Newell, "Emma's Legacy," 10.
59. Emma Smith to Lewis Bidamon, 7 Jan. 1850, CCLA.
60. D&C 124:60.
61. Helene Holt, "Nauvoo House," *Encyclopedia of Mormonism*, ed. Daniel H. Ludlow, 4 vols. (New York City: Macmillan, 1992), 3:997; "Nauvoo House, Nauvoo, Illinois," Places, JSP.
62. Chambers, "Recollections of Nauvoo."
63. Helene Holt, "Nauvoo House."
64. Edmund C. Briggs, "A Visit to Nauvoo in 1856," *Journal of History* 9 (Oct. 1916): 453–54.
65. Valeen Tippetts Avery, "Last Years of the Prophet's Wife: Emma Hale Smith Bidamon and the Establishment of the Reorganized Church of Jesus Christ of Latter Day Saints," MA thesis, Northern Arizona University, 1981, 20.
66. Avery, "Emma's Legacy," 16–17.
67. Mary Audentia Smith Anderson, "The Memoirs of President Joseph Smith (1832–1914)," *The Saints' Herald* (5 May 1936): 559.
68. Emma Smith Bidamon to Joseph Smith III, 2–3 Feb. 1866; Emma Smith Bidamon to Joseph Smith III, 19 Aug. 1866, CCLA.
69. Emma Smith Bidamon to Joseph Smith III, 1 Aug. [1867–1872], CCLA.
70. Emma Smith Bidamon to Joseph Smith III, 1 Aug. 1868, CCLA.
71. Frederick Alexander Smith, in Youngreen, *Reflections of Emma*, 105.
72. Emma Smith Bidamon to Joseph Smith III, 27 Dec. 1868, CCLA.
73. Emma Smith Bidamon to Joseph Smith III, 17 [?] 1869, CCLA.
74. Emma Smith Bidamon to Joseph Smith III, 2 Dec. 1867, CCLA.
75. Emma Smith Bidamon to Joseph Smith III, 2 Dec. 1867, CCLA.
76. Emma Smith Bidamon to Joseph Smith III, 27 Dec. 1868, CCLA.
77. Edward Stevenson, "Correspondence, Cincinnati, Ohio, Aug. 9, 1872,"

Deseret News (21 Aug. 1872); Emma Smith McCallum, reminiscences, in Youngreen, *Reflections of Emma*, 59.
78. Joseph Smith III, personal journal, 22, 25, 27 April 1879, CCLA.
79. Alexander H. Smith, "Second Coming of Christ."
80. Lee Wiles, "Monogamy Underground: The Burial of Mormon Plural Marriage in the Graves of Joseph and Emma Smith," *Journal of Mormon History* 39, no. 3 (Summer 2013): 2.
81. *Deseret News*, 21 May 1879.
82. *WE* 7, no. 24 (Jul. 1879): 243.
83. See Maureen Ursenbach Beecher, Linda King Newel, and Valeen Tippetts Avery, "Emma and Eliza and the Stairs," *BYU Studies* 22, no. 1 (Winter 1982): 87–96.
84. Linda King Newell, "The Emma Smith Lore Reconsidered," *Dialogue: A Journal of Mormon Thought* 17, no. 3 (Autumn 1984): 91–95.
85. Brigham Young, address, 1 Oct. 1866, recorded by G. D. Watt, CHL.
86. "Remarks by Brigham Young, Made in the Old Tabernacle, G.S.L. City, Sunday, December 8th, 1867," *Deseret Evening News* 1, no. 21 (14 Dec. 1867); "Remarks by President Brigham Young, in the New Tabernacle, Afternoon, April 8, 1868," *Deseret News Weekly* 17, no. 14 (13 May 1868); *FFYRS*, 248–52, 262–65.
87. Salt Lake Stake Relief Society, 19 Jun. 1880, 49–51, CHL.
88. Eliza R. Snow, "Letter on Plural Marriage," *WE* 8, no. 11 (1 Nov. 1879): 84–85.
89. West Jordan Ward Relief Society, vol. 3, 7 Sep. 1868, 3–5, CHL.
90. See, for example, Cache Stake Relief Society, 18 May 1868, 190–95; Eleventh Ward Relief Society, vol. 1, 3 Mar. 1869, n.p., and 1 Jul. 1884, 2–4; Sugar House Ward Relief Society, v. 2, 10 Dec. 1873, 84–87; Clifton Relief Society, vol. 1, 7 Aug. 1879, 165–71, CHL.
91. Weber Stake, Ogden 2nd Ward Relief Society, vol. 2, 6 Feb. 1879, 22–25, CHL.
92. Weber Stake YLMIA, 10 Jun. 1881, 49, CHL. See also Spanish Fork Ward, Relief Society, vol. 2, 9 Nov. 1881, 233–34, CHL.
93. See, for example, Rockville Ward Relief Society, 4 Jan. 1881, vol. 1, n.p., CHL; Louisa Jones, "Beaver Stake," *WE* 18, no. 7 (1 Sep. 1889): 54. "Aunt Zina's Party," *WE* 29, no. 4–5 (15 Jul. & 1 Aug. 1900): 20.
94. Emmeline B. Wells, Diaries, vol. 15, 15 Mar. 1892. See *FFYRS*, 589–91.
95. J. S. Woolley, "Salt Lake Stake," *WE* 30, no. 9 (1 Jan. 1902): 66.

ABBREVIATIONS

Publications

BYU Studies	*Brigham Young University Studies.* Brigham Young University, Provo, Utah. Quarterly, 1959–present; available at byustudies.byu.edu.
CHTE	Church History Topics Essays; available online at https://www.churchofjesuschrist.org/study/history/topics.
D&C	Doctrine and Covenants of The Church of Jesus Christ of Latter-day Saints. Salt Lake City: The Church of Jesus Christ of Latter-day Saints, 2013.
FFYRS	*First Fifty Years of Relief Society: Key Documents in the History of Latter-day Saint Women.* Ed. Jill Mulvay Derr, Carol Cornwall Madsen, Kate Holbrook, and Matthew J. Grow. Salt Lake City, Utah: Church Historians Press, 2016.
GTE	Gospel Topics Essays; available online at https://www.churchofjesuschrist.org/study/manual/gospel-topics-essays.
JSP	The Joseph Smith Papers, Church Historian's Press; available online at josephsmithpapers.org.
NRSM	Female Relief Society of Nauvoo, minute book,

	1842–1844, CHL; available online at churchhistorianspress.org.
RIC	*Revelations in Context: The Stories behind the Sections of the Doctrine and Covenants.* Ed. Matthew McBride and James Goldberg. Salt Lake City: The Church of Jesus Christ of Latter-day Saints, 2016). Also available online at churchofjesuschrist.org.
T&S	*Times and Seasons.* Commerce and Nauvoo, Illinois, 1839–1846.
WE	*Woman's Exponent.* Salt Lake City, Utah, 1872–1914. Also available online at catalog.churchofjesuschrist.org.

Repositories and Collections

BYU	L. Tom Perry Special Collections, Harold B. Lee Library, Brigham Young University, Provo, Utah.
CHL	Church History Library, The Church of Jesus Christ of Latter-day Saints, Salt Lake City, Utah.
CCLA	Library and Archives, Community of Christ (formerly Reorganized Church of Jesus Christ of Latter Day Saints), Independence, Missouri.
FHL	Family History Library, Salt Lake City, Utah.
UofU	Special Collections, J. Willard Marriott Library, University of Utah, Salt Lake City, Utah.

Digital Archives

JSP	The Joseph Smith Papers. http://josephsmithpapers.org/.
CHP	Church Historians Press. Church History Department, The Church of Jesus Christ of Latter-day Saints. churchhistorianspress.org.

ADDITIONAL READING

Bushman, Richard Lyman. *Joseph Smith—Rough Stone Rolling: A Cultural Biography of Mormonism's Founder.* New York City: Knopf Books. 2005.

Derr, Jill Mulvay. "'Strength in Our Union': The Making of Mormon Sisterhood." In *Sisters in Spirit: Mormon Women in Historical and Cultural Perspective*, edited by Maureen Ursenbach Beecher and Lavina Fielding Anderson, 153–207. Urbana: University of Illinois Press. 1987.

Derr, Jill Mulvay and Carol Cornwall Madsen. "'Something Better' for the Sisters: Joseph Smith and the Female Relief Society of Nauvoo." In *Joseph Smith and the Doctrinal Restoration*, 123–43. Provo, UT: Brigham Young University, Religious Studies Center, 2005.

Grow, Matthew J. "'Thou Art an Elect Lady:' D&C 24, 25, 26, 27." In *Revelations in Context: The Stories behind the Sections of the Doctrine and Covenants*, edited by Matthew McBride and James Goldberg. Salt Lake City, Utah: The Church of Jesus Christ of Latter-day Saints, 2016. Available at churchofjesuschrist.org.

Hicks, Michael. *Mormonism and Music: A History.* Urbana: University of Illinois Press, 1989.

Leonard, Glen M. *Nauvoo: A Place of Peace, A People of Promise.* Salt Lake

City, UT and Provo, UT: Deseret Book Press and Brigham Young University Press, 2002.

Madsen, Carol Cornwall. "The 'Elect Lady' Revelation (D&C 25): Its Historical and Doctrinal Context." In *Sperry Symposium Classics: The Doctrine and Covenants*, edited by Craig K. Manscill, 117–33. Provo, UT: Religious Studies Center, Brigham Young University, 2004. Available online at https://rsc.byu.edu/books/all.

———. "Mormon Women and the Temple: Toward a New Understanding." *Sisters in Spirit: Mormon Women in Historical and Cultural Perspective*, edited by Maureen Ursenbach Beecher and Lavina Fielding Anderson, 80–110. Urbana: University of Illinois Press, 1987.

———. "'My Dear and Beloved Companion': The Letters of Joseph and Emma Smith." *Ensign*, September 2008. Available online at https://churchofjesuschrist.org/study/magazines.

Newell, Linda King. "Emma Hale Smith and the Polygamy Question." *The John Whitmer Association Journal* 4 (1984): 3–15.

Newell, Linda King and Valeen Tippetts Avery. *Mormon Enigma: Emma Hale Smith*. Urbana: University of Illinois Press, 1994.

Romig, Ronald E. *Emma's Nauvoo*. Independence, MO: John Whitmer Books, 2007.

Saints: The Standard of Truth, 1815–1846, vol. 1. Salt Lake City: The Church of Jesus Christ of Latter-day Saints, 2018. Available online at https://www.churchofjesuschrist.org/study/history/saints-v1.

Staker, Mark Lyman. "'A Comfort Unto My Servant, Joseph:' Emma Hale Smith, 1804–1879." In *Women of Faith in the Latter Days: Volume 1, 1775–1820*, edited by Richard E. Turley Jr. and Brittany A. Chapman [Nash]. Salt Lake City: Deseret Book, 2011.

———. *Hearken, O Ye People: The Historical Setting of Joseph Smith's Ohio Revelations*. Salt Lake City: Greg Kofford Books, 2009.

———. "Isaac and Elizabeth Hale in Their Endless Mountain Home." *Mormon Historical Studies* 15, no. 2 (Fall 2014): 1–105.

———. "Joseph and Emma's Susquehanna Home: Expanding

Mormonism's Headquarters." *Mormon Historical Studies* 16, no. 2 (Fall 2015): 69–118.

Ulrich, Laurel Thatcher. *A House Full of Females: Plural Marriage and Women's Rights in Early Mormonism, 1835–1870.* New York City: Knopf Books, 2017.

Youngreen, Buddy. *Reflections of Emma.* Orem, Utah: Keepsake Paperbacks, 1982.

INDEX

Abercrombie, Nancy, 48
Abrahamic covenant, 26, 29–30
Agape banquets, 113, 128
Alger, Fanny, 114, 120n48
Angell, Mary Ann, 163–64
"Asleep in Jesus," 100

Babbitt, Almon, 168
Baptism, of Emma Smith, 58–60
Bennett, John C., 114, 133–34
Bernhisel, John, 82, 164–65
Bible (JST), 81–82
Bidamon, Charles, 48
Bidamon, Lewis, xvi, 48, 145, 158, 166, 168–69
Bidamon, Mary Elizabeth, 48
Bidamon, Zerelda, 48
Blessing(s): last, given to Emma, 71–73; given by women, 76n57, 131, 178n30
Boggs, Lilburn W., 43, 107, 149
Book of Mormon: Emma as scribe for, 82–85; lost manuscript pages of, 83; Emma as witness of, 85–86
Boynton, John F., 25–26

Brannan, Samuel, 108
Briggs, Edmund C., 169
British immigrants, 129
Brown, Sarah, 129
Buck, Daniel, 9
Buckingham, Joseph T., 162

Cahoon, William, 110
Carlin, Thomas, 12, 149–51, 176
Carthage Jail, 100
Chapman, Salome, 129
Charity banquets, 113, 128
Church of Jesus Christ of Latter-day Saints, The, 4, 57–58, 127
Civic affairs, 115–17
Clayton, William, 29
Cleveland, Sarah M., 124, 125, 127, 129
Coles, Elvira A., 129
Collection of Sacred Hymns for the Church of Jesus Christ of Latter Day Saints, A, 93–96
Comfort, Emma as, 25, 62, 104
Community of Christ (RLDS), 4, 31, 82, 97–98, 169–72

Cook, Margaret, 123–24
Covenants and ordinances of Emma Smith, 57–58; baptism, 58–60; revelations directed at Emma, 60–64; confirmation, 64–65; patriarchal blessing, 65–67; temple covenants, 67–71; final blessing from Joseph, 71–73
Coverture, 142, 143–45
Cowdery, Oliver, 59, 83, 84, 93, 114, 146, 154

Doctrine and Covenants 25, 60–61
Doniphan, Alexander W., 42
Dream, about Emma Smith's children, 52
Durfee, Elizabeth, 126, 131

Elect Lady, Emma Smith as, 121–27
Elijah, 26
Ells, Hanna M., 127, 135
Endowment, 68–70, 130–32
Evening and the Morning Star, The, 93
Events: personal, 110–11; Church, 112–15
Extermination order, 43

Family celebrations, 111
Far West, Missouri, 42
Feme covert, 142
Feme sole, 142, 143
Foot washing ordinances, 67–68
Forscutt, Mark, 154

Gates, Susa Young, 76n57, 178n30
God: characteristics of, 61; relying on, 64–65
Gold plates: retrieval of, 79–80; Emma protects, 80–81; Emma's role in translation of, 82–85
Goldthwaite, Lydia, 25, 112

Gossip, 17, 114, 120n48, 133–34
Grapes, 167
Greene, John P., 31–32
Gurley, Samuel H., 169

Hale, Alva, 11, 12, 20, 80
Hale, David, 8, 10, 12
Hale, Elizabeth (Emma's mother), xi–xii, 7, 8, 9, 11, 12, 37, 45
Hale, Elizabeth (Emma's sister), 10
Hale, Isaac, xi–xii, 7–8, 9, 11, 17, 20, 143–44
Hale, Jesse, 8–9, 10, 12
Hale, Phebe, 10
Hale, Reuben, 84
Hale, Tryal, 10, 12
Harmony, Pennsylvania, 6–10, 20, 80–81, 143–44
Harris, Martin, 83, 84
Harris, Nathan, 112
Hawkes, Phebe Ann, 129
Healing, 108–10
Howe, Harriet, 112
Humility, 62–64, 72
Huntington, Zina, 47
Hyde, Orson, 164
Hymnal(s), 90; and Emma's musical background, 91; Emma's creation of, 91–98; influence of Emma's, 98–100

Independence, Missouri, temple site in, 4

Johnson, Benjamin F., 164
Joseph Smith Translation, 81–82

Kendall, Elizabeth, 47
Kennedy, Emma Smith, 162
Kimball, Sarah M., 123–24
Kimball, Vilate, 161

Kirtland, Ohio, 65, 144, 145–47
Kirtland Safety Society, 145–46
Kirtland Temple, 67–68, 93–94, 98–99
Knight, Joseph, 58–59, 84, 86–87n6
Knight, Newel, 25, 112
Knight, Sally, 64
Knight, Vinson, 147

Latter Day Saints' Messenger and Advocate, The, 93
Latter Day Saints' Selection of Hymns, The, 97–98
Lawrence, Maria, 27
Lawrence, Sarah, 27
Lee, Ann, 122
Lewis, Nathaniel, 7, 8, 9
Lewis, Sarah Cole, 7
Liberty Jail, 21, 43, 64, 106–7
Literary Firm, 92, 96
Lowell, Susan, 25–26

Madsen, Nels, 165
Maid of Iowa, 111, 144
Malaria, 44, 108–9
Manchester hymnal, 96, 97
Manning, Jane, 109
Mansion House, 44, 51, 111, 114, 144–45, 148, 160, 161, 163, 168
Marks, Rosannah, 145
Marks, William, 145, 152, 162, 170
Marriage: of Emma and Joseph, 10–11, 17–18; new and everlasting covenant of, 24–31, 69; Joseph versus Brigham Young's views on, 163–64. *See also* Plural marriage
Maudsley, Sutcliffe, 99–100
McCallum, Emma Smith, 50, 52, 109
McLellin, William E., 120n48
Meacham, Dorothy, 131
Measles, 41–42
Middleton, John, 49

Miller, James, 161
Money-digging, 16–17
Mulholland, James, 81
Murdock, John, 39, 40–41
Murdock, Julia Clapp, 39

Nauvoo, Illinois, 43–44, 108–9, 122–23, 136, 144–45, 147–48, 151, 159–60, 164
Nauvoo House, 145, 161, 169
Nauvoo Legion, 115–17
Nauvoo Relief Society. *See* Relief Society
Nauvoo Temple, 121, 136
Newell, Grandison, 147

Parrish, Warren, 25, 112
Partridge, Eliza, 27, 47
Partridge, Emily, 27, 47, 161
Patriarchal blessing, of Emma Smith, 37–38, 65–67, 106, 159
Patriarchal blessing meetings, 112–13
Peck, George, 9
Persecution: of Joseph Smith, 21, 105–6, 149–51; faced by Smith family, 42–43, 44, 106; of early Saints, 106–7; and Emma's political activism, 148–49
Phelps, William W., 92, 93, 100, 104, 135, 161
Pitt, William, 111
Plural marriage: and complexities of Emma Smith's life, 2; sealing and, 27–31; and women cared for by Emma, 47; endowment and, 70; and Emma as wife of Church President, 114–15; and problems in Relief Society, 133–35; Brigham Young and, 164; and Reorganized Church, 170; and conflicted memories of Emma, 174–75

Political activism, 142–43, 148–52
Poor, caring for, 113, 128
Pratt, Orson, 164
Pratt, Parley P. Jr., 165
Pratt, Parley P. Sr., 94
Prayer, 72, 78
Presidential campaign, 151–52
Priesthood: and Emma Smith's role in Restoration, 3; sealing and, 70–71; women's use of, 76n57, 131, 178n30; and Relief Society, 126
Property ownership, 142, 143–45

Racial inclusion, 109
Raymond, Martha H., 25, 112
Rebaptism, 59–60
Red Brick Store, 148, 166, 171
Relief Society, 121–22; organization of, 68, 123–26; hymns and, 99; historical context of, 122–23; and female authority, 123–27; name of, 125–26; service rendered by, 127–30; as temple preparation, 130–32; problems in, 132–36; reinstitution of, 136–37, 174–75; seeks protection for Joseph Smith, 149–50; and memories of Emma, 175–76; jubilee anniversary of, 176
Reorganized Church of Jesus Christ of Latter Day Saints. *See* Community of Christ (RLDS)
Restoration: Emma Smith's role in, 1–3, 78; defined, 4–5
Revelation(s): directed at Emma, 24–25, 28, 60–64, 74–75n22, 126, 176; concerning plural marriage, 29
Richards, Willard, 160
Rigdon, Sidney, 42, 146, 162
Rigdon, Smith & Co., 146
Riverside Mansion, 145, 169

Rogers, David, 96

Salvation, 26–27, 131
School of the Prophets, 113–14
Scott, Ann, 81
Sealing, 26–31; of Joseph and Emma, 69; endowment and, 70; and plural marriage, 114–15, 170
Second Great Awakening, 91
Service: rendered by Emma, 107–9, 128–29; and charity banquets, 113, 128; rendered by Relief Society, 127–30
Sewing, 105
Smith, Ada, 49
Smith, Agnes, 129
Smith, Alexander Hale, 42, 43, 45–46, 50–51, 171, 173
Smith, Alvin, 17, 79
Smith, Amanda Barnes, 149–50
Smith, Bathsheba, 70
Smith, Bertha, 49, 50
Smith, David Hyrum, 45–46, 50, 51–52, 97, 161, 171
Smith, Don Carlos (Joseph's brother), 44
Smith, Don Carlos (Joseph's son), 44–45, 52, 123
Smith, Frederick Alexander, 86, 151–52, 161
Smith, Frederick Granger Williams, 41, 44, 45–46, 50
Smith, George A., 68
Smith, Hyrum, 146, 160–61
Smith, John, 165
Smith, Joseph F., 165
Smith, Joseph III: and Reorganized Church, 30, 31, 49–50, 169–70; on persecution of Saints, 43, 44; and death of Joseph, 45–46; Emma's

council to, 64–65; nurses others during malaria epidemic, 109; on openness of Smith home, 109; on enmity between Emma and Brigham, 162; as Joseph's successor, 162; and Emma's financial problems, 166; on Joseph's plural marriages, 170; and death of Emma, 173

Smith, Joseph Jr.: family of, xii–xvi; and complexities of Emma Smith's life, 2–3; marriage of, 10–11, 17–18; Isaac Hale disapproves of, 11; arrest of, 12, 21, 59, 149–51; meets Emma, 16–17; and blending of Smith and Hale families, 18–19; disagreement between William and, 18–19; challenges in marriage of, 19–22; imprisonment in Liberty Jail, 21, 43, 64, 106–7; persecution of, 21, 42–43, 44, 105–6, 149–51; affection between Emma and, 22–24; and new and everlasting covenant of marriage, 24–31; marriages performed by, 25–26; and plural marriage, 27–31, 47, 114–15, 133–35, 170–71; death of, 31–32, 45–47, 117, 136, 152, 158, 159–62; and death of Emma, 32, 173; children of, 38–45; Emma's dream of, 52; confirms Emma and Sally Knight, 64; learns about patriarchs and patriarchal blessings, 65; organizes Relief Society, 68, 124, 126; and temple ordinances, 68–69; sealed to Emma, 69; gives final blessing to Emma, 71–73; and retrieval of gold plates, 79–80; and Book of Mormon translation, 82–85; and lost Book of Mormon manuscript pages, 83; and Kirtland Temple dedication, 98–99; imprisonment in Carthage Jail, 100; and Emma as wife of Church President, 104–17; brings Whitneys into home, 108, 128–29; on friendly gatherings, 110; events hosted by, 111; Church events attended by, 112–15; gossip concerning, 114, 120n48, 133–34; and civic affairs, 115–17; on organization of Church, 127; on Relief Society, 130–31; and women's temple covenants, 131–32; property owned by, 144–45; presidential campaign of, 151–52; successor to, 162–63; marital relationship between Emma and, 163–64; outstanding debts of, 165–66

Smith, Joseph Murdock, 39, 40

Smith, Joseph Sr., 17, 65–66

Smith, Julia Murdock, 39, 40–41, 43, 45–46, 49, 99–100

Smith, Lucy Mack: on Hale family home, 8; and marriage of Joseph and Emma, 17; Emma cares for, 19, 109; as example of motherhood, 37; as mother in Israel, 37; and retrieval of gold plates, 80; on lost Book of Mormon manuscript pages, 83; on Emma's public activity, 105; and Relief Society, 129–30; on trials faced by Emma, 159

Smith, Mary Fielding, 161

Smith, Samuel H. B., 165

Smith, Vida E., 50

Smith, William, 18–19, 162

Smith Bidamon, Emma Hale: pedigree chart for, xi–xii; family of, xii–xvi, 143; timeline for, xvii–xxv; impact of, 1–2; role in Restoration, 1–3, 78; and plural marriage, 2, 27–31, 47, 70, 114–15, 134–35, 164, 170–71, 175; complexities of life of, 2–3; written sources for information on, 3–4; life in Harmony, 6–7; childhood and early years of, 7–10; marries Joseph, 10–11, 17–18; rift and reunion with family, 11–12; meets Joseph, 16–17; and blending of Smith and Hale families, 18–19; challenges in marriage of, 19–22; illness of, 22; affection between Joseph and, 22–24; lost children of, 23, 37–38, 53n8, 123; revelations directed at, 24–25, 28, 60–64, 74–75n22, 126, 176; and new and everlasting covenant of marriage, 24–31; and death of Joseph, 31–32, 45–47, 117, 152, 159–62; death of, 32, 172–74; as mother in Israel, 37; patriarchal blessing of, 37–38, 65–67, 106, 159; children of, 38–45; as mother figure, 47–48; adult children and grandchildren of, 48–52; covenants and ordinances of, 57–58; baptism of, 58–60; confirmation of, 64–65; temple covenants of, 67–71; sealed to Joseph, 69; Joseph's final blessing to, 71–73; religious devotions of, 78; and retrieval of gold plates, 79–80; protects scriptures, 80–82; as Book of Mormon scribe, 82–85; musical background of, 91; compiles hymnal, 91–98; influence of hymns of, 98–100; as wife of Church President, 104–17; service rendered by, 107–9, 128–29; healing skill of, 108–10; racially inclusive perspective of, 109; events hosted by, 110–11; and civic affairs, 115–17; as Elect Lady, 121–27; as Relief Society President, 121–37; and female authority, 123–27; as teacher, 126; business acuity of, 142–43, 145–48; political activism of, 142–43, 148–52; property owned by, 143–45; activities following Joseph's death, 152–54, 158–59; and Joseph's successor, 162–63; hostility between Brigham Young and, 162–64, 174; Saints remain close to, 164–65; financial problems of, 165–66; work of, following Joseph's death, 166–68; final years of, 167–68; marries Lewis Bidamon, 168–69; and Reorganized Church, 169–72; conflicted memories of, 174–77

Snow, Eliza R., 29, 76n57, 100, 124, 127, 130, 135, 149–50, 161, 174, 175–76

Snow, Eunice Billings, 116

Spiritual gifts, 126

Staker, Mark, 14n18

Stowell, Josiah, 16–17

Strang, James J., 162

Susquehanna River, 6, 7, 16

Tarbell, Zachariah, 17–18

Taylor John, 37, 100, 124–25, 132, 135, 175

Temple covenants: of Emma Smith, 67–71; Relief Society as preparation for, 130–32

Tharpe, Nancy J., 116–17

Thompson, Mercy, 69, 129

Tracy, Nancy A., 113

27th Commandment, 61–64

Van Tuyl, Abram, 145
Virtue, 132

Walker, William Holmes, 99
Wasson, Benjamin, 81
Wasson, Lorenzo D., 11, 160
Wells, Emmeline B., 115–16, 127, 176
Wheeler, Phebe, 127, 135
Whitmer, David, 84
Whitney, Elizabeth Ann, 40, 94, 108, 113, 124, 125, 127, 128–29
Whitney, Helen Mar, 111
Whitney, Newel, 40, 68, 113, 128–29, 161, 164
Wilkinson, Jemima, 122
Williams, Frederick G., 41, 94
Winters, Elizabeth, 114

Women: and temple ordinances, 67–69; blessings given by, 76n57, 131, 178n30; and property ownership, 142, 143–45. *See also* Relief Society
Women's associations, 122–23. *See also* Relief Society
Woodruff, Phebe, 161
Woodruff, Wilford, 93, 161, 176
Word of Wisdom, 113–14
Worthiness, 132
Wright, Lucy M., 28

Young, Brigham, 96, 136, 162–66, 171, 174–75, 178n30
Young, Mary Ann Angell, 163–64
Young, Zina Jacobs, 136, 176